reading images

This second edition of the landmark textbook *Reading Images* builds on its reputation as the first systematic and comprehensive account of the grammar of visual design. Drawing on an enormous range of examples from children's drawings to textbook illustrations, photo-journalism to fine art, as well as three-dimensional forms such as sculpture and toys, the authors examine the ways in which images communicate meaning.

Features of this fully updated second edition include:

- new material on moving images and on colour
- a discussion of how images and their uses have changed through time
- websites and web-based images
- ideas on the future of visual communication.

Reading Images focuses on the structures or 'grammar' of visual design – colour, perspective, framing and composition – and provides the reader with an invaluable 'tool-kit' for reading images, which makes it a must for anyone interested in communication, the media and the arts.

Gunther Kress is Professor of English at the Institute of Education, University of London. **Theo van Leeuwen** has worked as a film and television producer in the Netherlands and Australia and as Professor in the Centre for Language & Communication Research at Cardiff University. He is currently Dean at the Faculty of Humanities and Social Sciences, University of Technology, Sydney. They have both published widely in the fields of language and communication studies.

Praise for the first edition

'*Reading Images* is the most important book in visual communication since Jacques Bertin's semiology of information graphics. It is both thorough and thought-provoking; a remarkable breakthrough.'

Kevin G. Barnhurst, *Syracuse University, USA*

'Fresh and stimulating. The sociocentric approach is by far the most penetrating approach to the subject currently available.'

Paul Cobley, *London Guildhall University*

'A useful text for all students who are involved in areas which rely on both language and visual images for their expression and articulation of ideas.'

Catriona Scott, *Middlesex University*

'This is the best detailed and sustained development of the "social semiotic" approach to the analysis of visuals. Clear, informative and theoretically developmental.'

Dr S. Cottle, *Bath HE College*

'Excellent – wide ranging – accessible – tutors' "Bible".'

Jan Mair, *Edge Hill University College of Higher Education*

'Extremely attractive and well laid out. Very useful bibliography.'

Dr M. Brottman, *East London University*

'Very clearly written – it makes good connections between different areas of visual practice – especially useful for students from a variety of backgrounds attempting "mixed" coursework.'

Amy Sargeant, *Plymouth University*

reading images

GUNTHER KRESS and
THEO van LEEUWEN

THE GRAMMAR
OF VISUAL DESIGN

SECOND EDITION

Routledge
Taylor & Francis Group

LONDON AND NEW YORK

First published 1996
by Routledge
2 Park Square, Milton Park, Abingdon, Oxon OX14 4RN

Simultaneously published in the USA and Canada
by Routledge
270 Madison Ave, New York, NY 10016

Second edition published 2006

Reprinted 2007

Routledge is an imprint of the Taylor & Francis Group, an informa business

© 1996, 2006 Gunther Kress and Theo van Leeuwen

Typeset in Bell Gothic by RefineCatch Ltd, Bungay, Suffolk
Printed and bound in Great Britain by
TJ International Ltd, Padstow, Cornwall

British Library Cataloguing in Publication Data
A catalogue record for this book is available from the British Library

Library of Congress Cataloging in Publication Data
Kress, Gunther R.
   Reading images : the grammar of visual design / Gunther Kress and Theo
van Leeuwen. – 2nd ed.
        p. cm.
     Includes bibliographical references and index.
    1. Communication in design.   I. Van Leeuwen, Theo, 1947–   II. Title.
NK1510.K64 2006
701–dc22   2006002242

ISBN10: 0–415–31914–5 (hbk)
ISBN10: 0–415–31915–3 (pbk)
ISBN10: 0–203–61972–2 (ebk)

ISBN13: 9–78–0–415–31914–0 (hbk)
ISBN13: 9–78–0–415–31915–7 (pbk)
ISBN13: 9–78–0–203–61972–8 (ebk)

CONTENTS

Preface to the second edition

The first edition of *Reading Images* has had a positive reception among a wide group from the professions and disciplines which have to deal with real problems and real issues involving images. This has gone along with a broader agenda of concern with 'multi-modality', a rapidly growing realization that representation is always multiple. We do not think for a moment that this book represents anything like a settled approach, a definitive 'grammar' of images, and at times we have been worried by attempts to treat it in that way. We see it as an early attempt, one among many others, and we would like to see it treated very much as a resource for beginning to make inroads into understanding the visual as representation and communication – in a semiotic fashion – and also as a resource in the development of theories and 'grammars' of visual communication. In that spirit we want to stress that we see everything we have written here simultaneously as our fully serious and yet entirely provisional sense of this field.

When we completed the first edition of this book we were aware of a number of 'omissions' – things we felt still needed doing. Some of these we have taken up in other ways, for instance in our attempt to develop a theory of multimodality; others we have tried to address in this second edition. Foremost among these have been the quite different issues of the moving image and of colour. The first of these has been constantly raised by those who have used the book, and rightly so. We hope that what we have said here can begin to integrate the field of moving images into our social semiotic approach to visual communication. The issue of colour was less frequently raised, yet constituted for us a kind of theoretical test case, as much to do with the issue of colour itself as to do with a theory of multimodal social semiotics much more widely considered. Here, too, we feel that we have provided just a first attempt for a different approach. In addition we have added a number of new examples from CD-ROMs and websites, domains of visual communication that had hardly begun to develop when we wrote the first edition, and are now of central importance for many users of this book.

One persistent criticism of the first edition from a group of readers has been that the book was (too) linguistic. The first comment we would make is to say that for us 'formality' in the domain of representation is not in any way the same as 'being linguistic'. So to some extent we think that that criticism rests on that kind of misunderstanding. We also think that there is a difference between explicitness and formality. We certainly have aimed for the former, and often (but not always) for the latter. Nor do we think that either explicitness or formality are the enemies of innovation, creativity, imagination: often all these latter rest on the former. It is the case that our starting point has been the systemic functional grammar of English developed by Michael Halliday, though we had and have attempted to use its general semiotic aspects rather than its specific linguistically focused features as the grounding for our grammar. As Ferdinand de Saussure had done at the beginning of the last century, we see linguistics as a part of semiotics; but we do not see linguistics as the discipline that can furnish a ready-made model for the description of semiotic modes other than language. Then we had thought, in our first attempt, that to show how visual communication works in comparison to language might be helpful in understanding either and both – but that, too, was misunderstood maybe as an attempt to impose linguistic categories on the visual. We have therefore tried to refine and clarify those sections of the book that deal with the relation between language and visual communication, and to delete or reformulate material which we think might have given rise to these misunderstandings, hopefully with no loss of clarity. A careful reading of this second edition of our book will show, we trust, that we are as concerned to bring out the differences between language and visual communication as we are the connections, the broader semiotic principles that connect, not just language and image, but all the multiple modes in multimodal communication.

In our growing understanding of this domain, reflected in the reworking of this book, we owe a debt of gratitude for support, comment and critique to many more people than we can mention or even than we actually know. But the names of some friends, colleagues, students, fellow researchers and critics who were not already acknowledged in our preface to the first edition have to be mentioned. Among these are Carey Jewitt, Jim Gee, Ron Scollon, Paul Mercer, Brian Street, Radan Martinec, Adam Jaworski, David Machin, Klas Prytz, Teal Triggs, Andrew Burn, Bob Ferguson, Pippa Stein, Denise Newfield, Len Unsworth, Lesley Lancaster and the many researchers whose work has both given us confidence and new ideas, and extended our understanding of this field – and of course, and crucially, we acknowledge the support from our publishers and editors at Routledge, Louisa Semlyen and Christabel Kirkpatrick.

Preface to the first edition

This book grew out of discussions about visual communication which spanned a period of seven years. Both of us had worked on the analysis of verbal texts, and increasingly felt the need of a better understanding of all the things that go with the verbal: facial expressions, gestures, images, music, and so on. This was not only because we wanted to analyse the whole of the texts in which these semiotic modes play a vital role rather than just the verbal part, but also to understand language better. Just as a knowledge of other languages can open new perspectives on one's own language, so a knowledge of other semiotic modes can open new perspectives on language.

In 1990 we published a first version of our ideas on visual communication, *Reading Images*, with Deakin University Press. It was written for teachers, and we concentrated on children's drawings and school textbook illustrations, although we also included examples from the mass media, such as advertisements and magazine layout. Since then we have expanded our research to other fields of visual communication: a much wider range of mass media materials; scientific (and other) diagrams, maps and charts; and the visual arts. We have also made a beginning with the study of three-dimensional communication: sculpture, children's toys, architecture and everyday designed objects. The present book therefore offers a much more comprehensive theory of visual communication than the earlier book.

In Australia, and increasingly elsewhere, our work has been used in courses on communication and media studies, and as a methodology for research in areas such as media representation, film studies, children's literature and the use of illustrations and layout in school textbooks. The present book has benefited greatly from the suggestions and comments of those who have used our work in these ways, and of our own undergraduate and postgraduate students, initially at the University of Technology and Macquarie University in Sydney, later at the Institute of Education and the London College of Printing in London, and also at the Temasek Polytechnic in Singapore.

We began our work on visual communication in the supportive and stimulating environment of the Newtown Semiotics Circle in Sydney; discussions with our friends, the members of this Circle, helped shape our ideas in more ways than we can acknowledge. If any two people from that first period were to be singled out, it would be Jim Martin, who gave us meticulous, detailed, extensive and challenging comments on several of the chapters of the earlier book, and Fran Christie, who had urged us to write it. But here we would also like to make a special mention of Bob Hodge, whose ideas appear in this book in many ways, even if not always obviously so.

Of those who used our book in teaching and research, and whose comments on the earlier book have helped us rethink and refine our ideas, we would like to mention the research team of the Disadvantaged Schools Programme in Sydney, in particular Rick Iedema, Susan Feez, Peter White, Robert Veel and Sally Humphrey; Staffan Selander, through whose Centre for Textbook Research in Härnösand our work came to be taken up by researchers in the field of textbook research in Sweden and several other European countries; the members of the 'Language and Science' research team at the Institute of Education, Isabel Martins, Jon Ogborn and Kieran McGillicuddy; Philip Bell; Basil Bernstein; Paul Gillen and Teun van Dijk.

Three writers influenced our ideas in different and fundamental ways. One is Roland Barthes. Although we see our work as going beyond his seminal writing on visual semiotics in several ways, he remains a strong inspiration. There is not a subject in semiotics on which Barthes has not written originally and inspiringly. He has provided for us a model of what semiotics can be, in the range of his interests, in the depth of his work, and in his engagement with the social and cultural world. Equally significant for us is Michael Halliday. His view of language as a social semiotic, and the wider implications of his theories, gave us the means to go beyond the structuralist approach of 1960s Paris School semiotics, and our work is everywhere influenced by his ideas. Then there is Rudolf Arnheim. The more we read his work, the more we realize that most of what we have to say has already been said by him, often better than we have done it, albeit it usually in commentaries on individual works of art rather than in the form of a more general theory. He is commonly associated with Gestalt psychology: we would like to claim him as a great social semiotician.

We would like to than our editor, Julia Hall, for her encouragement and invaluable help in producing this book. Jill Brewster and Laura Lopez-Bonilla were involved in various stages of the book; their encouragement and help made the work possible and enjoyable.

Acknowledgements

Plate 3 *Joshua Smith* by William Dobell, 1943, © DACS 2004.

Plate 5 *Cossacks* by Vassily Kandinsky, 1910–1911. © ADAGP, Paris and DACS, London 2004. Photography © Tate, London 2005.

Plate 6 Historic Colours by Colin Poole, reproduced by kind permission of PhotoWord Syndication Ltd.

Plate 7 Palgrave colour scheme reproduced with permission of Palgrave Macmillan.

1.1+1.13 'My bath' from *Baby's First Book* by B. Lewis, illustrated by H. Wooley, copyright © Ladybird Books Ltd., 1950.

1.2 Bird in tree from *On My Walk,* by Dick Bruna, 1988. Illustration Dick Bruna © Mercis bv, 1972.

1.4 Magazine cover with naturalistic photograph, cover of *Newsweek*, April 9, 2004 © 2004 Newsweek, Inc. Photograph by Karim Sahib-AFP-Getty Images. Reprinted by permission.

1.5 Magazine cover with conceptual photograph, cover of *Newsweek,* November 12, 2001 © 2001 Newsweek, Inc. Reprinted by permission.

1.6 Image from 'Interactive Physics'. Courtesy of MSC Software.

2.5 Communication model from Watson, J. and Hill, A. (1980) *A Dictionary of Communication and Media Studies*, London, Arnold, p. 143. Reproduced by permission of Hodder Headline PLC.

2.6 Two Communication Models from Watson, J. and Hill, A. (1980) *A Dictionary of Communication and Media Studies*, London, Arnold p. 147. Reproduced by permission of Hodder Headline PLC.

2.10 *Beat the Whites with the Red Wedge* by El Lissitzky, 1919–20. © DACS 2004.

2.11 Kasimir Malevich (1878–1935) "Suprematist Composition: Red Square and Black Square", 1914, New York, Museum of Modern Art (MoMA) © 2004, Digital image, The Museum of Modern Art, New York/Scala, Florence.

2.17 Gulf War Diagram, *Sydney Morning Herald*, 14 February, 1991 reproduced by permission of *Sydney Morning Herald*.

2.18 Speech circuit from *Saussure's Course in General Linguistics*, 1974, F. de Saussure, translated by Roy Harris by permission of Gerald Duckworth & Co.

2.20 Vittel advertisements reproduced by kind permission of Nestlé Group.

2.22 Communication Model from Watson, J. and Hill, A. (1980) *A Dictionary of Communication and Media Studies*, London, Arnold p. 147. Reproduced by permission of Hodder Headline PLC.

2.23 Arctic tundra system, fig. 7.5, p.172 from Sale, C., Friedman, B. and Wilson, G. *Our Changing World*, Book 1, Pearson Education Australia. Reproduced by permission of the publisher.

2.24 Communication Model from Watson, J. and Hill, A. (1980) *A Dictionary of Communication and Media Studies*, London, Arnold p. 54. Reproduced by permission of Hodder Headline PLC.

3.1 Guide interface from 'Dangerous Creatures', 1994. Screenshot reprinted by permission from Microsoft Corporation.

3.2 Sekonda advertisement reproduced by kind permission of Sekonda/Time Products.

3.3 Sources of signs from Eco, U. (1976) *A theory of semiotics,* Bloomington, Indiana University Press, p.177. Reproduced by permission of the publisher.

3.5 Semantic field diagram from Eco, U. (1976) *A theory of semiotics*, Bloomington, Indiana University Press, p.78. Reproduced by permission of the publisher.

3.7 Network from Sharples, M. and Pemberton, 'Representing writing: external representations and the writing process' in N. Williams and P. Holt, eds *Computers and Writing*. Reproduced by kind permission of Intellect Ltd, www.intellectbooks.com

3.13 Resort wear, *Australian Women's Weekly*, December 1987. © Australian Women's Weekly/ACP Syndication. Reproduced with permission.

3.19 Electrical circuit diagram from J. Hill, 1980, *Introductory Physics*. Reproduced by permission of Taylor & Francis Group.

3.20 The place of linguistics on the map of knowledge from Halliday, M.A.K. (1978) *Language as Social Semiotic*, London, Arnold. Reproduced by permission of Hodder Headline PLC.

3.21 'Women at work', Fig. III–6, p. 29, from *Pictographs and Graphs: How to Make and Use Them* by Rudolf Modley and Dyno Lowenstein. © 1952 by Harper & Brothers. Copyright renewed 1980 by Peter M. Modley and Marion E. Schilling. Reprinted by permission of HarperCollins Publishers Inc.

3.28 'Fun with fungi', *Sydney Morning Herald*, 18 June 1992, reproduced by permission of *Sydney Morning Herald*.

4.2 ATM screen reproduced by kind permission of National Australia Bank.

4.4 The murder of Dr Chang, *Sydney Morning Herald*, 5 July 1991, reproduced by permission of *Sydney Morning Herald*.

4.5 Playstation website reproduced by kind permission of Sony Computer Entertainment Europe Ltd.

4.7 New look Ford Mondeo from www.ford.co.uk reproduced by kind permission of Ford.

4.8 Fiesta 'Rock solid' website reproduced by kind permission of Ogilvy Group Holdings Ltd and Ford.

4.16 'Prison Guard' by Danny Lyon, 1969, from *Conversations with the dead.* © Danny Lyon.Magnum Photos. Reproduced with permission.

4.19 Gulf war map, *Sydney Morning Herald,* 22 January 1991, reproduced by permission of *Sydney Morning Herald.*

4.20 An increase in tourism, *Sydney Morning Herald,* 22 January 1991, reproduced by permission of *Sydney Morning Herald.*

4.22 Detail from a fourteenth-century Spanish nativity, from Rudolf Arnheim, *Art and Visual Perception: A Psychology of the Creative Eye. The New Version.* © 1974 The Regents of the University of California. Reproduced by permission of University of California Press.

5.1 Speech circuit from *Saussure's Course in General Linguistics,* 1974, F. de Saussure, translated by Roy Harris by permission of Gerald Duckworth & Co.

5.2 Schematized speech circuit from *Saussure's Course in General Linguistics,* 1974, F. de Saussure, translated by Roy Harris by permission of Gerald Duckworth & Co.

5.6 *Card-players* (Van Doesburg, 1916–17) photograph/picture: Tim Koster, ICN, Rijswijk/Amsterdam. Reproduced with permission of Institut Collectie Nederland.

5.7 *Composition 9* (Van Doesburg, 1917). Collection of the Gemeentemuseum Den Haag. Reproduced with permission.

5.8 Colour Project for the Schröder Residence (Gerrit Rietveld, 1923–4) © DACS 2005.

5.9 Photograph of the Schröder Residence, Gerrit Rietveld, © DACS 2004.

5.11 © Oxford University Press from *The Young Geographer Investigates: Mountains* by Terry Jennings (OUP, 1986), reprinted by permission of Oxford University Press.

5.12 Drawing by Newton. By permission of the Warden and Fellows, New College, Oxford, and The Bodleian Library, University of Oxford. MS 361, vol. 2, fol. 45V.

5.13 Drawing of Stretton's experiment, figure 8.1 (p.141) from *The Eye and Brain: Psychology of Seeing 5/e* by Richard Gregory, 1998, reproduced by permission of Oxford University Press. Gregory, Richard, *Eye and Brain.* Reprinted by permission of Princeton University Press.

6.2 Gold-diggers, *Australian Women's Weekly,* November 1987. © Australian Women's Weekly/ACP Syndication. Reproduced with permission.

6.3 Sony Middle East website reproduced by kind permission of Sony Gulf FZE.

6.9 Gerbner's communication model from Watson, J. and Hill, A. (1980) *A Dictionary of Communication and Media Studies*, London, Arnold. Reproduced by permission of Hodder Headline PLC.

6.10 Royal couple. H.M. The Queen's wedding, photograph by Baron, Camera Press, London. H.M. The Queen and Prince Philip, photograph by H.R.H. Prince Andrew, Camera Press, London. Reproduced with permission.

6.12 Buddhist painting from Rudolf Arnheim, *Art and Visual Perception: A Psychology of the Creative Eye. The New Version.* © 1974 The Regents of the University of California. Reproduced by permission of University of California Press.

6.13 'Going on holiday' from Prosser, R. (2000) *Leisure, Recreation and Tourism,* London, Collins Educational. Reprinted by permission of HarperCollins Publishers Ltd © R. Prosser, 2000.

6.14 Andersch et al.'s communication model from Watson, J. and Hill, A. (1980) *A Dictionary of Communication and Media Studies*, London, Arnold. Reproduced by permission of Hodder Headline PLC.

6.16 Vertical triptych from the website of Oxford University reproduced by kind permission of Oxford University.

6.23 Screenshot from CD-ROM '3D Body Adventure', Knowledge Adventure, 1993 provided courtesy of Knowledge Adventure, Inc.

7.1 Roy Lichtenstein, *Big Painting, 1965.* © The Estate of Roy Lichtenstein/DACS 2004.

8.1 *Jacob and the Angel* (Jacob Epstein, 1940) © The Estate of Jacob Epstein/Tate, London 2005. Image supplied by and reproduced by permission of Granada TV.

8.2 *People in the Wind* (Kenneth Armitage, 1952). Reproduction courtesy of Kenneth Armitage Estate. Photography © Tate, London 2005.

8.5 *Woman* by Joan Miró, 1970 © Successio Miro, DACS 2004.

8.6 Les Heures des Traces (*Hour of the Traces*) by Alberto Giacometti, 1930 © ADAGP, Paris and DACS, London 2004. Photography © Tate, London 2005.

8.7 *Jacob and the Angel* (Jacob Epstein, 1940) © The Estate of Jacob Epstein/Tate, London 2005. Image supplied by and reproduced by permission of Granada TV.

8.8 Playmobil 'family set' and 'ethnic family' from Playmobil catalogue. Reproduced by kind permission of Playmobil UK Ltd.

8.9 *Recumbent Figure* by Henry Moore, 1938. Illustrated on p. 250; has been reproduced by permission of the Henry Moore Foundation. Photography © Tate, London 2005.

8.10 *King and Queen* by Henry Moore, 1952–3. Illustrated on p. 253; has been reproduced by permission of the Henry Moore Foundation. Photography © Tate, London 2005.

8.11 Church of Santa Maria Della Spina from Rudolf Arnheim, *Art and Visual Perception: A Psychology of the Creative Eye. The New Version.* © 1974 The Regents of the University of California. Reproduced by permission of University of California Press.

8.12 Connected and disconnected narrative process, pp. 83–84 from S. Goodman and D. Graddol, *Redesigning English – new texts, new identities*, London, Routledge, 1997. Reproduced by permission of the publisher.

8.13 Overshoulder shot in computer game, *Delta Force*. Image courtesy of NovaLogic Inc. © 2004. All rights reserved.

8.14 Dynamic interpersonal relations in the opening scene of *The Big Sleep* (Howard Hawks, 1947), pp. 91–92 from S. Goodman and D. Graddol, *Redesigning English – new texts, new identities*, London, Routledge, 1997. Reproduced by permission of the publisher.

Introduction: the grammar of visual design

The subtitle of this book is 'the grammar of visual design'. We hesitated over this title. Extensions of the term 'grammar' often suggest 'rules'. In books with titles like *The Grammar of Television Production* one learns, for instance, about the rules of continuity; knowing these rules is then what sets the 'professional' apart from the 'amateur'. What we wish to express is a little different. In our view, most accounts of visual semiotics have concentrated on what might be regarded as the equivalent of 'words' – what linguists call 'lexis' – rather than 'grammar', and then on the 'denotative' and 'connotative', the 'icono-graphical' and 'iconological' significance of the elements in images, the individual people, places and things (including abstract 'things') depicted there. In this book, by contrast, we will concentrate on 'grammar' and on syntax, on the way in which these elements are combined into meaningful wholes. Just as grammars of language describe how words combine in clauses, sentences and texts, so our visual 'grammar' will describe the way in which depicted elements – people, places and things – combine in visual 'statements' of greater or lesser complexity and extension.

We are by no means the first to deal with this subject. Nevertheless, by comparison to the study of visual 'lexis', the study of visual 'grammar' has been relatively neglected, or dealt with from a different perspective, from the point of view of art history, or of the formal, aesthetic description of composition, or the psychology of perception, or with a focus on more pragmatic matters, for instance the way composition can be used to attract the viewer's attention to one thing rather than another, e.g. in such applied environments as advertising or packaging. All these are valid approaches, and in many places and many ways we have made use of the insights of people writing from these different perspectives. Yet the result has been that, despite the very large amount of work done on images, not much attention has been paid to the meanings of regularities in the way image elements are used – in short, to their grammar – at least not in explicit or systematic ways. It is this focus on meaning that we seek, above all, to describe and capture in our book. We intend to provide usable descriptions of major compositional structures which have become estab-lished as conventions in the course of the history of Western visual semiotics, and to analyse how they are used to produce meaning by contemporary image-makers.

What we have said about visual 'grammar' is true also of the mainstream of linguistic grammar: grammar has been, and remains, 'formal'. It has generally been studied in isolation from meaning. However, the linguists and the school of linguistic thought from which we draw part of our inspiration – linguists following the work of Michael Halliday – have taken issue with this view, and see grammatical forms as resources for encoding interpretations of experience and forms of social (inter)action. Benjamin Lee Whorf argued the point in relation to languages from different cultures. In what he called 'Stand-ard Average European' languages, terms like 'summer', 'winter', 'September', 'morning', 'noon', 'sunset' are coded as nouns, as though they were things. Hence these languages make it possible to interpret time as something you can count, use, save, etc. In Hopi, a North American Indian language, this is not possible. Time can only be expressed as 'subjective duration-feeling'. You cannot say 'at noon', or 'three summers'. You have to say something like 'while the summer phase is occurring' (Whorf, 1956).

The critical linguists of the East Anglia School, with whom one of us was connected, have shown that such different interpretations of experience can also be encoded using the resources of the same language, on the basis of different ideological positions. Tony Trew (1979: 106–7) has described how, when the Harare police – in what was in 1975 still Rhodesia – fired into a crowd of unarmed people and shot thirteen of them, the *Rhodesia Herald* wrote, 'A political clash has led to death and injury', while the *Tanzanian Daily News* wrote, 'Rhodesia's white suprematist police ... opened fire and killed thirteen unarmed Africans.' In other words, the political views of newspapers are not only encoded through different vocabularies (of the well-known 'terrorist' vs 'freedom fighter' type), but also through different grammatical structures; that is, through the choice between coding an event as a noun ('death', 'injury') or a verb ('kill'), which for its grammatical completion requires an active subject ('police') and an object ('unarmed Africans').

> Grammar goes beyond formal rules of correctness. It is a means of representing patterns of experience. . . . It enables human beings to build a mental picture of reality, to make sense of their experience of what goes on around them and inside them.
>
> (Halliday, 1985: 101)

The same is true for the 'grammar of visual design'. Like linguistic structures, visual structures point to particular interpretations of experience and forms of social interaction. To some degree these can also be expressed linguistically. Meanings belong to culture, rather than to specific semiotic modes. And the way meanings are mapped across different semiotic modes, the way some things can, for instance, be 'said' either visually or verbally, others only visually, again others only verbally, is also culturally and historically specific. In the course of this book we will constantly elaborate and exemplify this point. But even when we can express what seem to be the same meanings in either image-form or writing or speech, they will be *realized* differently. For instance, what is expressed in language through the choice between different word classes and clause structures, may, in visual communication, be expressed through the choice between different uses of colour or different compositional structures. And this will affect meaning. Expressing something verbally or visually makes a difference.

As for other resonances of the term 'grammar' ('grammar' as a set of rules one has to obey if one is to speak or write in 'correct', socially acceptable ways), linguists often protest that they are merely describing what people do, and that others insist on turning descriptions into rules. But of course to describe is to be involved in producing knowledge which others will transform from the descriptive into the normative, for instance in education. When a semiotic mode plays a dominant role in public communication, its use will inevitably be constrained by rules, rules enforced through education, for instance, and through all kinds of written and unwritten social sanctions. Only a small elite of experimenters is allowed to break the rules – after all, breaking rules remains necessary to keep open the possibility of change. We believe that visual communication is coming to be less and less the domain of specialists, and more and more crucial in the domains of public communication. Inevitably this will lead to new, and more rules, and to more formal, normative teaching. Not being 'visually literate' will begin to attract social sanctions. 'Visual literacy' will begin to be a matter of survival, especially in the workplace.

We are well aware that work such as ours can or will help pave the way for developments of this kind. This can be seen negatively, as constraining the relative freedom which visual communication has so far enjoyed, albeit at the expense of a certain marginalization by comparison to writing; or positively, as allowing more people greater access to a wider range of visual skills. Nor does it have to stand in the way of creativity. Teaching the rules of writing has not meant the end of creative uses of language in literature and elsewhere, and teaching visual skills will not spell the end of the arts. Yet, just as the grammar creatively employed by poets and novelists is, in the end, the same grammar we use when writing letters, memos and reports, so the 'grammar of visual design' creatively employed by artists is, in the end, the same grammar we need when producing attractive layouts, images and diagrams for our course handouts, reports, brochures, communiqués, and so on.

It is worth asking here what a linguistic grammar is a grammar *of*. The conventional answer is to say that it is a grammar of 'English' or 'Dutch' or 'French' – the rules that define English as 'English', Dutch as 'Dutch', and so on. A slightly less conventional answer would be to say that a grammar is an inventory of elements and rules underlying culture-specific forms of *verbal* communication. 'Underlying' here is a shorthand term for something more diffuse and complex, more like 'knowledge shared more or less by members of a group, explicitly and implicitly'. This brings in subtle matters of what knowledge is and how it is held and expressed, and above all the social question of what a 'group' is. That makes definitions of grammar very much a social question, one of the knowledges and practices shared by groups of people.

We might now ask, 'What is our "visual grammar" a grammar *of*?' First of all we would say that it describes a social resource of a particular group, its explicit and implicit knowledge about this resource, and its uses in the practices of that group. Then, second, we would say that it is a quite general grammar, because we need a term that can encompass oil painting as well as magazine layout, the comic strip as well as the scientific diagram. Drawing these two points together, and bearing in mind our social definition of grammar, we would say that 'our' grammar is a quite general grammar of contemporary visual design in 'Western' cultures, an account of the explicit and implicit knowledge and practices around a resource, consisting of the elements and rules underlying a culture-specific form of visual communication. We have quite deliberately made our definition a social one, beginning with the question 'What is the group? What are its practices?' and from there attempting to describe the grammar at issue, rather than adopting an approach which says, 'Here is our grammar; do the practices and knowledges of this group conform to it or not?'

In the book we have, by and large, confined our examples to visual text-objects from 'Western' cultures and assumed that this generalization has some validity as it points to a communicational situation with a long history that has evolved over the past five centuries or so, alongside writing (quite despite the differences between European languages), as a 'language of visual design'. Its boundaries are not those of nation-states, although there are, and very much so, cultural/regional variations. Rather, this visual resource has spread, always interacting with the specificities of locality, wherever global Western culture is the dominant culture.

This means, first of all, that it is not a 'universal' grammar. Visual language is not – despite assumptions to the contrary – transparent and universally understood; it is culturally specific. We hope our work will continue to provide some ideas and concepts for the study of visual communication in non-Western forms of visual communication. To give the most obvious example, Western visual communication is deeply affected by our convention of writing from left to right (in chapter 6 we will discuss this more fully). The writing directions of cultures vary: from right to left or from left to right, from top to bottom or in circular fashion from the centre to the outside. Consequently different values and meanings are attached to such key dimensions of visual space. These valuations and meanings exert their influence beyond writing, and inform the meanings accorded to different compositional patterns, the amount of use made of them, and so on. In other words, we assume that the elements, such as 'centre' or 'margin', 'top' or 'bottom', will play a role in the visual semiotics of any culture, but with meanings and values that are likely to differ depending on that culture's histories of use of visual space, writing included. The 'universal' aspect of meaning lies in semiotic principles and processes, the culture-specific aspect lies in their application over history, and in specific instances of use. Here we merely want to signal that our investigations have been restricted, by and large, to Western visual communication. Even though others have begun to extend the applications of the principles of this grammar, we make no *specific* claims for the application of our ideas to other cultures. Within Western visual design, however, we believe that our theory applies to all forms of visual communication. We hope that the wide range of examples we use in the book will convince readers of this proposition.

Our stress on the unity of Western visual communication does not exclude the possibility of regional and social variation. The unity of Western design is not some intrinsic feature of visuality, but derives from a long history of cultural connection and interchange, as well as now from the global power of the Western mass media and culture industries and their technologies. In many parts of the world, Western visual communication exists side by side with local forms. Western forms might be used, for instance, in certain domains of public communication, such as public notices, sites of public transport, the press, advertising, and the visual arts, as well as in somewhat more 'private' domains, in the home, and in markets and shops, for instance. Often the relation is hierarchical, with one form overlaid on another (see Scollon and Scollon, 2003; Kress, 2003), and often – as in advertising, for instance – the two are mutually transformed and fused. Where Western visual communication begins to exert pressure on local forms, there are transitional stages in which the forms of the two cultures mix in particular ways. In looking at advertisements in English-language magazines from the Philippines, for instance, we were struck by the way in which entirely conventional Western iconographical elements were integrated into designs following the rules of a local visual semiotic. In advertisements on the MTR in Hong Kong, some advert-isements conform to the 'Eastern' directionality, others to the Western, yet others mix the two. As with the Filipino advertisements, discourses and iconography can be 'Western', mixed in various ways with those of the 'East', while colour schemes can, at the same time, be distinctly non-Western. The situation there is in any case complicated (as it is, differ-ently, in Japan) by the fact that directionality in the writing system has become compli-cated in several ways: by the adoption, in certain contexts, of 'Western' directionality and the Roman alphabet alongside the continued use of the more traditional directionalities and forms of writing. And as economic (and now often cultural) power is re-weighted, the trend can go in both or more directions: the influence of Asian forms of visual design is becoming more and more present in the 'West'. Superimposed on all this are the increas-ingly prominent diasporic communities – of Greeks, Lebanese, Turks, of many groups of the Indian subcontinent, of new and older Chinese communities (for instance, Hong Kong Chinese around the Pacific Rim) – which seemingly affect only the members of this diaspora, and yet in reality are having deep influences well beyond them.

Within Europe, increasing regionality counterbalances increasing globalization. So long as the European nations and regions still retain different ways of life and a different ethos, they will use the 'grammar of visual design' distinctly. It is easy, for example, to find examples of the contrasting use of the left and right in the composition of pages and images in the British media. It is harder to find such examples in, for instance, the Greek or the Spanish or the Italian media, as students from these countries have assured us and demonstrated in their work – after trying to do the assignments we had set them at home during their holidays. In the course of our book we will give some examples of this, for instance in connection with newspaper layout in different European countries. However, we are not able to do more than touch on the subject; and the issue of different 'dialects' and 'inflections' needs to be explored more fully in the future.

In any case, the unity of languages is a social construct, a product of theory and of social and cultural histories. When the borders of (a) language are not policed by acad-emies, and when languages are not homogenized by education systems and mass media, people quite freely combine elements from the languages they know to make themselves understood. Mixed languages ('pidgins') develop in this way, and in time can become the language of new generations ('creoles'). Visual communication, not subject to such policing, has developed more freely than language, but there has nevertheless been a dominant language, 'spoken' and developed in centres of high culture, alongside less highly valued regional and social variants (e.g. 'folk art'). The dominant visual language is now controlled by the global cultural/technological empires of the mass media, which dissemin-ate the examples set by exemplary designers and, through the spread of image banks and computer-imaging technology, exert a 'normalizing' rather than explicitly 'normative' influence on visual communication across the world. Much as it is the primary aim of this book to describe the current state of the 'grammar of visual design', we will also discuss the broad historical, social and cultural conditions that make and remake the visual 'language'.

A SOCIAL SEMIOTIC THEORY OF REPRESENTATION

Our work on visual representation is set within the theoretical framework of 'social semiotics'. It is important therefore to place it in the context of the way 'semiotics' has developed during, roughly, the past 75 years. In Europe, three schools of semiotics applied ideas from the domain of linguistics to non-linguistic modes of communication. The first was the Prague School of the 1930s and early 1940s. It developed the work of Russian Formalists by providing it with a linguistic basis. Notions such as 'foregrounding' were applied to language (e.g. the 'foregrounding', for artistic purposes, of phonological or syntactic forms through 'deviation' from standard forms, for artistic purposes) as well as to the study of art (Mukarovsky), theatre (Honzl), cinema (Jakobson) and costume (Bogatyrev). Each of these semiotic systems could fulfil the same communicative functions (the 'referential' and the 'poetic' functions). The second was the Paris School of the 1960s and 1970s, which applied ideas from de Saussure and other linguists to painting (Schefer), photography (Barthes, Lindekens), fashion (Barthes), cinema (Metz), music (Nattiez), comic strips (Fresnault-Deruelle), etc. The ideas developed by this School are still taught in countless courses of media studies, art and design, etc., often under the heading 'semiology', despite the fact that they are at the same time regarded as having been overtaken by post-structuralism. Everywhere students are learning about 'langue' and 'parole'; the 'signifier' and the 'signified'; 'arbitrary' and 'motivated' signs; 'icons', 'indexes' and 'symbols' (these terms come from the work of the American philosopher and semiotician Charles Sanders Peirce, but are often incorporated in the framework of 'semiology'), and so on. Generally this happens without students being given a sense of, or access to, alternative theories of semiotics (or of linguistics). We will compare and contrast this kind of semiotics with our own approach, in this introduction as well as elsewhere in the book. This third, still fledgling, movement in which insights from linguistics have been applied to other modes of representation has two sources, both drawing on the ideas of Michael Halliday, one growing out of the 'Critical Linguistics' of a group of people working in the 1970s at the University of East Anglia, leading to the outline of a theory that might encompass other semiotic modes (Hodge and Kress), the other, in the later 1980s, as a development of Hallidayan systemic-functional linguistics by a number of scholars in Australia, in semiotically oriented studies of literature (Threadgold, Thibault), visual semiotics (O'Toole, ourselves) and music (van Leeuwen).

The key notion in any semiotics is the 'sign'. Our book is about signs – or, as we would rather put it, about sign-making. We will be discussing forms ('signifiers') such as colour, perspective and line, as well as the way in which these forms are used to realize meanings ('signifieds') in the making of signs. But our conception of the sign differs somewhat from that of 'semiology', and we wish therefore to compare the two views explicitly. In doing so we use the term 'semiology' to refer to the way in which the Paris School semiotics is generally taught in the Anglo-Saxon world, through the mediation of influential textbooks such as the series of media studies textbooks edited by John Fiske (Fiske and Hartley, 1979; Dyer, 1982; Fiske, 1982; Hartley, 1982; O'Sullivan *et al.*, 1983). In doing this we do not seek to repudiate those who went before us. We see a continuity between their work and ours, as should be clear from our main title, *Reading Images,* which echoes that of the first volume in Fiske's series, *Reading Television* (Fiske and Hartley, 1979).

We would like to begin with an example of what we understand by 'sign-making'. The drawing in figure 0.1 was made by a three-year-old boy. Sitting on his father's lap, he talked about the drawing as he was doing it: 'Do you want to watch me? I'll make a car . . . got two wheels . . . and two wheels at the back . . . and two wheels here . . . that's a funny wheel. . . .' When he had finished, he said, 'This is a car.' This was the first time he had named a drawing, and at first the name was puzzling. How was this a car? Of course he had provided the key himself: 'Here's a wheel.' A car, for him, was defined by the criterial characteristic of 'having wheels', and his representation focused on this aspect. What he represented was, in fact, 'wheelness'. Wheels are a plausible criterion to choose for three-year-olds, and the wheel's action, on toy cars as on real cars, is a readily noticed and describable feature. In other words, this three-year-old's interest in cars was, for him, most plausibly condensed into and expressed as an interest in wheels. Wheels, in turn, are most plausibly represented by circles, both because of their visual appearance and because of the circular motion of the hand in drawing/representing the wheel's action of 'going round and round'.

To gather this up for a moment, we see representation as a process in which the makers of signs, whether child or adult, seek to make a representation of some object or entity, whether physical or semiotic, and in which their interest in the object, at the point of making the representation, is a complex one, arising out of the cultural, social and psycho-logical history of the sign-maker, and focused by the specific context in which the sign-maker produces the sign. That 'interest' is the source of the selection of what is seen as the criterial aspect of the object, and this criterial aspect is then regarded as adequately representative of the object in a given context. In other words, it is never the 'whole object' but only ever its criterial aspects which are represented.

These criterial aspects are represented in what seems to the sign-maker, at the moment of sign-making, the most apt and plausible fashion, and the most apt and plausible repre-sentational mode (e.g. drawing, Lego blocks, painting, speech). Sign-makers thus 'have' a

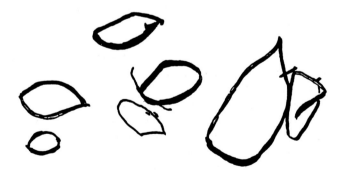

⬤ **Fig 0.1 Drawing by a three-year-old child**

meaning, the signified, which they wish to express, and then express it through the semiotic mode(s) that make(s) available the subjectively felt, most plausible, most apt form, as the signifier. This means that in social semiotics the sign is not the pre-existing conjunction of a signifier and a signified, a ready-made sign to be recognized, chosen and used as it is, in the way that signs are usually thought to be 'available for use' in 'semiology'. Rather we focus on the process of sign-making, in which the signifier (the form) and the signified (the meaning) are relatively independent of each other until they are brought together by the sign-maker in a newly made sign. To put it in a different way, using the example just above, the process of sign-making is the process of the constitution of a sign/metaphor in two steps: 'a car is (most like) wheels' and 'wheels are (most like) circles'.

Putting it in our terms: the sign-maker's interest at this moment of sign-making has settled on 'wheelness' as the criterial feature of 'car'. He constructs, by a process of analogy, two metaphors/signs: first, the signified 'wheel' is aptly represented by the signifier 'circle' to make the motivated sign 'wheel'; second, the signified 'car' is aptly represented by the signifier 'many wheels' to make the motivated sign 'car'. The resulting sign, the drawing glossed 'this is a car', is thus a motivated sign in that each conjunction of signifier and signified is an apt, motivated conjunction of the form which best represents that which is to be meant. This sign is thus the result of a double metaphoric process in which analogy is the constitutive principle. Analogy, in turn, is a process of classification: x is like y (in criterial ways). Which metaphors (and, 'behind' the metaphors, which classifications) carry the day and pass into the semiotic system as conventional, and then as naturalized, and then as 'natural', neutral classifications, is governed by social relations of power. Like adults, children are engaged in the construction of metaphors. Unlike adults, they are, on the one hand, less constricted by culture and its already-existing and usually invisible metaphors, but, on the other hand, usually in a position of less power, so that their metaphors are less likely to carry the day.

It follows that we see signs as motivated – not as arbitrary – conjunctions of signifiers (forms) and signifieds (meanings). In 'semiology' motivation is usually not related to the act of sign-making as it is in our approach, but defined in terms of an intrinsic relation between the signifier and the signified. It is here that Peirce's 'icon', 'index' and 'symbol' make their appearance, incorporated into 'semiology' in a way which in fact contradicts some of the key ideas in Peirce's semiotics. The 'icon' is the sign in which 'the signifier–signified relationship is one of resemblance, likeness' (Dyer, 1982: 124) – i.e. objective likeness, rather than analogy motivated by 'interest', establishes the relation. The 'index' is the sign in which 'there is a sequential or causal relation between signifier and signified' (Dyer, 1982: 125); that is, a logic of inference, rather than analogy motivated by 'interest'. The third term in the triad, 'symbol', by contrast, is related to sign production, as it 'rests on convention, or "contract"' (Dyer, 1982: 125), but this very fact makes it 'arbitrary', 'unmotivated', a case of meaning by decree rather than of active sign-making.

In our view signs are never arbitrary, and 'motivation' should be formulated in relation to the sign-maker and the context in which the sign is produced, and not in isolation from the act of producing analogies and classifications. Sign-makers use the forms they consider apt for the expression of their meaning, in any medium in which they can make signs. When children treat a cardboard box as a pirate ship, they do so because they consider the material form (box) an apt medium for the expression of the meaning they have in mind (pirate ship), and because of their conception of the criterial aspects of pirate ships (containment, mobility, etc.). Language is no exception to this process of sign-making. All linguistic form is used in a mediated, non-arbitrary manner in the expression of meaning. For children in their early, pre-school years there is both more and less freedom of expression: more, because they have not yet learned to confine the making of signs to the culturally and socially facilitated media, and because they are unaware of established conventions and relatively unconstrained in the making of signs; less, because they do not have such rich cultural semiotic resources available as do adults. So when a three-year-old boy, labouring to climb a steep hill, says, 'This is a heavy hill', he is constrained by not having the word 'steep' as an available semiotic resource. The same is the case with the resources of syntactic and textual forms.

'Heavy', in 'heavy hill', is, however, a motivated sign: the child has focused on particular aspects of climbing a hill (it takes a lot of energy; it is exhausting) and uses an available form which he sees as apt for the expression of these meanings. The adult who corrects by offering 'steep' ('Yes, it's a very steep hill') is, from the child's point of view, not so much offering an alternative as a synonym for the precise meaning which he had given to 'heavy' in that context. Both the child and the parent make use of 'what is available'; it happens that different things are available to each. But to concentrate on this is to miss the central aspect of sign-making, especially that of children. 'Availability' is not the issue. Children, like adults, make their own resources of representation. They are not 'acquired', but made by the individual sign-maker.

In 'semiology', countless students across the world are introduced to the terms 'langue' and 'parole', with 'langue' explained, for instance, as 'the abstract potential of a language system . . . the shared language system out of which we make our particular, possibly unique, statements' (O'Sullivan *et al.*, 1983: 127) or, in our terms, as a system of available forms already coupled to available meanings, and with 'parole' defined as:

> an individual utterance that is a particular realization of the potential of langue. . . .
> By extension we can argue that the total system of television and film conventions and practices constitutes a langue, and the way they are realized in each programme or film a parole.
>
> (O'Sullivan *et al.*, 1983: 127)

We clearly work with similar notions, with 'available forms' and 'available classifications' ('langue') and individual acts of sign-making ('parole'), and we agree that such notions can usefully be extended to semiotic modes other than language. But for us the idea of 'potential' (what you can mean and how you can 'say' it, in whatever medium) is not limited by a system of 'available meanings' coupled with 'available forms', and we would like to use a slightly less abstract formulation: a semiotic 'potential' is defined by the semiotic resources available to a specific individual in a specific social context. Of course, a description of semiotic potential can amalgamate the resources of many speakers and many contexts.

But the resulting 'langue' (the langue of 'English' or of 'Western visual design') is in the end an artefact of analysis. What exists, and is therefore more crucial for understanding representation and communication, are the resources available to real people in real social contexts. And if we construct a 'langue', a meaning potential for 'Western visual design', then it is no more and no less than a tool which can serve to describe a variety of sign-making practices, within boundaries drawn by the analyst. It follows that we would not draw the line between 'langue' and 'parole' as sharply as it is usually done. Describing a 'langue' is describing a specific set of semiotic resources available for communicative action to a specific social group.

Here are some antecedents of the car drawing. Figure 0.2 is a drawing made by the same child, some ten months earlier. Its circular motion is expressive of the child's exuberant, enthusiastic and energetic actions in making the drawing. In figure 0.3, made about three months later, the circular motion has become more regular. The exuberance and energy are still there, but the drawing has acquired more regularity, more interest in shape: 'circular motion' is beginning to turn into 'circle'. In other words, the meanings of figure

▲ Fig 0.2 Drawing by a two-year-old child

🔺 **Fig 0.3 Drawing by a two-year-old child**

0.2 persist in figure 0.3, transformed, yet with significant continuity: figure 0.3 gathers up, so to speak, the meanings of figure 0.2, and then transforms and extends them.

Figure 0.4, finally, shows a series of circles, each drawn on a separate sheet, one circle to each sheet. The movement from figure 0.2 to figure 0.4 is clear enough, as is the conceptual and transformative work done by the child over a period of fourteen months (figure 0.4 dates from the same period as figure 0.1). Together the drawings show how the child *developed* the representational resources available to him, and why circles seemed such an apt choice to him: the expressive, energetic physicality of the motion of figure 0.2 persisted as the child developed this representational resource, so that the circular *motion* remained part of the meaning of circle/wheel. But something was added as well: the transformation of representational resources was also a transformation of the child's subjectivity, from the emotional, physical and expressive disposition expressed in the act of representing 'circular motion' to the more conceptual and cognitive disposition expressed in the act of representing a 'car'.

Children, like all sign-makers, make their 'own' representational resources, and do so as

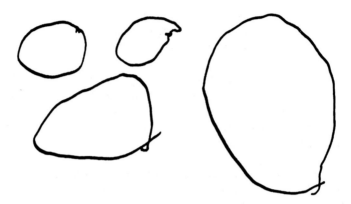

Fig 0.4 Drawing by a three-year-old child

part of a constant production of signs, in which previously produced signs become the signifier-material to be transformed into new signs. This process rests on the *interest* of sign-makers. This transformative, productive stance towards sign-making is at the same time a transformation of the sign-makers' subjectivity – a notion for which there was little place in a 'semiology' which described the relation between signifiers and signifieds as resting on inference or objective resemblance, or on the decrees of the social 'contract'.

We have used children's drawings as our example because we believe that the production of signs by children provides the best model for thinking about sign-making. It applies also to fully socialized and acculturated humans, with the exception of the effects of 'convention'. As mature members of a culture we have available the culturally produced semiotic resources of our societies, and are aware of the conventions and constraints which are socially imposed on our making of signs. However, as we have suggested, in our approach adult sign-makers, too, are guided by interest, by that complex condensation of cultural and social histories and of awareness of present contingencies. 'Mature' sign-makers produce signs out of that interest, always as transformations of existing semiotic materials, therefore always in some way newly made, and always as motivated conjunctions of meaning and form. The effect of convention is to place the pressure of constant limitations of conformity on sign-making; that is, the way signifiers have been combined with signifieds in the history of the culture, acts as a constantly present constraint on how far one might move in combining signifiers with signifieds. Convention does not negate new making; it attempts to limit and constrain the semiotic scope of the combinations.

This, then, is our position vis-à-vis 'European' semiology: where de Saussure had (been assumed to have) said that the relation of signifier and signified in the sign is arbitrary and conventional, we would say that the relation is always motivated and conventional. Where he had seemingly placed semiotic weight and power with the social, we wish to assert the effects of the transformative role of individual agents, yet also the constant presence of the social: in the historical shaping of the resources, in the individual agent's social history, in the recognition of present conventions, in the effect of the environment in which representation and communication happen. Yet it is the transformative action of individuals, along the contours of social givens, which constantly reshapes the resources, and makes possible the self-making of social subjects.

One of the now taken-for-granted insights of socially oriented theories of language is the variation of language with the variation of social context. The accounts of this variation differ, ranging from correlation ('language form x relates to social context y') to determination ('language form x is produced by social actors y or in social context y'). A social semiotic approach takes the latter view, along the following lines.

(1) Communication requires that participants make their messages maximally understandable in a particular context. They therefore choose forms of expression which they believe to be maximally transparent to other participants. On the other hand, communication takes place in social structures which are inevitably marked by power differences, and this affects how each participant understands the notion of 'maximal understanding'. Participants in positions of power can force other participants into greater efforts of interpretation, and their notion of 'maximal understanding' is therefore different from that of participants who do their best to produce messages that will require a minimal effort of interpretation, or from that of participants who, through lack of command of the representational system, produce messages that are harder to interpret (e.g. children, learners of a foreign language). The other participants may then either make the effort required to interpret these messages or refuse to do so, whether in a school or in a railway station in a foreign country.

(2) Representation requires that sign-makers choose forms for the expression of what they have in mind, forms which they see as most apt and plausible in the given context. The examples above instantiate this: *circles* to stand for *wheels*, and *wheels* to stand for *cars; heavy* to stand for *significant effort*, and *significant effort* to stand for *climbing a steep slope*. Speakers of a foreign language use exactly the same strategy. They choose the nearest, most plausible form they know for the expression of what they have in mind. The requirements of communication are no different in more usual circumstances, they are simply less apparent. The interest of sign-makers, at the moment of making the sign, leads them to choose an aspect or bundle of aspects of the object to be represented as being criterial, at that moment, for representing what they want to represent, and then choose the most plausible, the most apt form for its representation. This applies also to the interest of the social institutions within which messages are produced, and there it takes the form of the (histories of) conventions and constraints.

APPLICATIONS

In the previous section we have focused on the theoretical background of our work, but our aims are not just theoretical. They are also descriptive and practical. We seek to develop a descriptive framework that can be used as a tool for visual analysis. Such a tool will have its use for practical as well as analytical and critical purposes. To give some examples of the former, educationalists everywhere have become aware of the increasing role of visual communication in learning materials of various kinds, and they are asking themselves what kind of maps, charts, diagrams, pictures and forms of layout will be most effective for learning. To answer this question they need a language for speaking about the forms and meanings of these visual learning materials. Within the media, visual design is less and less the province of specialists who had generally seen little need for methodical and analytic- ally explicit approaches, and had relied instead on creative sensibilities honed through experience. But where media forms are relatively recently introduced – as is the case, for example, with advertising in Eastern Europe and parts of Asia – there is no such resistance to combining systematic analysis and practice. And with the advance of easy to use soft- ware for desktop publishing, the production of diagrams and charts, image manipulation, etc., visual design becomes less of a specialist activity, something many people will do alongside other activities. This has already led to rapid growth in the number of courses in this area – and designing such courses requires more of an analytical grasp of principles than learning on the job by example and osmosis. Last, and maybe at bottom at the root of much of this change, is 'globalization', which – maybe nearly paradoxically – demands that the cultural specificities of semiotic, social, epistemological and rhetorical effects of visual communication must be understood everywhere, since semiotic entities from anywhere now appear and are 'consumed' everywhere.

Analysing visual communication is, or should be, an important part of the 'critical' disciplines. Although in this book we focus on displaying the regularities of visual com- munication, rather than its ('interested', i.e. political/ideological) uses, we see images of whatever kind as entirely within the realm of the realizations and instantiations of ideol- ogy, as means – always – for the articulation of ideological positions. The plain fact of the matter is that neither power nor its use has disappeared. It has only become more difficult to locate and to trace. In that context there is an absolute need in democratic terms for making available the means of understanding the articulations of power anywhere, in any form. The still growing enterprise of 'critical discourse analysis' seeks to show how lan- guage is used to convey power and status in contemporary social interaction, and how the apparently neutral, purely informative (linguistic) texts which emerge in newspaper report- ing, government publications, social science reports, and so on, realize, articulate and disseminate 'discourses' as ideological positions just as much as do texts which more explicitly editorialize or propagandize. To do so we need to be able to 'read between the lines', in order to get a sense of what discursive/ideological position, what 'interest', may have given rise to a particular text, and maybe to glimpse at least the possibility of an alternative view. It is this kind of reading for which critical discourse analysis seeks to provide the ways and means. So far, however, critical discourse analysis has mostly been confined to language, realized as verbal texts, or to verbal parts of texts which also use other semiotic modes to realize meaning. We see our book as a contribution to a broadened critical discourse analysis, and we hope that our examples will demonstrate its potential for this kind of work.

Our examples include 'text-objects' of many kinds, from works of art to entirely ordinary, banal artefacts such as maps, charts, pages of different kinds, including those of websites, etc. We have included works of art not just because of their key role in the history of conventions and constraints, hence in the formation of the 'grammar of visual design', but also because they, too, articulate ideological positions of complex and potent kinds, and they, too, should be approached from the point of view of social critique.

As is perhaps already obvious from what we have said so far, we believe that visual design, like all semiotic modes, fulfils three major functions. To use Halliday's terms, every semiotic fulfils both an 'ideational' function, a function of representing 'the world around and inside us' and an 'interpersonal' function, a function of enacting social interactions as social relations. All message entities – texts – also attempt to present a coherent 'world of the text', what Halliday calls the 'textual' function – a world in which all the elements of the text cohere internally, and which itself coheres with its relevant environment. Whether we engage in conversation, produce an advertisement or play a piece of music, we are simultaneously communicating, doing something to, or for, or with, others in the here and now of a social context (swapping news with a friend; persuading the reader of a magazine to buy something; entertaining an audience) and representing some aspect of the world 'out there', be it in concrete or abstract terms (the content of a film we have seen; the qualities of the advertised product; a mood or melancholy sentiment or exuberant energy conveyed musically), and we bind these activities together in a coherent text or communicative event. The structure of our book reflects this. Chapters 2 and 3 deal with the *patterns of representation* which the 'grammar of visual design' makes available, and hence with the ways we can encode experience visually. Chapters 4 and 5 deal with the *patterns of interaction* which the 'grammar of visual design' makes available, and hence with the things we can do to, or for, each other with visual communication, and with the relations between the makers and viewers of visual 'texts' which this entails. Chapter 6 deals with the 'textual' function, with the way in which representations and communicative acts cohere into meaningful wholes. Chapter 7 deals with the materiality of visual signs – the tools we make them with (ink, paint, brushstrokes, etc.) and the materials we make them on (paper, canvas, computer screens, etc.); these, too, contribute to the meaning of visual texts. Chapter 8 extends the previous chapters into the domain of three-dimensional visuals and moving images. Again we assume that there is something like a Western 'grammar of three-dimensional visual design', a set of available forms and meanings used in sculpture as well as, for instance, in three-dimensional scientific models, or in children's toys – and a Western 'grammar of the moving image'.

We will begin, however, by discussing some of the broader themes we have touched on in this introduction.

1 The semiotic landscape: language and visual communication

In the early years of schooling, children are constantly encouraged to produce images, and to illustrate their written work. Teachers comment on these illustrations as much as they do on the written part of the text, though perhaps not quite in the same vein: unlike writing, illustrations are not 'corrected' nor subjected to detailed criticism ('this needs more work', 'not clear', 'spelling!', 'poor expression', and so on). They are seen as self-expression, rather than as communication – as something which the children can do already, spontaneously, rather than as something they have to be taught.

By the time children are beyond their first two years of secondary schooling, illustrations have largely disappeared from their own work. From here on, in a somewhat contradictory development, writing increases in importance and frequency and images become specialized. This is made more problematic by the facts of the present period, in which writing and image are in an increasingly unstable relation. We might characterize the situation of say twenty or thirty years ago in this way: texts produced for the early years of schooling were richly illustrated, but towards the later years of primary school images began to give way to a greater and greater proportion of written text. In as much as images continued, they had become representations with a technical function, maps, diagrams or photographs illustrating a particular landform or estuary or settlement type in a geography textbook, for instance. Thus children's own production of images was channelled in the direction of specialization – away from 'expression' and towards technicality. In other words, images did not disappear, but they became specialized in their function.

In many ways the situation in school remains much the same, with two profoundly important provisos. On the one hand all school subjects now make much more use of images, particularly so in the years of secondary schooling. In many of these subjects, certainly in the more technical/scientific subjects such as (in England) Science, Information Technology or Geography, images have become the major means of representing curricular content. In the more humanistic subjects – for example, History, English and Religious Studies – images vary in their function between illustration, decoration and information. This trend continues, and it is the case for worksheets, in textbooks and in CD-ROMs. On the other hand, there is no teaching or 'instruction' in the (new) role of images (though in England, in the school subject Information Technology, there is teaching in desktop publishing). Most importantly, assessment continues to be based on writing as the major mode. Students are called upon to make drawings in Science, Geography and History; but, as before, these drawings tend not to be the subject of the teacher's attention, judging by their (written) comments on the children's work. In other words, materials provided *for* children make intense representational use of images; in materials demanded *from* children – in various forms of assessment particularly – writing remains the expected and dominant mode.

Outside school, however, images play an ever-increasing role, and not just in texts for children. Whether in the print or electronic media, whether in newspapers, magazines, CD-ROMs or websites, whether as public relations materials, advertisements or as informational materials of all kinds, most texts now involve a complex interplay of written text, images and other graphic or sound elements, designed as coherent (often at the first level visual rather than verbal) entities by means of layout. But the skill of producing multi-modal texts of this kind, however central its role in contemporary society, is not taught in schools. To put this point harshly, in terms of this essential new communication ability, this new 'visual literacy', institutional education, under the pressure of often reactionary political demands, produces illiterates.

Of course, writing is itself a form of visual communication. Indeed, and paradoxically, the sign of the fully literate social person is the ability to treat writing completely as a visual medium – for instance by not moving one's lips and not vocalizing when one is reading, not even 'subvocalizing' (a silent 'speaking aloud in the head', to bring out the full paradox of this activity). Readers who move their lips when reading, who subvocalize, are regarded as culturally and intellectually tainted by having to take recourse to the culturally less valued mode of spoken language when reading visual script. This 'old' visual literacy, writing, has for centuries now been one of the most essential achievements and values of Western culture, and one of the most essential goals of education, so much so that one major and heavily value-laden distinction made by Western cultures has been that between literate (advanced) and non-literate (oral and primitive) cultures. No wonder that the move towards a new literacy, based on images and visual design, can come to be seen as a threat, a sign of the decline of culture, and hence a particularly potent symbol and rallying point for conservative and even reactionary social groupings.

The fading out of certain kinds of texts by and for children, then, is not a straightforward disvaluation of visual communication, but a valuation which gives particular prominence to one kind of visual communication, writing, and to one kind of visual literacy, the 'old' visual literacy. Other visual communication is either treated as the domain of a very small elite of specialists, or disvalued as a possible form of expression for articulate, reasoned communication, seen as a 'childish' stage one grows out of. This is not a valuation of *language* as such over visual communication, because even now the structures, meanings and varieties of spoken language are largely misunderstood, and certainly not highly valued *in their variety* in the education system (with some exceptions, such as in formal 'debating') or in public forums of power.

To sum up: the opposition to the emergence of the visual as a full means of representation is not based on an opposition to the visual as such, but on an opposition in situations where it forms an alternative to writing and can therefore be seen as a potential threat to the present dominance of verbal literacy among elite groups.

In this book we take a fresh look at the question of the visual. We want to treat forms of communication employing images as seriously as linguistic forms have been. We have come to this position because of the now overwhelming evidence of the importance of visual communication, and the now problematic absence of the means for talking and thinking about what is actually communicated by images and by visual design. In doing so, we have to move away from the position which Roland Barthes took in his 1964 essay 'Rhetoric of the image' (1977: 32–51). In this essay (and elsewhere, as in the introduction to *Elements of Semiology*; Barthes, 1967a), he argued that the meaning of images (and of other semiotic codes, like dress, food, etc.) is always related to and, in a sense, dependent on, verbal text. By themselves, images are, he thought, too 'polysemous', too open to a variety of possible meanings. To arrive at a definite meaning, language must come to the rescue. Visual meaning is too indefinite; it is a 'floating chain of signifieds'. Hence, Barthes said, 'in every society various techniques are developed intended to *fix* the floating chain of signifieds in such a way as to counter the terror of uncertain signs; the linguistic message is one of these techniques' (1977: 39). He distinguished between an image–text relation in which the verbal text *extends* the meaning of the image, or vice versa, as is the case, for example, with the speech balloons in comic strips, and an image–text relation in which the verbal text *elaborates* the image, or vice versa. In the former case, which he called *relay*, new and different meanings are added to complete the message. In the latter case, the same meanings are restated in a different (e.g. more definite and precise) way, as is the case, for example, when a caption identifies and/or interprets what is shown in a photograph. Of the two, elaboration is dominant. Relay, said Barthes, is 'more rare'. He distinguished two types of elaboration, one in which the verbal text comes first, so that the image forms an *illustration* of it, and one in which the image comes first, so that the text forms a more definite and precise restatement or 'fixing' of it (a relation he calls *anchorage*).

Before approximately 1600 (the transition is, of course, very gradual), Barthes argued, 'illustration' was dominant. Images elaborated texts, more specifically the founding texts of the culture – mythology, the Bible, the 'holy writ' of the culture – texts, therefore, with which viewers could be assumed to be familiar. This relation, in which verbal texts formed a source of authority in society, and in which images disseminated the dominant texts in a particular mode to particular groups within society, gradually changed to one in which nature, rather than discourse, became the source of authority. In the era of science, images, ever more naturalistic, began to function as 'the book of nature', as 'windows on the world', as 'observation', and verbal text served to identify and interpret, to 'load the image, burdening it with a culture, a moral, an imagination'.

This position does explain elements of communication. Any one of the image–text relations Barthes describes may at times be dominant, although we feel that today there is a move away from 'anchorage'. Compare, for example, the 'classic' documentary film in which the viewer is first confronted with 'images of nature', then with the authoritative voice of a narrator who identifies and interprets the images, with the modern 'current affairs' item, in which the viewer is first confronted with the anchorperson's verbal discourse and, either simultaneously or following on from the verbal introduction, with the 'images of nature' that illustrate, exemplify and authenticate the discourse. But Barthes' account misses an important point: the visual component of a text is an independently organized and structured message, connected with the verbal text, but in no way dependent on it – and similarly the other way around.

One important difference between the account we develop in this book and that of earlier semioticians is our use of work in linguistic theories and descriptions. This is a difficult argument to make, but worth making clearly. We think that this book would not have been possible without the achievements of linguistics, yet we do not, in the way some critics of our approach have suggested, see our approach as a linguistic one. So what have we used from linguistics, and how have we used it? And, equally, what have we not used from linguistics? To start with the latter question, we have not imported the theories and methodologies of linguistics directly into the domain of the visual, as has been done by others working in this field. For instance, we do not make a separation of syntax, semantics and pragmatics in the domain of the visual; we do not look for (the analogues of) sentences, clauses, nouns, verbs, and so on, in images. We take the view that language and visual communication can both be used to realize the 'same' fundamental systems of meaning that constitute our cultures, but that each does so by means of its own specific forms, does so differently, and independently.

To give an example, the distinction between 'subjective' and 'objective' meanings has played an important role in Western culture ever since the physical sciences began to develop in the sixteenth century. This distinction can be realized (that is, given concrete, material expression, hence made perceivable and communicable) with linguistic as well as visual means. The terms 'subjective' and 'objective' can therefore be applied to both: they belong to the meaning potential of a culture and its society. But the way the distinction is realized in language is quite different from the way it is realized in images. For example, in language an idea can be realized subjectively by using a 'mental process verb' like *believe* in the first person (e.g. *We believe that there is a grammar of images*); or objectively through the absence of such a form (e.g. *There is a grammar of images*). Visual representation, too, can realize both subjectivity, through the presence of a perspectival angle, and objectivity, through its absence, a point which will be discussed more fully in chapter 4. Mental process clauses and nominalization are unique to language. Perspective is unique to images. But the *kinds of meaning* expressed are from the same broad domain in each case; and the forms, different as they are, were developed in the same period, in response to the same cultural changes. Both language and visual communication express meanings belonging to and structured by cultures in the one society; the semiotic processes, though not the semiotic means, are broadly similar; and this results in a considerable degree of congruence between the two.

At the same time, however, each medium has its own possibilities and limitations of meaning. Not everything that can be realized in language can also be realized by means of images, or vice versa. As well as a broad cultural congruence, there is significant difference between the two (and other semiotic modes, of course). In a language such as English one needs to use a verb in order to make a full utterance (*believe, is*); and language has to use names to refer to whatever is to be represented (*a grammar of images, believe, we*). But language does not have or need angles of vision to achieve perspective, nor does it have or need spatial dispositions of elements to achieve the meanings of syntactic relations: images have and need both. The meaning potentials of the two modes are neither fully conflated nor entirely opposed. We differ from those who see the meaning of language as inherent in the forms and the meaning of images as derived from the context, or the meanings of language as 'conscious' and the meanings of images as 'unconscious'.

To return to the first of our two questions – What have we used from linguistics, and how have we used it? – perhaps the most significant borrowing is our overall approach, an 'attitude' which assumes that, as a resource for representation, images, like language, will display regularities, which can be made the subject of relatively formal description. We call this a 'grammar' to draw attention to culturally produced regularity. More specifically, we have borrowed 'semiotic orientations', features which we taken to be general to all human meaning-making, irrespective of mode. For instance, we think that the distinction between 'objectivity' and 'subjectivity' is a general cultural/semiotic issue which can be realized linguistically as well as visually, though differently so, as we have said. Or, as another instance, we have taken Michael Halliday's social semiotic approach to language as a model, as a source for thinking about general social and semiotic processes, rather than as a mine for categories to apply in the description of images. His model with its three functions is a starting point for our account of images, not because the model works well for language (which it does, to an extent), but because it works well as a source for thinking about all modes of representation.

Maybe most to the point is this: our approach to communication starts from a social base. In our view the meanings expressed by speakers, writers, printmakers, photographers, designers, painters and sculptors are first and foremost social meanings, even though we acknowledge the effect and importance of individual differences. Given that societies are not homogeneous, but composed of groups with varying, and often contradictory, interests, the messages produced by individuals will reflect the differences, incongruities and clashes which characterize social life. It is likely, and in our experience often the case, that the different modes through which texts are constructed show these social differences, so that in a multimodal text using images and writing the writing may carry one set of meanings and the images carry another. In an advertisement, for instance, it may be that the verbal text is studiously 'non-sexist', while the visual text encodes overtly sexist stereotypes. Given the still prevalent sense about the meaning of images, it is possible to pretend that the meaning carried in the image is there only 'in the eye of the beholder', something that it would not be possible to assert about verbally realized meanings.

Our examples in this book are quite deliberately drawn from very many domains, and from different historical periods. We hope that our ideas will help anyone interested in communication to see in images not only the aesthetic and expressive, but also the structured social, political and communicative dimensions. We will draw examples from the kinds of texts which are already fully based on the new visual literacy and play a dominant role in any public sphere, magazine articles, advertisements, textbooks, websites and so on. This is not because we want to promote these texts as a kind of model which should replace other kinds of texts, but because their role in the lives of children and adults is so important that we simply cannot afford to leave the ability to think and talk about them (and, indeed, to produce them) to a handful of specialists. We have a particular interest in the place of the visual in the lives of children, and we hope to show that children very early on, and with very little help (despite all the encouragement), develop a surprising ability to use elements of the visual 'grammar' – an ability which, we feel, should be understood better and developed further, rather than being cut off prematurely as is, too often, the case at present; and an ability that should also be available to adults.

AN UNCONVENTIONAL HISTORY OF WRITING

The dominance of the verbal, written medium over other visual media is firmly coded and buttressed in conventional histories of writing. These go something like this. Language in its spoken form is a natural phenomenon, common to all human groups. Writing, however, is the achievement of only some (historically, by far the minority of) cultures. At a particular stage in the history of certain cultures, there developed the need to make records of transactions of various kinds, associated usually with trade, religion or (governing) power. These records were initially highly iconic; that is, the relation between the object to be recorded and the forms and means of recording was close and transparent. For instance, the number of notches in a stick would represent the number of objects stored or traded or owed. The representation of the object would usually also be transparent: a wavy line eventually became the Chinese ideogram for 'water'; the hieroglyphic image of the ox's head which initially 'stood for' 'ox' eventually became the letter aleph ($\aleph$), alpha (α), a. This example illustrates what in these histories is regarded as the rarest of all achievements, the invention of alphabetic writing.

Alphabetic writing developed, it seems clear, out of iconic, image-based scripts. In these original script forms, an object was initially represented by an image of that object. Over time, in the use of the script by different groups, speaking different languages, the image of the object came to stand for the name of the object and then for its initial letter. Aleph, 'ox' in Egyptian hieroglyphics, after centuries of travel and constant transformation through the cultures and languages of the eastern Mediterranean, became the letter *alpha*, and eventually the letter *a* in the Roman alphabet. Clearly this was a process where each step involved considerable abstraction, so much so that, seemingly, alphabetic writing has been invented only once in the history of human cultures. All present alphabetic scripts, from India to the Middle East to Europe, are developments of that initial step from Egyptian (or possibly Sumerian) iconic hieroglyphic representation to the Phoenician alphabet, and from there westward to the Greek-speaking world, and eastward to the Indian subcontinent, or, in the region of its origin, developing into the Arabic version of the alphabet.

This is indeed an impressive cultural history, impressive enough to have stood as the accepted historical account of the achievement of (alphabetic) writing, unquestioned for centuries. Within this account, all cultures with forms of visual representation that are not directly connected to language are treated as cultures without writing. However, it is worth investigating this history, and in particular the crucial step from visual representation to the link with language, a little more closely. Prior to this step (in reality a development spanning millennia) there were two separate and independent modes of representation. One was language-as-speech; the other, the visual image, or visual marks. Each served a particular set of purposes such as the construction of histories and myths, the recording of genealogies and transactions, and the recording and measurement of objects. In the case of some cultures, however, the one form of representation 'took over' the other, as a means of recording; that is, visual representation became specialized – one could say, reduced – to function as a means of the visual representation of speech, perhaps in highly organized and bureaucratized societies. At this point the visual was subsumed, taken over, by the verbal as its means of recording. Consequently its former public uses, possibilities and potentials for independent representation disappeared, declined and withered away.

In the case of other cultures, however, this development did not occur. Here the visual continued, along with the verbal means of representation. Instances of this abound: from the one extreme of the Inca quipu strings (sensorily the tactile mode of representation) to Australian Aboriginal drawings, sand-paintings and carvings. These encode, in a manner not at all directly dependent on, or a 'translation' of, verbal language, meanings of the culture which are deemed to be best represented in visual form. They are *connected with* language, or language with them, so that wall-paintings or sand-paintings, for instance, are accompanied by verbal recounts of geographical features, journeys, ancestor myths, and so on. However, in these cases there is no question of the priority of the one over the other mode, and the visual has certainly not become subsumed to the verbal as its form of representation.

In this connection it is interesting to consider the history of two words which in a sense are synonymous with Western notions of literacy, the words *grammar* and *syntax*. *Grammar* derives from the Greek *grammatike* ('the art of reading and writing', 'grammar', 'alphabet'); related words were *gramma* ('sign', 'letter', 'alphabet'), *grammatikos* ('literate', '(primary) teacher', 'grammarian'). This etymology records the state of things in the Hellenistic period (from approximately 300BC); in earlier times the meaning 'sign', as in 'painted or drawn [etc.] mark' was the primary meaning. In Homer, for example, the verb *graphein* still means 'scratch', 'scratch in', as in engraving, and from there it comes to mean *both* 'writing' and 'drawing', 'painting'. *Syntaxis*, in pre-Hellenistic times, meant 'contract', 'wage', 'organization', 'system', 'battle formation', with *syntagma*, for instance, 'contingent of troops', 'constitution (of a state)', 'book or treatise'. Only in the Hellenistic period does *syntaxis* come to mean (among its other meanings) 'grammatical construction'. The verb *syntasso*, again, means both 'arrange battle formations' and 'concentrate (one's thoughts)', 'organize', 'write', 'compose'.

While we do not wish to place too much emphasis on etymology, nevertheless the history of these two words which are so crucial to our notions of literacy points to forms of social *organization* and *order*, on the one hand, and to visual '*markings*' on the other. Together they indicate the initially quite independent organization of the mode of images and the mode of verbal language. At the same time, the subsequent history of the word *grammar* brings out clearly the subordination of the visual medium to the medium of verbal language. Cultures which still retain the full use of both media of representation are, from the point of view of 'literate cultures', regarded as illiterate, impoverished, underdeveloped, when in fact they have a richer array of means of representation than that overtly and consciously available to literate cultures. Nevertheless, as we pointed out earlier, literate cultures do make use of means of visual communication other than writing, be it that they are seen as uncoded replicas of reality or as a means of individual expression by children or artists. In other words, they are not treated as either the expressions of, or accessible to means of reading based on, articulated, rational and social meanings.

Our unconventional history of writing is one that treats the coming together of visual and verbal representation as only one possibility, and one, furthermore, that brings with it not just those benefits of writing which are well enough understood, but also the negative aspects incurred in the loss of an independent form of representation, the diminution of modes of expression and representation. From that point of view cultures such as Australian Aboriginal cultures are seen as having both modes of representation: the visual (or perhaps a whole set of visual forms of representation) and the verbal. The point of this history is not only the political one of undermining the notion of 'illiterate culture' (or 'merely oral culture'), but also the attempt to see to what extent the conventional history blinds us to the facts and uses of visual communication in so-called literate cultures.

In this book we develop the hypothesis that in a literate culture the visual means of communication are rational expressions of cultural meanings, amenable to rational accounts and analysis. The problem which we face is that literate cultures have systematically suppressed means of analysis of the visual forms of representation, so that there is not, at the moment, an established theoretical framework within which visual forms of representation can be discussed.

THE 'OLD' AND THE 'NEW' VISUAL LITERACY IN BOOKS FOR THE VERY YOUNG

So far we have distinguished two kinds of visual literacy: one in which visual communication has been made subservient to language and in which images have come to be regarded as unstructured replicas of reality (the 'old visual literacy', in our terms); and another in which (spoken) language exists side by side with, and independent of, forms of visual representation which are openly structured, rather than viewed as more or less faithful duplicates of reality (the 'new', in our terms). We have looked at these as historical and cultural alternatives. But they also exist side by side, at least in contemporary Western culture, and we suggest that we are in the middle of a shift in valuation and uses from the one mode to the other, from the 'old' to the 'new' visual literacy, in many important social contexts. The examples we will now discuss suggest that the very first books children encounter may already introduce them to particular kinds of visual literacy.

Figure 1.1 shows a typical two-page spread from *Baby's First Book*, a book which, on its inside cover, declares that 'the text and illustrations, though oversimple to grown-ups, will satisfy their [i.e. the toddlers'] cravings for the repetition of what they already know, and will help them associate the words with the objects'. When we wrote the first version of this chapter, in 1989, it was still widely distributed, and today it is already making a comeback as an object of nostalgia.

Figure 1.2 shows a typical page from Dick Bruna's *On My Walk*. This book is one of a set of four, the others being *In My Home*, *In My Toy Cupboard* and *On the Farm*. It consists of eight pages and, with the exception of the front and back covers, the pages contain no words whatsoever.

Compared to the picture of the bird in the tree, the picture of the bath is realistic, detailed and complex. If we were to analyse it into its components, if we were to try

Bath

Every night
I have my bath
before I go
to bed.

Fig 1.1 **My bath (from *Baby's First Book*, Ladybird)**

and identify all the different elements of this picture, we might encounter problems. Are the ripples in the water to be counted as components? Are the shadows, cast by the tub and towel? And if we were to try and identify the relations between these components, what would we have to say, for example, about the relation between the duck and the soap? We ask these questions because they are the kinds of questions with which one might start if one wanted to show that images are structured messages, amenable to constituent analysis. Isn't the structure here that of the cultural object 'bathroom', rather than one imposed by the conventions of a visual code? Isn't this picture unproblematically, transparently readable (recognizable), provided one knows what bathrooms look like?

This is the line Paris School semioticians such as Roland Barthes and Christian Metz took in the 1960s. Commenting on photography, Barthes said:

> In order to move from the reality to its photograph it is in no way necessary to divide up this reality into units and to constitute these units as signs, substantially different from the object they communicate. . . . Certainly, the image is not the reality but at least it is its perfect *analogon* and it is exactly this analogical perfection which, to commonsense, defines the photograph. Thus can be seen the special status of the photographic image: *it is a message without a code.*

> (Barthes, 1977: 17)

○ Fig 1.2 Bird in tree (Bruna, 1988)

And he extends this argument to other pictorial modes, albeit with a qualification:

> Are there other messages without a code? At first sight, yes: precisely the whole range of analogical reproductions of reality – drawings, paintings, cinema, theatre. However, each of those messages develops in an immediate and obvious way a supplementary message . . . which is what is commonly called the style of the reproduction.
>
> (Barthes, 1977: 17)

The picture of the bird in the tree, on the other hand, is much less naturalistic, much less detailed and much simpler than the picture of the bathroom. It is stylized and conventional, and quite clearly a 'coded' image. No depth, no shadows, no subtle nuances of colour: everything is plain and bold and simple. And the structure of the image, with its one central and four marginal images, does not imitate anything in the real world. It is a conventional visual arrangement, based on a visual code. As a result the components of the whole stand out as separate, distinct units, and the picture would seem quite amenable to constituent analysis. This is not just a matter of style: the structure of this picture could also be realized in more detailed styles. Bruna's book dates from 1953, well before the era of computer 'imaging', but the picture of the bird in the tree could have been composed with a computer, aligning ready-made simple icons in a compositional configuration – it is in fact quite similar to the computer-drawn dinner invitation in figure 1.3.

▲ **Fig 1.3 Computer-drawn dinner invitation**

Second, the picture of the bathroom is part of a two-page layout, and accompanied by words. Language comes first, authoritatively imposing meaning on the image, turning it into a typical instance of a bathroom by means of the generic label 'Bath'. As a result the picture could be replaced by other images of bathrooms without much loss of meaning (one verbal text, many images, many possible illustrations). Here language is general, bestowing similarity and order on the diverse, heterogeneous world of images. Thus the book presents, on the one hand, an 'uncoded', naturalistic representation ('the world as it is' – empirical, factual, specific) and, on the other hand, a specific, authoritatively pre-scribed way of reading this 'uncoded' naturalistic picture. We will show later that, contrary to what Barthes and others argued in the 1960s, pictures of this kind are also structured, whether they are photographs, drawings, paintings or other kinds of pictures. For the moment, however, the important point is that they are not usually interpreted as such, that awareness of the structuredness of images of this kind is, in our society, suppressed and not part of 'common sense'.

In Dick Bruna's *On My Walk*, by contrast, there are no words to authoritatively impose meaning on the image, and the image is no longer an illustration: the image carries the meaning, the words come second. Parents who read this book with their children could all tell a different story, could even use different languages (one image, many verbal texts).

The world of 'one image, many different verbal texts' ('commentaries') imposes a new mode of control over meaning, and turns the image, formerly a record of nature or a playground for children and artists, into a more powerful, but also more rigorously controlled and codified public language, while it gives language, formerly closely policed in many social institutions, a more private and less controlled, but also less powerful, status. The 'readings' which parents produce when they read *On My Walk* with their children may all be different, yet these different readings will necessarily have common elements, deriving from their common basis – the elements included in the image, and the way these elements are compositionally brought together.

Whatever story parents will tell about the page with the bird in the tree, it will necessarily have to be a story that creates a relation between, for instance, birds and aeroplanes (nature and technology) and birds and cats (prey and predator). It will also have to be a story in which the bird, safely in its tree, is the central character, literally and figuratively. In how many ways can cats and birds be related? Not that many, at least not if one assumes that books like *On My Walk* serve to introduce children to the world around them, rather than to the possible worlds of fantasies and utopias. Cats can 'hunt', 'torture', 'kill' and 'eat' birds. Birds can 'escape' cats or fail to do so. There are not that many stories to choose from. On the other hand, parents and their children can choose the order in which they want to deal with the various elements: the page is 'non-linear'. It does not impose a sequential structure. And they can choose whether to tell the story of the bird and the cat as a political story, a story of powerful predators coming from another continent and native birds killed and threatened with extinction (as might be done, for instance, in Australia), or as a story that legitimizes the survival of the fittest. The story of the bird and the aeroplane, similarly, may be told from an environmentalist point of view, or as a story of evolutionary triumphs and human technological progress. Even where such discourses are not explicitly invoked, they will still communicate themselves to children through the parents' attitudes towards the characters and the actions.

Not only the elements on the individual pages, but also the pages themselves must be brought in relation to each other. The book as a whole must be readable as a coherent sequence. This is prompted by the title (*On My Walk*) as well as by the picture on the front cover, which shows all the elements together. We have investigated this a little further in connection with another book in the Bruna series, *On the Farm*. This book contains the following central pictures: house, farmer, cat, dog, apple tree, rooster, lamb, cow. Listing the ways in which these pictures can plausibly be linked to each other, we found that some (e.g. the apple tree and the house) can only be linked in spatial, locative terms (e.g. the apple tree is next to the house). Others (e.g. the animals and the house) can be related by verbs of 'dwelling' (e.g. the cow lies under the apple tree) or by the verbs of 'motion' (e.g. the cat climbs up the apple tree). Two of the animals (the cat and the dog) can relate to the other animals and to each other by means of antagonistic or co-operative actions (e.g. the dog barks at the cow; the dog leads the sheep). Only the farmer can relate to all the other elements in an agentive way. He can buy them, own them, build them, grow them, keep them, raise them, harvest them, shear them, slaughter them, and so on. In other words, whatever way the parents read these pictures, they will, in the end, have to deal with the theme of spatial order, the theme of social interaction (projected on to animals) and the theme of human mastery over nature (as well as, via the marginal pictures, with the theme of procreation), and they will have to do all this in terms of the elements pre-selected by the book. An analysis of the way the elements can be opposed to each other shows that, whatever the classifications parents may construct, they will not be able to avoid engaging with the Western cultural distinctions between 'untamed nature', 'domesticated/cultivated nature' and 'human technology'. And they will also have to recognize the distinction between animate and inanimate, flora and fauna, and between pets, farm animals and wild animals.

It should be noted, however, that every page in the book (and in Bruna's other books) contains at least one relation that does not easily fit the received classifications, that forms somewhat of a challenge and a puzzle. What, for example, is the relation between a rabbit and a basket of flowers? A beetle and a fence? Such visual enigmas can challenge parents and children to exercise their imagination, to include in their thinking elements that do not easily fit in with the traditional order of things, to tolerate some ambiguity, to allow the inclusion of the 'other' in their construction of the world.

The two books, then, are very different in their stance towards the image. The Bruna stance presents highly processed, essentialized and idealized representations, and provides parents and, later, children with the opportunity to talk about the images in ways which are or seem appropriate to them, to apply specific values, specific discourses to these relatively abstract images. The Ladybird stance presents ostensibly less processed, more naturalistic visual representations and provides parents (and, later on, children) with a specific verbally realized way of reading the image. The Ladybird book is open and interactive from the perspective of the image, and authoritarian from the perspective of writing; the Bruna book works in the opposite way. The closure in the Bruna book lies in the limits which selection, form and structure of the images impose on the apparently open readings – these enter the discourses which are already 'in' the socialized parents, so that the whole, once orally transmitted to the children, will appear spontaneous and 'natural' to parents and children alike. Are they not, after all, merely engaged in an innocent reading of 'what is there' in the pictures? Thus the two books represent two different forms of social control over meaning. One is openly and explicitly located in the text itself; the other lies, perhaps more covertly and implicitly, in the way the book presents itself less as a text than as an organized resource for *making* texts, jointly with the parental discourses that will inevitably enter the text as well.

These discourses, however, are not themselves part of Bruna's books, of the public text meant to transcend their diversity. Instead they are relegated to the realm of the private, of 'lifestyles' where they do not threaten the order of the larger social world. There is never just 'heteroglossia' (many meanings), nor ever just 'homoglossia' (one authoritative meaning). Instead there is a role distribution among the different semiotics, a role distribution in which some semiotics are given a great deal of social power, but at the price of being subjected to greater institutional (and technological) control, while others are allowed relative freedom from control, but pay for this with diminished power. Today, we seem to move towards a decrease of control over language (e.g. the greater variety of accents allowed on the public media, the increasing problems in enforcing normative spelling), and towards an increase in codification and control over the visual (e.g. the use of image banks from which ready-made images can be drawn for the construction of visual texts, and, generally, the effect of computer imaging technology).

The two forms of control over meaning can be found elsewhere also. Compare, for example, the classic documentary film – in which an authoritative 'voice of God' narrator explains and interprets images of recorded reality – to the more modern 'direct cinema' documentary, in which control over meaning lies in the selection of images and in the sometimes hardly noticeable ways in which these images are edited together. Or think of the way in which, in the field of 'cultural studies', an emphasis on analysing 'what the text says' is gradually being replaced by an emphasis on 'how different audiences read the same text', an emphasis, in other words, on the apparent freedom of interpretation which, by diverting attention away from the text itself, allows the limitations which the text imposes on this 'freedom of reading' to remain invisible, and therefore, perhaps, all the more efficacious and powerful.

In this connection the background of the Bruna book is worth brief mention. It was first printed in 1953, in Amsterdam, and reprinted many times in its country of origin. The first British printing was in 1978. The time lag is perhaps no accident. Unlike the British, the Dutch had, early in the twentieth century, recognized that their country did not have a 'common culture', but was divided into groups characterized by different and often opposing ideologies, *zuilen* (literally 'columns', 'pillars'), as the Dutch have called them. Dutch broadcasting, for example, had from its inception in the late 1920s a system in which different *levensbeschouwelijke* groups (i.e. 'groups orientated towards a particular view of life') ran broadcasting organizations which were allotted air time according to the size of their membership. Thus the same events would, on radio and later on television, be interpreted from a variety of different discursive ideological positions, while most other European countries had centralized, usually government-run, broadcasting organizations with one authoritative message. For a message to reach, in this context, the whole population, it had to be adaptable to a variety of cultural and ideological constructions and, as we have seen, the Bruna books use the visual medium to achieve exactly that. Perhaps the belated success of the series in countries like Britain and Australia shows that there is now, in these countries too, an increasing awareness that they no longer have a 'common culture', and that, instead, they have become complex, diverse and discursively divided, and therefore in need of new forms of communication (although the Dutch *zuilen* system went in decline from the 1960s onwards).

The changing distributions of meaning between language and image, which we suggest is now in full flow, was foreshadowed by various experiments in the Soviet Union of the early 1920s. While linguists and literary scholars like Voloshinov and Bakhtin wrote of language as socially divided, 'multi-accentual' and 'heteroglossic', constructivist artists like Malevich, El Lissitzky and Rodchenko, and film-makers like Eisenstein, rejected naturalism and began to elaborate a new visual language, capable of communicating new, revolutionary ideas visually. Then, as now, images became more stylized, more abstract and more obviously *coded*: the new visual language was explicitly compared with language, with hieroglyphic writing, with the stylized masks of kabuki theatre. Then, as now, visual communication was also seen as *transparent*: colours and shapes were thought to have a direct, unmediated, 'psychological' impact, a non-semiotic capacity for stirring the emotions of the 'masses'. Then, as now, visual communication was to be *removed from the sphere of art*, to become part of the more powerful and more public sphere of industrial production, of typography, design, architecture. This semiotic revolution was allied to the political revolution: constructivist posters and films had a propagandistic purpose – they sought to help bring about a cultural revolution, and they had to get their message across to a socially and linguistically heterogeneous population. The visual, thought to be able to produce an emotive immediacy, was to be the medium that could achieve this. In the end, the new semiotic order failed to establish itself permanently. It was crushed by Stalin. Old-fashioned centralist and repressive control over meaning (and with it a return to naturalist, 'bourgeois' art) prevailed over control by means of a form of propaganda that could allow pluralism and ideological cohesion to coexist. This time – though with very different political, social, technological and economic conditions – it may not fail.

The semiotic shifts we have exemplified in our discussion of the two children's books can be observed elsewhere, too. The shift from 'uncoded' naturalistic representations to stylized, conceptual images can be seen, for instance, on the covers of news magazines, which used to be dominated by documentary photographs – photographs recording events, or portraying newsworthy people. Occasionally this still happens, as in figure 1.4, but increasingly the photographs on magazine covers are contrived and posed, using conventional symbols to illustrate the essence of an *issue*, rather than documenting newsworthy *events*, as in figure 1.5, where a padlock and a United States flag, against a neutral background, illustrate the issue of tightened border control. Unlike the picture of the 'Bird in Tree' (figure 1.2), these are still photographic images, but they might as well be drawings.

As an example of the changing relation between language and image, consider an extract from a Science CD-ROM for the lower years of high school (figure 1.6). Here language has here been displaced by the visual as decisively as in the Bruna book. Instead of the major medium of information, with the visual as 'illustration', it has become a medium for comment or labelling, with the visual as the central source of information. Two questions need asking: one is the question of implicit changes in notions and practices of reading, and of reading science in particular; the other is the question of changes in the constitution of what is represented here, science itself. The students/viewers/users of the science CD-ROM are no longer addressed via the hierarchically complex structures of scientific writing, with its specific demands for cognitive processing, and its need to 'translate' verbal forms to their three-dimensional or visual equivalents (as on the page reproduced in figure 1.7). They are addressed largely in the visual mode, and either as 'scientists' who understand abstraction from the empirically real, or as people focusing on the empirically real with the intention to understand the regularities lying 'behind' that reality. In other words, even though the visual mode might seem to provide direct access to the world, it is as amenable to realizing theoretical positions as is the verbal.

More complex is the question whether, in this dramatic shift from the verbal to the visual, the very constitution of the school subject Science is undergoing a transformation.

▲ Fig 1.4 Magazine cover with naturalistic photograph (*Newsweek*, 19 April 2004)

Can everything that was communicable in the formation of scientific writing be said in these visually constructed forms? Conversely, are there possibilities of scientific communication in the visual which were not available in the mode of writing? And which of these is a more apt medium for scientific theory? Will scientific theories change as the form of expression shifts from the written to the visual mode? We cannot take up these questions here, but if we are to make ourselves conscious of the far-reaching implications of these changes in the semiotic landscape, they need at least to be asked.

Implicit in this is a central question, which needs to be put openly, and debated seriously: is the move from the verbal to the visual a loss or a gain? Our answer at this stage in our thinking is multiple. There are losses, and there are gains. Our argument throughout this book is that different semiotic modes – the visual, the verbal, the gestural, etc. – each have their potentialities and their limitations. A move from a central reliance on one mode to a central reliance on another will therefore inevitably have effects in both directions. But that is not the end of the story. We also have to consider what is represented. It may be that visual representation is more apt to the stuff of science than language ever was, or even that a science which is constructed visually will be a different kind of science. The world represented visually on the screens of the 'new media' is a differently constructed world to that which had been represented on the densely printed pages of the print media of some

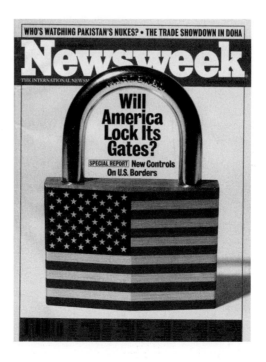

Fig 1.5 Magazine cover with conceptual photograph (*Newsweek*, 12 November 2001)

thirty or forty years ago. The resources it offers for understanding and for meaning-making differ from those of the world represented in language, and so do the citizens it produces.

These are far-reaching questions and they can only be answered by considering the interconnections between the changing political, economic and cultural conditions gathered up under the label of globalization and the new possibilities for representation afforded by the new media of production and dissemination. We have barely hinted at these kinds of questions in our discussion of the Bruna and Ladybird books. Could it be the case that information is now so vast, so complex, that perhaps it *has* to be handled visually, because the verbal is no longer adequate?

Mere nostalgia, mere social and cultural regrets or pessimism cannot help here. We, all of us, have our particular standpoints and our particular values carried forward from yesterday or from the day before yesterday. The first most important challenge is to understand this shift, in all of its detail, and in all of its meaning. From that understanding, we can hope to begin the task of constructing adequate new value systems.

To summarize:

(1) Visual communication is always coded. It seems transparent only because we know the code already, at least implicitly – but without knowing what it is we know, without

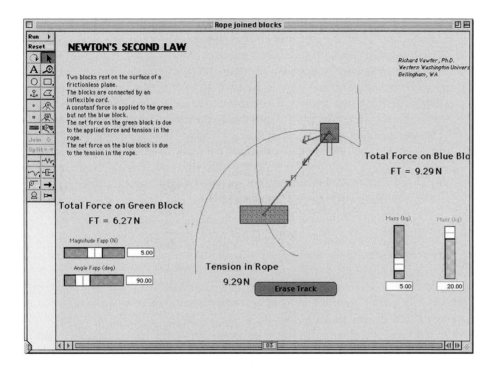

Fig 1.6 Contemporary science CD-ROM

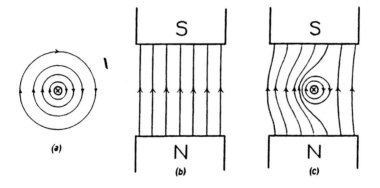

Fig 1.7 Early twentieth-century science textbook (McKenzie, 1938)

having the means for talking about what it is we do when we read an image. A glance at the 'stylized' arts of other cultures should teach us that the myth of transparency is indeed a myth. We may experience these arts as 'decorative', 'exotic', 'mysterious' or 'beautiful', but we cannot understand them as communication, as forms of 'writing' unless we are, or become, members of these cultures.

(2) Societies tend to develop explicit ways for talking only about those semiotic resources which they value most highly, and which play the most important role in controlling the common understandings they need in order to function. Until now, language, especially written language, has been the most highly valued, the most frequently analysed, the most prescriptively taught and the most meticulously policed mode in our society. If, as we have argued, this is now changing in favour of more multiple means of representation, with a strong emphasis on the visual, then educationalists need to rethink what will need to be included in the curricula of 'literacy', what should be taught under its heading in schools, and consider the new and still changing place of writing as a mode within these new arrangements.

If schools are to equip students adequately for the new semiotic order, if they are not to produce people unable to use the new resources of representation actively and effectively, then the old boundaries between the mode of writing on the one hand, and the 'visual arts' on the other, need to be redrawn. The former had traditionally been that form of literacy without which people could not adequately function as citizens or as workers; the latter had been either a marginal subject for the specially gifted, or a subject with limited and specialized applications, as in 'technical drawing'. The newly defined area will have to involve the technologies of the 'new screens' – the electronic technologies of information and communication, central now to the semiotic landscape. But above all, such a curriculum is crucially dependent on having the means of analysis, the means for talking about the 'new literacy', about what it is we do when we produce and read images. As Iedema (1994: 64) notes, in the 'post-Fordist' workplace,

> Workers must be multi-skilled, articulate and 'self-steering'. . . . [They] negotiate their jobs as members of 'quality circles' and consultative committees. This requires that workers are not merely capable of *doing* their work, but also that they are capable of talking and thinking about their work and its effectiveness.

Elsewhere (Kress, 2000; Kress and van Leeuwen, 2001) we have talked of the need for the introduction of the concept of *design*, both as a category with general significance in representation and communication, and as a crucial category for developing the curricula of institutionalized education, whether in the traditional school or other formal sites of learning. This is implicit also in the description we have given earlier in this chapter of the new forms of reading. This is not the place to develop that point, though it is essential to draw attention to its unavoidable significance as part of the urgent need for developing adequate ways and talking about the visual.

THE SEMIOTIC LANDSCAPE

The place of visual communication in a given society can only be understood in the context of, on the one hand, the range of forms or modes of public communication available in that society and, on the other hand, their uses and valuations. We refer to this as 'the semiotic landscape'. The metaphor is worth exploring a little, as is its etymology. The features of a landscape (a field, a wood, a clump of trees, a house, a group of buildings) only make sense in the context of their whole environment and of the history of its development ('waste land' has meaning only in that context, as has 'field' or 'track'; 'village' has meaning only as a group of buildings that is part of a history of ways of working the land). In the same way, particular features and modes of communication should be seen in the history of their development, and in the environment of all the other modes of communication which surround them. The use of the visual mode is not the same now as it was even fifty years ago in Western societies; it is not the same from one society to another; and it is not the same from one social group or institution to another.

Each feature of a landscape has its history, as does the landscape as a whole, and each is subject to constant remaking. It is here that the etymology of the word *landscape* is revealing. To the casual beholder a landscape simply is, and may even have a timeless appearance ('the timeless beauty of the English, or Spanish, countryside'). Yet it is in fact a product of social action and of a social history, of human work on the land, on nature: *–scape*, with its relation to *shape* in English and *schaffen* (both 'to work' and 'to create') in German, indicates this. And this applies also to the 'semiotic landscape'. Metaphoric excursions of this kind can be stretched too far; however, we will allow ourselves one other point of comparison. Landscapes are the result, not just of human social work, but also of the characteristics of the land itself. The flat land by the river is most suitable for the grazing of cattle or the growing of wheat; the hillsides for vineyards or forestry. At the same time, the characteristic values of a culture may determine which of the potential uses of the land are realized, whether the hillsides are used for vineyards or forestry, for example. And cultural values may even induce people to go against the grain of the land, to use the steep hillside for growing rice, for example, which opposes the 'natural potential' of the land almost to the limit.

Semiotic modes, similarly, are shaped both by the intrinsic characteristics and potentialities of the medium and by the requirements, histories and values of societies and their cultures. The characteristics of the medium of air are not the same as those of the medium of stone, and the potentialities of the speech organs are not the same as those of the human hand. Nevertheless, cultural and social valuations and structures strongly affect the uses of these potentialities. It is not an accident that in Western societies written language has had the place which it has had for the last three or four millennia, and that the visual mode has in effect become subservient to language, as its mode of expression in writing. Western linguistic theories have more or less naturalized the view that the use of air and the vocal organs is the natural, inevitable semiotic means of expression. But even speech is, in the end, cultural. We are not biologically predisposed to use speech as our major mode of communication. The parts of the body that we call the 'speech organs' are an adaptation of physical organs initially developed to prevent humans from choking while breathing and eating. When the need arises, we can and do use other means of expression, as in the highly articulated development of gesture in sign languages, and also in theatrical mime and certain Eastern forms of ballet. And, while these are at present restricted to relatively marginal domains, who is to say that this will always remain so in the future development of humankind? It is salutary to consider how other cultures 'rank' modes of communication, and to bring that knowledge into the mainstream of 'Western' thinking (see, for instance, Finnegan, 2002).

The new realities of the semiotic landscape are brought about by social, cultural and economic factors: by the intensification of linguistic and cultural diversity within the boundaries of nation states; by the weakening of these boundaries within societies, due to multiculturalism, electronic media of communication, technologies of transport and global economic developments. Global flows of capital and information of all kinds, of commodities, and of people, dissolve not only cultural and political boundaries but also semiotic boundaries. This is already beginning to have the most far-reaching effects on the characteristics of English (and Englishes) globally, and even within national boundaries.

The place, use, function and valuation of language in public communication is changing. It is moving from its former, unchallenged role as *the* mode of communication, to a role as one mode among others, to the function, for instance, of being a mode for comment, for ratification, or for labelling, albeit more so in some domains than in others, and more rapidly in some areas than in others. Although this is a relatively new phenomenon in public communication, children do it quite 'naturally' in their text-making.

New ways of thinking are needed in this field. Here we use, once more, children's representation as a metaphor to suggest some directions. The drawings reproduced in figure 1.8 were made by a five-year-old boy. On a summer Sunday afternoon, while his parents were entertaining friends, the child took a small, square notepad from near the telephone and drew a picture on each of six pages. His father had not noticed this until he came across him in the hall of their house, where the child was putting the cards 'in order', as shown in figure 1.8. Asked what he was doing, the child's account was as follows: for pictures 1 and 2 together 'Me and the dog are in life, so they're in the correct order'; on pictures 3 and 4 'The flying bomb is in the air and the plane is in the air, so they're in the correct order'; and on 5 and 6 'The patterns are in the correct order'.

The whole process, involving sign-making, representation and classification, had proceeded through the visual medium. It was only when the parent came along with his question that the child was forced to use words. The metaphoric processes of sign-making, the acts of representation and classification, each involving quite complex analogies, took place in the visual mode. Language, as speech, entered when communication with the parent became necessary. Speech was the mode used for 'ratifying' and for describing what had taken place without it.

Some two weeks later, at the end of the summer term of his primary school, the child brought home some of his exercise books. Among these was the page shown in figure 1.9. Clearly, here the task was one of classification, and it had been undertaken at school, prior to the making and ordering of the drawings in figure 1.8, at home. A whole sequence of

"ME AND THE DOG ARE IN LIFE, SO THEY'RE IN THE CORRECT ORDER"

"THE FLYING BOMB IS IN THE AIR AND THE PLANE IS IN THE AIR, SO THEY'RE IN THE CORRECT ORDER"

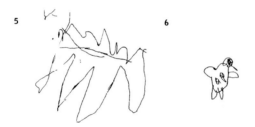

"THE PATTERNS ARE IN THE CORRECT ORDER"

▲ **Fig 1.8 Six drawings by a five-year-old boy**

semiotic activities is thus involved, a sequence of production, transformation and development, moving from the initial task of joining images of the same objects – a classificatory, cognitive, conceptual, semiotic and manual task – to that of producing complex and dissimilar images, and finding likeness in them (or imposing likeness on them) through an intermediary task of abstraction and generalization. If we think about this period of two weeks, the child's production of signs involved a series of distinct semiotic modes, and of translations between such modes. First the teacher spoke with the children about the task (mode: language as speech); then she introduced the book and showed them what was at issue (mode: 3D physical object, and visual mode); then the children used their pencils to draw the connecting lines (mode: manual action and visual mode of drawing); then the teacher engaged the children in *spoken* discussion, and made evaluative comments on their

Draw a line to join the things which are the same.

work. This was followed by a long period of 'silence', a fortnight or so when nothing was seen or heard, but when, we assume, the series of transformative acts of the child continued 'internally', 'mentally'. Finally the internal activity became visible, literally, through the child's unprompted production of the drawings, his unprompted classificatory activity (spatially shown) and his spoken commentary in response to his father's question.

Of course, while all this took place the child, as do all of us, would no doubt have experienced constantly shifting affective, emotional states. He might have been enthused by the task in the class and praised by the teacher for his success; he might have had a difficult time with his friends in the playground, or at home, and so on, and all of this would have influenced how he 'read' the activity and how it was 'taken up' by him. If we see it like this, it makes it impossible to think of affect and cognition as distinct, as separable. In other words, here – as always – the affective aspects are always one with, and act continuously as a 'modality' on, cognitive semiotic processes.

In part in response to the representational, semiotic and cognitive resources made available by the teacher, and her demands made in the class, though afterwards prompted by his own interests, the child used a series of different representational modes (including, of course, 'internal representations') in a constantly productive sequence of semiotic activities. Some happened within the same mode (linking the images of the object by a line, for instance), some took place by a shift across modes (the shift from the spatially performed classification to the spoken commentary on it). Such processes are constantly transformative (the name we use for such processes within one mode) and transductive (our name for such processes across modes). All these, we assume, have effects on 'inner resources', which constantly reshape (transform) the subjectivity of the child.

As we have indicated, the visual, actional and spatial modes, rather than speech, seemed to be the central representational and cognitive resources. Speech was used for communication with adults, as a means for translation, for comment and for ratification. It may well be that the complexities realized in the six images and their classification were initially beyond the child's capacity of spoken expression, conception and formulation, but that the visual mode offered him semiotic and cognitive resources which were not available to him in the verbal mode. However, once expressed in the visual mode, once classified *through* the visual/spatial mode, the meanings which the child had produced became available as externalized, objective expression; this in turn may have made them differently available for verbal expression, for the verbal ratification of semiotic, affective/cognitive processes that had already taken place.

This incessant process of 'translation', or 'transcoding' – *transduction* – between a range of semiotic modes represents, we suggest, a better, a more adequate understanding of representation and communication. In the example we have discussed here, language is not at the centre. In many areas of public communication the same is either the case already, or rapidly coming to be the case. And clearly it matters which semiotic modes of representation and communication are dominant, most frequent, most valued in the public domains in which we act.

Figure 1.10 comes from work done by two (13-year-old) students in Science, in the early years of secondary school in England. Two questions can be asked. The first is, What is the effect of the mode of representation on the epistemology of science?, and the second: 'Do different modes of representation facilitate, or rule out, different accounts of natural phenomena?' To answer both, we need to compare two differing modal representations of 'the same' issue.

This time our question is not 'What is the status of written language in these texts?' but rather 'What is the effect of the different modal realizations in terms of epistemology, in terms of the students' perspective on knowledge?' If we compare figure 1.10 with just one example from another exercise for assessment – the task 'to write a story of the journey of a red blood cell around the body' – we can see the rudiments of that difference. Here is a brief extract from one such 'story', in this case written in the genre of 'diary':

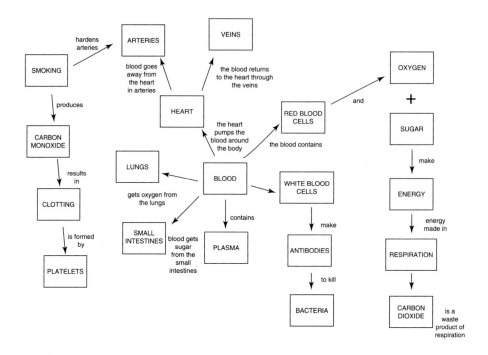

◭ **Fig 1.10 Concept map: 'blood circulation'**

Dear Diary, I have just left the heart. I had to come from the top of the right chamber of the heart (Right atrium) and squeeze my way through to the Right ventricle where the heartbeat got stronger, and I left the heart.

Dear Diary, I am currently in the lungs, it is terribly cramped in here as the capillaries are tiny and there are millions of us. We have just dropped off oxygen and we picked up some carbon dioxide.

Dear Diary, we have entered the liver where we had a thorough wash.

Dear Diary, we have just left the kidney where we dropped off some water which will be turned into urine.

Dear Diary, I have finished my journey around the body by stopping off at the heart.

In the diary, the fundamental organizational principle, or logic, is that of 'sequence in time', and the fundamental representational principle is that of action or event or, less frequently, states of affairs. Objects are related to other objects by actions represented by verbs ('we have entered the liver', 'we have just left the kidney'). The actions and events themselves are arranged in temporal sequence, mirroring that of the imagined events as they happened in the world. In the concept map, on the other hand, the fundamental organizational principle is that of a conceptual order, realized by the spatial arrangements of the individual concepts. Here objects are related, not by actions, but by hierarchy, by significance deriving from relation of 'priority' of various kinds.

All these examples reveal what has in fact always been the case: language, whether in speech or writing, has always existed as just one mode in the ensemble of modes involved in the production of texts, spoken or written. A spoken text is never just verbal, but also visual, combining with modes such as facial expression, gesture, posture and other forms of self-presentation. A written text, similarly, involves more than language: it is written *on* something, on some material (paper, wood, vellum, stone, metal, rock, etc.) and it is written *with* something (gold, ink, (en)gravings, dots of paint, etc.); with letters formed as types of font, influenced by aesthetic, psychological, pragmatic and other considerations; and with layout imposed on the material substance, whether on the page, the computer screen or a polished brass plaque. Yet the multimodality of written texts has, by and large, been ignored, whether in educational contexts, in linguistic theorizing or in popular common sense. Today, in the age of 'multimedia', it can suddenly be perceived again.

We can summarize this discussion in the form a set of hypotheses: (a) human societies use a variety of modes of representation; (b) each mode has, inherently, different representational potentials, different potentials for meaning-making; (c) each mode has specific social valuation in particular social contexts; (d) different potentials for meaning-making may imply different potentials for the formation of subjectivities; (e) individuals use a range of representational modes, and therefore have available a range of means of meaning-making, each affecting the formation of their subjectivity; (f) the different modes of representation are not held discretely, separately, as strongly bounded autonomous domains in the brain, or as autonomous communicational resources in culture, nor are they deployed discretely, either in representation or in communication; (g) affective aspects of human beings and practices are not discrete from other cognitive activity, and therefore never separate or absent from representational and communicative behaviour; (h) each mode of representation has a continuously evolving history, in which its semantic reach can contract or expand or move into different areas of social use as a result of the uses to which it is put.

None of these hypotheses would, we imagine, attract significant disagreement, especially when put singly. Jointly they represent a challenge to the existing common sense on the relations between language and thought and in mainstream theories and practices in all areas of public communication. This is a crucial feature of the new semiotic landscape.

A NOTE ON A SOCIAL SEMIOTIC THEORY OF COMMUNICATION

In order to function as a full system of communication, the visual, like all semiotic modes, has to serve several representational and communicational requirements. We have adopted the theoretical notion of 'metafunction' from the work of Michael Halliday for this purpose. The three metafunctions which he posits are the *ideational*, the *interpersonal* and the *textual*. In the form in which we gloss them here they apply to all semiotic modes, and are not specific to speech or writing.

The ideational metafunction

Any semiotic mode has to be able to represent aspects of the world as it is experienced by humans. In other words, it has to be able to represent objects and their relations in a world outside the representational system. That world may of course be, and most frequently is, already semiotically represented.

In doing so, semiotic modes offer an array of *choices*, of different ways in which objects, and their relations to other objects and to processes, can be represented. Two objects may be represented as involved in a process of interaction which could be visually realized by vectors:

⬥ **Fig 1.11 Vector**

But objects can also related in other ways, for instance in terms of a classification. They would be connected, not by a vector but, for instance, by a 'tree' structure:

⬥ **Fig 1.12 Tree structure**

In chapters 2 and 3 we will investigate precisely which ideational choices are available for visual sign-making in this way.

The interpersonal metafunction

Any semiotic mode has to be able to project the relations between the producer of a (complex) sign, and the receiver/reproducer of that sign. That is, any mode has to be able to represent a particular social relation between the producer, the viewer and the object represented.

As in the case of the ideational metafunction, modes offer an array of choices for representing different 'interpersonal' relations, some of which will be favoured in one form of visual representation (say, in the naturalistic image), others in another (say, in the diagram). A depicted person may be shown as addressing viewers directly, by looking at the camera. This conveys a sense of interaction between the depicted person and the viewer. But a depicted person may also be shown as turned away from the viewer, and this conveys the absence of a sense of interaction. It allows the viewer to scrutinize the represented characters as though they were specimens in a display case.

In chapters 4 and 5 we will discuss these and other interpersonal choices, both in terms of the kinds of interactions that can be represented, and in terms of the visual features that realize these interactions.

The textual metafunction

Any semiotic mode has to have the capacity to form *texts*, complexes of signs which cohere both internally with each other and externally with the context in and for which they were produced. Here, too, visual grammar makes a range of resources available: different compositional arrangements to allow the realization of different textual meanings. In figure 1.1, for example, the text is on the left and the picture on the right. Changing the layout (figure 1.13) would completely alter the relation between written text and image and the meaning of the whole. The image, rather than the written text, would now serve as point of departure, as 'anchor' for the message. In chapter 6 we will discuss such left–right relationships and other compositional resources.

▲ Fig 1.13 Altered layout of figure 1.1 (left–right reversal)

Our focus is on the description of these ideational, interpersonal and textual resources as they are realized in the visual mode. We recognize that in doing this work we are engaged in more than 'mere description', and participate ourselves in the reshaping of the semiotic landscape; and we realize also that this is a highly political enterprise.

2 Narrative representations: designing social action

INTRODUCTION

The pictures shown in figure 2.1 are taken from an Australian primary-school social studies textbook (Oakley *et al.*, 1985). One represents the traditional technology of the Australian Aborigines, the other the superior technology of those who invaded their territory ('The British had a technology that was capable of changing the face of the earth. Their tools were able to work faster than those of the Aborigines and their weapons were much more powerful'). The former has three main elements (an axe, a basket and a wooden sword), the latter four (the 'British', as they are called in the caption, their guns, the Aborigines and the landscape). But the two pictures differ not only in what each includes and excludes (the left picture, for instance, excludes the *users* of the technology, the right picture includes them), they differ also in structure: they relate their elements to each other differently. The elements of the left picture are arranged symmetrically, against a neutral background: axe, basket and wooden sword are represented as equal in size, placed at equal distance from each other and oriented in the same way towards the horizontal and the vertical axes, so that the picture as a whole creates a relation of similarity between the three elements. The picture says, as it were, that this axe, this basket and this wooden

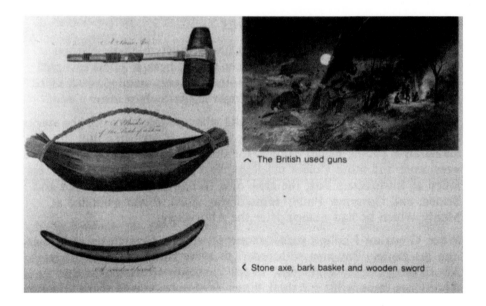

▲ The British used guns

‹ Stone axe, bark basket and wooden sword

△ Fig 2.1 The British used guns (Oakley *et al.*, 1985)

sword all belong to the same overarching category (a category, incidentally, which is only implied, and which conflates the notion of 'tools' and the notion of 'weapons').

The right picture represents technology in action. Where the left picture is impersonal, this picture is personal. Where the left picture is static, this picture is dynamic. Where the left picture is dry and conceptual, this picture is dramatic. It relates the British and the Aborigines through a transactional schema in which the British play the role of 'Actor', the ones who do the deed, and the Aborigines the role of 'Goal', the ones to whom the deed is done – the British *stalk* the Aborigines, one could say. It also relates the landscape to the British and the Aborigines in a 'locative' way (the British and the Aborigines are *in* the landscape), and the gun to the British in an 'instrumental' way (the British stalk the Aborigines *with* their guns).

These relations can be transformed into linguistic form, as we have just done, but the point is that here they are realized by visual means. The transactional relation between the British and the Aborigines is realized by the vector that links them, namely the oblique lines formed by the glances and outstretched arms of the British and by their guns. The locative relation is realized by overlapping, by the gradients of focus, the degrees of colour saturation and so on, which create the contrast between foreground and background. And the instrumental relation is realized by the gesture of holding, where the object held is a tool.

The important point at this stage is not the detail of the analysis, but the observation that the semiotic modes of writing and visual communication each have their own quite particular means of realizing what may be quite similar semantic relations. What in language is realized by words of the category 'action verbs' is visually realized by elements that can be formally defined as *vectors*. What in language is realized by locative prepositions is visually realized by the formal characteristics that create the contrast between foreground and background. This is not to say that all the relations that can be realized linguistically can also be realized visually – or vice versa, that all the relations that can be realized visually can also be realized linguistically. Rather, a given culture has a range of general, possible relations which is not tied to expression in any particular semiotic mode, although some relations can only be realized visually and others only linguistically, or some more easily visually and others more easily linguistically. This distribution of realization possibilities across the semiotic modes is itself determined historically and socially as well as by the inherent potentialities and limitations of a semiotic mode.

To return to the two pictures in figure 2.1, they can be said to represent an aspect of the experiential world, technology. But through the different design patterns selected in each, through the manner in which each brings its individual elements together into a coherent and meaningful whole, they represent the technology of Aborigines very differently from the technology of the British. Nothing about Aboriginal technology necessitates it to be represented as a static, conceptual taxonomy, nor is there anything intrinsic about British technology that requires it to be represented in a personalized and dramatized way. British technology is just as capable of being represented by a classificatory scheme as is Aboriginal technology, and it is just as possible to tell dramatic stories of Aborigines stalking their invaders with spears or wooden swords as it is to tell such stories about the British, even if the former kind of story does not usually form part of mainstream Australian history. In other words, the representation is mediated, visually, through two distinct discourses: that of anthropology for Aboriginal people – who 'know no history'; and that of history for the whites – who are not subjects of anthropology.

Imagine a reversal of those relations. Imagine on the left a catalogue of British tools and weapons, and on the right a picture in which Aborigines point their wooden swords at a small group of British in the background. Suddenly a representation of colonization as the transition from a fixed, stable ('primitive') order of things to the dynamic unfolding of history is changed into something like the revenge of the 'primitive' on the West's technological order. This may be suitable for a fiction film, perhaps, set safely in an apocalyptic future, but not for a primary-school textbook in contemporary Australia.

The two design patterns in figure 2.1, the classificatory pattern and the transactional pattern, are only two of several possible patterns. In the course of this chapter we will introduce others, and try to give an overview of the visual structures that can realize ways of representing the world. Our emphasis is not on *depiction*, nor on the question of *recognition*, on how we come to see configurations of pencil marks or brushstrokes or pixels as pictures of trees, or on how pictures of trees may connote or symbolize meanings and values over and above what they literally represent. This aspect of the pictorial has already received a good deal of attention in the writings of philosophers (e.g. Goodman, 1969; Hermeren, 1969), semioticians (e.g. Eco, 1976a; Barthes, 1977), media analysts (Williamson, 1978) and art historians (e.g. Panofsky, 1970). At this stage of our work on visual communication we have little to add to what has been said in these areas.

The question of visual structuring, on the other hand, has, in our opinion, been dealt with less satisfactorily. Visual structuring has either been treated as simply reproducing the structures of reality (e.g. Metz, 1974a, 1974b), rather than as creating meaningful propositions by means of visual syntax, or it has been discussed in formal terms only (e.g. Arnheim, 1974, 1982, who in his actual analyses offers many insights on the semantic dimension of visual structuring). Our example of the representation of Aboriginal and British technology has, we hope, made clear why neither of these approaches satisfies us. Visual structures do not simply reproduce the structures of 'reality'. On the contrary, they produce images of reality which are bound up with the interests of the social institutions within which the images are produced, circulated and read. They are ideological. Visual structures are never merely formal: they have a deeply important semantic dimension.

PARTICIPANTS

In chapter 1 we defined the ideational metafunction as the ability of semiotic systems to represent objects and their relations in a world outside the representational system or in the semiotic systems of a culture. In the introduction to the present chapter we tried to show how two design patterns can produce two different representations of broadly the same aspect of the world. Instead of 'objects' or 'elements' we will, from now on, use the term 'participants' or, more precisely, 'represented participants'. This has two advantages: it points to the relational characteristic of 'participant *in* something'; and it draws attention to the fact that there are two types of participant involved in every semiotic act, *interactive participants* and *represented participants*. The former are the participants in the act of communication – the participants who speak and listen or write and read, make images or view them, whereas the latter are the participants who constitute the subject matter of the communication; that is, the people, places and things (including abstract 'things') represented in and by the speech or writing or image, the participants about whom or which we are speaking or writing or producing images.

The situation is of course more complex than this, for the real interactive participants, the real image-producers and -viewers, cannot be taken to be identical with the 'implied' producer who 'silently instructs us, through the design of the whole' (Chatman, 1978: 148) and the 'implied' viewer. It may also be that the producers and/or viewers are themselves explicitly represented in the image, causing the two categories to shade into each other, complexities which have been studied extensively in the field of literary narratology (e.g. Iser, 1978; Bal, 1985; Rimmon-Kenan, 1983). We will return to these in the next chapter; for the purposes of this chapter the basic distinction will suffice.

In the case of abstract visuals such as diagrams, it does not seem too difficult to determine who or what the represented participants are. Shannon and Weaver's famous 'communication model' (figure 2.2), for instance, is made up of boxes and arrows (Shannon and Weaver, 1949). The boxes represent participants (people and/or things, the distinction being blurred by objectifying labels like 'information source' and 'destination'); the arrows represent the processes that relate them. If we wanted to translate this into language, we could say that the boxes are like nouns, the arrows like verbs (e.g. 'send' or 'transmit'), and that, together, they form clauses (e.g. 'an information source sends [information] to transmitter').

In the case of more detailed naturalistic images, however, it may be difficult, even futile, to try and identify the represented participants. Take 'The British used guns', for instance (figure 2.1). Do we include the hats and kerchiefs worn by the two men? Every single tree, every single one of the rocks strewn about in the foreground? The analogy with language loses its relevance here. In language, words such as *man, gun, tree, rocky ground* abstract away from details of this kind. In naturalistic images this does not happen. They are 'worth a thousand words'.

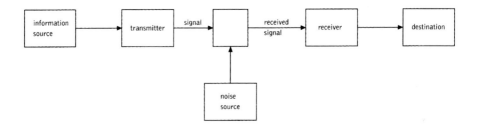

Fig 2.2 Shannon and Weaver's communication model

Yet we think that naturalistic images can be analysed into participants and processes much in the same way as diagrams. There are two different, but in the end compatible, ways of arguing this. The first is the way of formal art theory (e.g. Arnheim, 1974, 1982). The language of this kind of theory is, for the most part, formalistic, and grounded in the psychology of perception. Participants are called 'volumes' or 'masses', each with a distinct 'weight' or 'gravitational pull'. Processes are called 'vectors' or 'tensions' or 'dynamic forces'. But, and this is what matters for the purpose of identifying participants, these 'volumes' are perceived as distinct entities which are salient ('heavy') to different degrees because of their different sizes, shapes, colour, and so on. Thus the two men in figure 2.1 stand out as a distinct entity because of the tonal contrast between their silhouettes and the light of the fire. And what is more, we recognize their shapes on the basis of visual schemas not unlike those that are realized in diagrams. Artists have long learned their craft by reducing the visible world to simple geometric forms (see Gombrich, 1960). According to Arnheim (1974: ch. 4), children learn to draw in the same way, building up a repertoire of basic forms, and then, gradually, 'fusing the parts'. If the perception of pictures does indeed operate on the basis of the same principles as the production of pictures, we might grasp the overall structure of a picture like 'The British used guns' according to a schema that is not so different from that of Shannon and Weaver's communication model, as shown in figure 2.3.

The second way of identifying participants is that of functional semiotic theory (see Halliday, 1978, 1985). The conceptual apparatus of this kind of theory has, so far, been

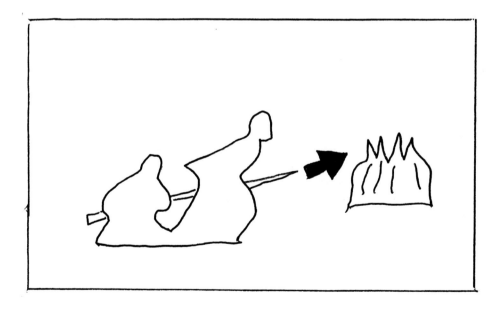

Fig 2.3 Schematic reduction of figure 2.1, showing vector

applied only to language, the most frequently and methodically analysed semiotic system. It is oriented towards the semantic functions rather than towards the forms of the participants. It uses terms like 'Actor', 'Goal' and 'Recipient' rather than terms like 'volume' and 'mass'. Yet the two approaches are compatible. The most salient 'volumes' in 'The British used guns' are not only perceptually most conspicuous, they also play the most crucial roles in the grammatical structure that constitutes the meaning of the picture: the two men (the participant from which the vector emanates) have the role of *Actor*, and the Aborigines (the participant at which the vector points) have the role of *Goal* in a structure that represents their relation as a *Transaction*, as something *done by* an Actor *to* a Goal. The same terms ('Actor', 'Goal', 'Transaction') are used in functional linguistics. This is possible because they are semantic-functional, rather than formal, terms. Our use of these terms does not imply that images and diagrams work in the same way as language; only that they can 'say' (some of) the same things as language – in *very different ways:* what in language is realized by means of syntactic configurations of certain classes of nouns and certain classes of verbs is visually realized, made perceivable and communicable, by the vectorial relations between volumes. In Arnheim's words, 'We shall distinguish between volumes and vectors, between being and acting' (1982: 154).

The transactional structure is not the only kind of structure that can be realized visually. We have already discussed an example of a classificatory structure (a subject which we will take up in more detail in a later section; see pp. 79–87). In the picture in figure 2.4, taken from the same social studies textbook as figure 2.1 (Oakley *et al.*, 1985), the structure is 'analytical'. Here the participants have the roles not of 'Actor' and 'Goal' but of 'Carrier' and 'Attribute'. This picture is not about something which participants are *doing* to other participants, but about the way participants *fit together* to make up a larger whole. It has the structure of a map. Just as in maps a larger participant, the 'Carrier', represents the 'whole' (say, Australia), and a number of other participants, the 'Possessive Attributes', represent the 'parts' (say, the states of Australia), so the Antarctic explorer functions as 'Carrier', and the balaclava, the windproof top, the fur mittens, etc. function as 'Possessive Attributes', as the parts that make up the whole. The closest linguistic translation here – were we to attempt one – would not be an action clause like 'The British point their guns at the Aborigines', but a 'possessive attributive' clause like 'The outfit of the Antarctic explorer consists of a balaclava, a windproof top, fur mittens . . . [etc.]'

We can now look at the abundance of detail in naturalistic images in a new way. The naturalistic image, whatever else it may be about, is always also about detail. It contains a multitude of *embedded* 'analytical' processes. It may, at the most salient level, say, 'The British point their guns at the Aborigines', but it will also, at less immediately conspicuous levels, say things like 'The men's outfits consist of hats, kerchiefs . . . [etc.]' and 'The trees have clumps of leaves.' In language, prepositional phrases (*two men* with hats and kerchiefs) and subordinate clauses (*two men*, wearing hats and kerchiefs) fulfil the same function of adding detail at a 'secondary' or even more deeply embedded level.

Embedding can also occur in diagrams. Take the 'communication model' in figure 2.5, a model drawn up, not by two telecommunication engineers, as in the case of Shannon and Weaver (figure 2.2), but by two sociologists, Riley and Riley (1959). As a whole, the

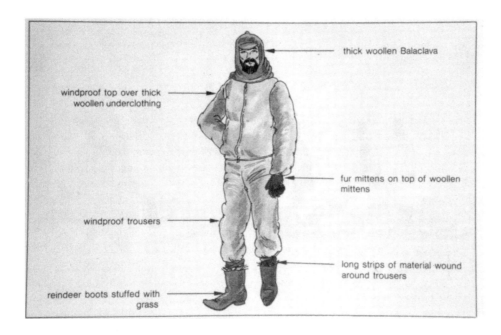

thick woollen Balaclava

windproof top over thick
woollen underclothing

fur mittens on top of woollen
mittens

windproof trousers

long strips of material wound
around trousers

reindeer boots stuffed with
grass

⬥ Fig 2.4 Antarctic explorer (Oakley *et al.*, 1985)

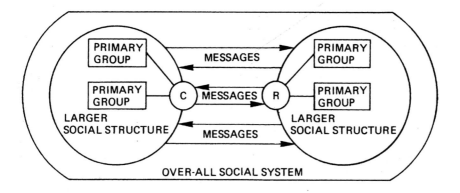

⬥ Fig 2.5 Communication model (from Watson and Hill, 1980: 143)

diagram is 'analytical'; it is a kind of abstract map. It shows that the 'over-all social system' consists of 'larger social structures' which in turn consist of 'primary groups'. It also features two individuals, 'C' ('Communicator') and 'R' ('Recipient'). These are depicted as half in, half out of the 'larger social structures', and they are connected to, though not part of, the 'primary groups'. Embedded within this analytical structure is a

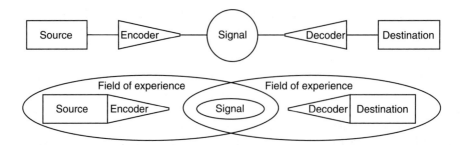

Fig 2.6 Two communication models (from Watson and Hill, 1980: 147)

transactional structure: the 'larger social structures' and the individuals 'C' and 'R' are represented as involved in an active process of communication, realized by vectors.

When we look at 'The British used guns' (in figure 2.1) as a transactional structure, the two men form one participant: together they have the role of 'Actor'. When we look at the two men as an 'analytical' structure, they form two distinct participants, linked by the lines formed by the hand of the man on the right and the gun of the man on the left. Diagrams allow further possibilities, as can be seen in the two communication models in figure 2.6, both drawn by Schramm (1954), a social psychologist writing about mass communication. In the first model, 'source' and 'encoder' are separate entities, *conjoined* by a line, just as are the two men in 'The British used guns'. We will argue later that lines without arrow heads realize a particular kind of 'analytical' structure:

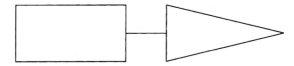

Fig 2.7 Conjoining participants

In the second model, 'source' and 'encoder' are *compounded*, welded together yet still distinct components of the whole:

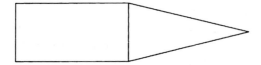

Fig 2.8 Compounding of participants

The third possibility would be a complete fusion between 'source' and 'encoder'. The shape of Riley and Riley's 'overall social system' (figure 2.5) can be interpreted as such a fusion – a fusion of two circles and a box. Apparently participants can lose their separate identity to different degrees. When they are conjoined, the process, the act of connecting them, is still explicit, realized by a line. When they are compounded, their identities remain distinct, but there is no longer an explicitly expressed process to connect them. When they are fused, even their separate identities have disappeared. In speech and writing, with somewhat different means – for instance, stress and intonation – we can move from, say, The *bird is black*, which has two distinct participants as well as a connecting process ('is'); to the *black bird*, which has *black* and *bird* still as different words, but removes the process; to the *blackbird,* in which two words have been fused to become one semantic entity/noun. Each successive step further obscures the act of predication, the explicit act of bringing the two participants together, until the structure is no longer 'analytical', no longer analysed or analysable. We make the point at some length because of the (ideological) significance of this semiotic resource in configuring the represented world.

Fig 2.9 Fusion of participants

As with many other kinds of diagram, the communication models we have used to illustrate this section are explained or paraphrased in the written texts that accompany them. But by no means everything that is expressed in the diagrams is also expressed in the written texts. Not all of the meanings conveyed visually are also conveyed verbally. The meanings of the visual shapes, the boxes and circles and triangles that give the participants their volume, for example, are almost always left unexplained. Older, common sense or theoretical notions, such as 'illustration' (images 'illustrating' verbal texts) or 'explanation' (words 'explaining' diagrams) are no longer an adequate account of the relations between words and pictures, here as in other instances. Why, in figure 2.6, is the 'signal' a circle, the 'source' a rectangle, the 'encoder' a triangle? Why, in figure 2.5, is the 'primary group' a rectangle, while the 'larger social structure' and the individuals 'C' and 'R' are circles? Why do Shannon and Weaver (figure 2.2) prefer angularity, while Riley and Riley prefer curvature (figure 2.5)?

There can be little doubt that such choices are charged with meaning. Basic geometrical shapes have always been a source of fascination, even of religious awe. Our scientific age is no exception. Circles, squares and triangles have been regarded as pure, quasi-scientific 'atoms' of the visible world, a 'pure manifestation of the elements', the 'universal-as-the-mathematical', as Mondrian said (quoted in Jaffé, 1967: 54–5). And they have been thought to have the power to directly affect our nervous system, for instance by the constructivist artist Gabo: 'The emotional force of an absolute shape is unique and not replaceable by any other means. . . . Shapes exult and shapes depress, they elate and make desperate' (quoted in Nash, 1974: 54). As we are here primarily concerned with the relations between participants, this subject falls somewhat outside our main concern; it deserves a separate study. But given the semiotic and ideological (mythical) significance of these aspects, we will at least indicate the issues with which such a study might be concerned.

In contemporary Western society, squares and rectangles are the elements of the mechanical, technological order, of the world of human construction. They dominate the shape of our cities, our buildings, our roads. They dominate the shape of many of the objects we use in daily life, including our pictures, which nowadays rarely have a round or oval frame, though other periods were happy to use these to frame more intimate portraits in particular. Unlike circles, which are self-contained, complete in themselves, rectangular shapes can be stacked, aligned with each other in geometrical patterns: they form the modules, the building blocks with which we construct our world, and they are therefore the dominant choice of builders and engineers, and of those who think like builders and engineers. In art, they are the choice of geometrical abstractionists, artists for whom art has to be, above all, rational. As Mondrian wrote in the 1920s,

> In all fields life grows increasingly abstract while it remains real. More and more the *machine* displaces natural power. In fashion we see a characteristic tensing of form and intensification of colour, signifying the departure from the natural.
>
> *In modern dance steps* (boston, tango, etc.) the same tensing is seen: the curved line of the old dance (waltz etc.) has yielded to the straight line, and each movement is immediately neutralized by a counter-movement – signifying the search for equilibrium. Our *social life* shows this too: autocracy, imperialism with its (natural) rule of power, is about to fall – if it has not fallen already – and yields to the (spiritual) power of law.
>
> Likewise the new spirit comes strongly forward in *logic, science* and *religion*. The imparting of veiled wisdom yields to the wisdom of pure reason; and knowledge shows increasing exactness. The old religion, with its mysteries and dogmas, is increasingly thrust aside by a clear relationship to the universal.
>
> (quoted in Jaffé, 1967: 64)

Glosses in 'dictionaries of visual symbols' and similar publications tend to express the meaning of geometrical shapes in terms of intrinsic, abstract qualities, but they point in the same direction. According to Dondis (1973: 44), the square represents 'honesty, straightness and workmanlike meaning'; according to Thompson and Davenport (1982: 110), it 'represents the world and denotes order'.

Circles are glossed very differently in such dictionaries, as denoting 'endlessness, warmth, protection' (Dondis, 1973: 44), or as 'the traditional symbol of eternity and the heavens' (Thompson and Davenport, 1982: 110). But such descriptions can be multiplied endlessly: the more abstract the sign, the greater its semantic extension; or, to put it in our terms, the greater its potential range of uses as a signifier in signs. We need to look for the principles that unite these meanings, and for the fundamental oppositions between square and circle, between the angular and the curved. In nature, squareness does not exist. Mondrian admitted that his method of 'abstracting the curve' made it difficult to represent nature: 'In painting a tree, I progressively abstracted the curve; you can understand that very little "tree" remained' (quoted in Jaffé, 1967: 120). Circles and curved forms generally are the elements we associate with an organic and natural order, with the world of organic nature – and such mystical meanings as may be associated with them derive from this. Angularity we associate with the inorganic, crystalline world, or with the world of technology, which is a world we have made ourselves, and therefore a world we can, at least in principle, understand fully and rationally. The world of organic nature is not of our making, and will always retain an element of mystery. Curved forms are therefore the dominant choice of people who think in terms of organic growth rather than mechanical construction, in terms of what is natural rather than in terms of what is artificial. In art, it is the choice of what is sometimes called 'biomorphic abstractionalism' – the curves, blobs and bulges in the paintings of Hans Arp or the sculptures of Henry Moore.

The values attached to these poles of meaning – that is, the actual signs produced with the signifiers of the 'technological' and the 'natural' – do, of course, differ. The square can connote the 'technological' positively, as a source of power and progress, or negatively, as a source of oppression which, literally and figuratively, 'boxes us in'. In Riley and Riley's communication model (figure 2.5) society is represented as a natural order, organically evolved rather than humanly constructed. But the 'primary groups' are depicted as rectangles. Perhaps this betrays an unconscious bias in favour of modern urban society, a view in which the small, close-knit community in which everyone knows everything about everyone is seen as oppressive, and the 'larger social structure' as liberating, providing the individual with anonymity, and thereby with autonomy and self-containment, choice and freedom. For Riley and Riley, individuals hail from 'primary groups' (and are still connected to them, albeit tenuously), but then go their own way, leaving the 'primary groups' behind, and moving freely in and out of the 'larger social structures', in a socially mobile world. This example shows that diagrams, rational and scientific as they may seem, can convey meanings visually that are not necessarily also conveyed verbally.

The triangle is angular, like the square – an element of the mechanical, technological order. But, unlike the square, the triangle, especially when tilted, is a (fused structure of a) participant and a vector, because it can convey directionality, point at things. The meanings it attracts are therefore less like 'qualities of being' than like processes, as in the well-known revolutionary poster by El Lissitzky (figure 2.10), in which the revolution, represented by a red triangle, is an active, dynamic force, wedging itself into the inert, self-contained, 'organic' society of White Russia.

In diagrams, triangles can similarly introduce a sense of process. The triangles in figure 2.6, for instance, could be seen as 'focusing' or 'aiming' the 'message' (we have already indicated why it is so difficult to give verbal transcodings of visual processes and we will discuss this more fully later). Not surprisingly, glosses of the meanings of triangles in visual dictionaries reflect this dynamic quality. Triangles are 'a symbol of generative power'

● Fig 2.10 *Beat the Whites with the Red Wedge* (El Lissitzky, 1919–20) (from Nash, 1974)

(Thompson and Davenport, 1982: 110), and represent 'action, conflict, tension' (Dondis, 1973: 44).

The meanings of the basic geometrical shapes, then, are motivated in two ways. First, they derive from the properties of the shapes or, rather, from the values given to these properties in specific social and cultural contexts. The straight line, for instance, means what it literally is: 'straight'. This 'straightness' may then be used to carry any one of a vast range of meanings compatible with that. It may be positively valued in one context (e.g. the 'straight and narrow path', or Mondrian's association of straightness with the 'spiritual power of law'), less positively in another (e.g. 'the straight man' as opposed to the 'funny man', or 'straight' as opposed to 'gay'). The producers of an image have their interests in making the visual sign, and this makes the meaning of the image quite specific for the producer; it colours in and makes specific the abstract meanings that derive from the inherent properties of the shapes and from the histories of their cultural uses. Rectangles can be stacked – and, again, this may be positively valued in one context, say in urban planning, or in geometric abstractionism; and less positively in another, say in counter-cultures that dream of living in geodesic domes, or in biomorphic abstractionism.

Second, these meanings derive from the common qualities we may detect in such objects in our environment as would be circular or rectangular when abstracted to their underlying basic shape, and from the values attached to these qualities in different social contexts. The sun, the moon, the belly of the pregnant woman, are curved. The skyscraper, the executive desk, the expensive briefcase, are rectangular. Such common qualities as we may see in these groups of objects (say, 'nature's cycles' and 'male power') will evidently be read and valued differently in different social contexts – and the groupings of objects from which we derive these meanings are likely to be made selectively, so as to obtain the common qualities sought.

Finally, our argument suggests that the semiotic genesis of diagrams lies, not just in technical drawing, but also in art, and specifically in the abstract art movements of our century, which no longer fill out and corporealize the schematic reductions which natural-istic artists have used for centuries, and which, if the Gestaltists are right, underlie all visual representation.

From the basic shapes other geometrical shapes can be derived: square, circle and triangle can be horizontally or vertically elongated to different degrees; and the square, the triangle and all elongated shapes can be tilted, either towards the right or towards the left. *Vertical elongation* creates a more pronounced distinction between top and bottom, and hence a bias towards hierarchy, and towards 'opposition' generally (what is most import-ant or otherwise dominant goes on top, what is less important or dominant is relegated to the bottom). *Horizontal elongation* causes a shape to lean towards the kind of structure in which what is positioned on the left is presented as 'Given', as information that is already familiar to the reader and serves as a 'departure point' for the message, while what is positioned on the right is presented as 'New', as information not yet known to the reader, and hence deserving his or her special attention. The shape of Schramm's 'field of experi-ence' and 'signal' in the second diagram of figure 2.6, for instance, suggests that these participants are, at least potentially, endowed with such an information structure. *Tilting*, finally, creates oblique lines and hence a sense of vectoriality. In Malevich's *Supremacist Composition: Red Square and Black Square* (figure 2.11) the participants are represented as squares. But because the red square is tilted, the painting is structurally more similar to El Lissitzky's *Beat the Whites with the Red Wedge* (figure 2.10) than, for instance, to Mondrian's compositions of red, yellow and blue squares: it is about dynamic' action, whereas Mondrian's compositions are about a stable order, a 'search for equilibrium' – the red square seems to move away from the oppressively large black square.[1]

Finally, it is important to stress the essential *interchangeability* of visual and verbal participants in diagrams, and, indeed, in many other visual genres. Although the processes and structures in diagrams are always visual, the participants which they relate to each other may be of different kinds: pictures, naturalistic or schematic; abstract shapes, with or without verbal labels; words, either enclosed or not enclosed in boxes or other shapes; letters; and so on. The same thing can be seen in page layout: the participants are hetero-geneous. They can be verbal (headlines, blocks of copy, etc.), but the semiotic means which bring them together into a coherent semantic structure are always visual. The key to understanding such texts therefore lies above all in an understanding of the visual semiotic means which are used to weld these heterogeneous elements into a coherent whole, into a text. Visual structures relate visual elements to each other; these visual elements, however, may themselves be heterogeneous – a word as a visual element, a block of written text as

Fig 2.11 *Suprematist Composition: Red Square and Black Square* (Kasimir Malevich, 1914) (from Nash, 1974)

a visual element, an image as a visual element, a number or an equation as a visual element.

NARRATIVE PROCESSES

When participants are connected by a vector, they are represented as *doing* something to or for each other. From here on we will call such vectorial patterns *narrative* – in Kress and van Leeuwen (1990) we used the term 'presentational' – and contrast them to *conceptual* patterns (see figure 2.12). Where conceptual patterns represent participants in terms of their class, structure or meaning, in other words, in terms of their generalized and more or less stable and timeless essence, narrative patterns serve to present unfolding actions and events, processes of change, transitory spatial arrangements.

The hallmark of a narrative visual 'proposition' is the presence of a vector: narrative structures always have one, conceptual structures never do. In pictures, these vectors are formed by depicted elements that form an oblique line, often a quite strong, diagonal line, as in 'The British used guns' (in figure 2.1), where the guns and the outstretched arms of the British form such a line. The vectors may be formed by bodies or limbs or tools 'in action', but there are many other ways to turn represented elements into diagonal lines of action. A road running diagonally across the picture space, for instance, is also a vector, and the car driving on it an 'Actor' in the process of 'driving'. In abstract images such as diagrams, narrative processes are realized by abstract graphic elements – for instance, lines with an explicit indicator of directionality, usually an arrowhead. Such features of directionality must always be present if the structure is to realize a narrative representation: connecting lines without an indicator of directionality form a particular kind of analytical structure, and mean something like 'is connected to', 'is conjoined to', 'is related to'.

The 'Actor' is the participant from whom or which the vector departs, and which may be *fused* with the vector to different degrees. In *Beat the Whites with the Red Wedge* (figure 2.10), for instance, the red triangle is both participant and vector, and represents both the 'wedge' and the act of wedging in (or 'beating', as the title has it). In figure 2.13, taken from a factual children's book about France (Bender, 1988), the Actors are realized by the colour of the arrows (the 'Gulf Stream' vector is red, the 'Mistral' vector blue), and by their volume (they are not just thin lines), and the narrative processes are realized by

⬥ **Fig 2.12 Main types of visual representational structure**

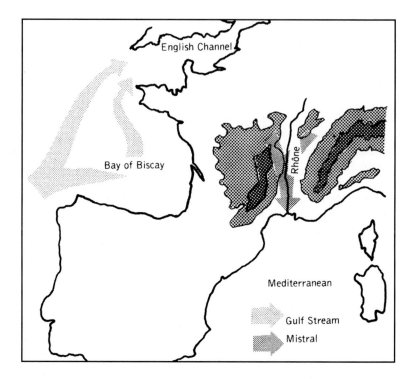

English Channel

Fig 2.13 Gulf Stream and Mistral (Bender, 1988)

their vectoriality. In Shannon and Weaver's (1949) communication model (figure 2.2), on the other hand, Actor and process are realized by separate visual elements, the Actor by a box ('information source'), the process by an arrow. Pictures like 'The British used guns' (in figure 2.1) occupy, perhaps, an intermediate position.

In the case of 'realist' images, the context usually makes clear what kind of action the vectors represent. 'The British used guns' (in figure 2.1) can be translated – should we wish or need to do so – not so much with 'used', as the caption has it, as with something like 'The British stalk the Aborigines with their guns'. Other possibilities exist, but the field is limited. The vectors in abstract pictures are more difficult to transcode. One first needs to formulate what they, literally, formally, do. This can then help to circumscribe the field of possible readings. The triangle in El Lissitzky's *Beat the Whites with the Red Wedge* (figure 2.10) literally *wedges itself into* the white circle. This opens up a perhaps large, but by no means infinite, range of possible readings: the triangle can be said to 'pierce' or 'infiltrate' or 'destabilize' the circle. In fact it does all these things – the process represents a field of possible meanings. In the case of Malevich's *Suprematist Composition: Red Square and Black Square* (figure 2.11), the red square literally *tilts away from* the black square above it. How can we transcode this? Does the red square 'flee from' or 'point away from' the black square? Is it 'ejected from' or 'discarded by' it? All these readings are legitimate. The point is that each reading will have the small red square as the mobile participant, however much it is dominated by the big, heavy black square, and the black square as static, motionless and monolithic. The picture tells the story of an 'underling' escaping from, or being expelled from, the monolithic power of the black square. Who or what this underling or these forces are the readers will produce in the process of reading, although the shapes and colours will point them in a certain direction, make certain readings more plausible, more like those of the producer's than others.

In the case of diagrams it is also difficult to say in words just what kind of action the vectors represent. The common sense view of the function of images as 'illustration' and 'explanation' would be that the accompanying verbal text explains what is not made clear visually. But usually this is not so. Usually the process is represented only visually, and the written text either does not paraphrase it at all, or provides contradictory or even misleading glosses. The Shannon and Weaver communication model has been 'quoted' and verbally explained in many books and articles, for instance in Watson and Hill's *Dictionary of Communication and Media Studies* (1980), which has a 250-word entry about the model, and in a *Scientific American* article by Pierce, a telecommunications engineer (1972). The first gives the following indications of the meaning of the vectors: the authors say that the model 'can be applied to any information *transfer* system' and they call it a '*process* centred model' (1980: 149, our italics) – two rather oblique references, one a broad gloss ('process'), the other only slightly more specific ('transfer'). Pierce's explanations are contradictory. On the one hand, he calls the model a 'system' (as do Watson and Hill in the dictionary) and paraphrases it in terms of an analytical rather than a narrative structure: 'The system *consists* of an information source, a transmitter, a communication channel, a noise source, a receiver and a message destination' (1972: 32, our italics) – note that he lists only the participants, not the processes. On the other hand, when he gives an example, he paraphrases the vectors by means of active verbs:

> A human being may *type* a message consisting of the letters and spaces on the keyboard of a teletypewriter. The teletypewriter serves as a transmitter that *encodes* each character as a sequence of electrical pulses, which may be 'on' or 'off', 'current' or 'no current'. These electrical pulses are *transmitted* by a pair of wires to another teletypewriter that acts as a receiver and *prints* out the letters and spaces.
>
> (Pierce, 1972: 33, our italics)

These are just two examples where others are possible. The meaning potential of diagrammatic vectors is broad, abstract and hence difficult to put into words. The accompanying texts tend to be much more explicit about participants, about things existing in space (or represented as though they are), than about processes, events and actions. Scientific and bureaucratic writing, and many forms of expository writing generally, put most of their meaning in the nouns rather than in the verbs. Verbs, in these forms of language, remain restricted to a relatively small set of (logical) connectors ('is', 'has', 'leads to', 'causes', 'generates', 'develops into', and so on), almost as though they were 'function words', like articles and pronouns, rather than 'content words'. In his book *Factual Writing* (1985: 40), Martin gives an example:

> There is little doubt that television coverage of a domestic slaughtering operation, conducted in a government approved abattoir, which involved the slaughter of lambs, calves and swine, would generate a good deal of public revulsion and protest.

In this extract most of the specific actions appear in noun form, and some have been *nominalized*; that is, turned into nouns from prior full clausal forms ('doubt', 'coverage', 'slaughtering operation', 'slaughter', 'revulsion', 'protest'). In a text of thirty-seven words, there are only two main verbs ('is' and 'generate'), both very general. Doings and happenings have been turned into things. The dynamics of action has been changed into a static of relations. Diagrams do something similar. They represent events which take place over time as *spatial configurations*, and so turn 'process' into 'system' – or into something ambiguously in between, something that can be called either 'system-centred' or 'process-centred'. In this respect diagrams are akin to certain forms of nominalizing writing, while naturalistic images, with their human participants and their more concrete, specific processes, are more akin to story-writing. Like many naturalistic images, stories are about human or animate beings and the things they do, and in stories much more meaning is put into verbs than in most non-narrative forms of writing.

Because their meaning is so abstract and general, vectors can represent fundamentally different processes as though they were the same (for instance, 'humans typing letters and spaces on a keyboard' and 'teletypewriters transmitting electrical pulses'). Diagrams of the Shannon and Weaver type can impose two models of interpretation on one situation or perhaps one model on many; here the two models are 'transport' and 'transformation'. Figure 2.2 represents what is going on either as *transport*, movement from one place to another, or as the more or less causally determined *transformation* from one thing into another. And because one sign, the arrow, can represent both, the two meanings often become conflated: movement, transport *is* transformation; mobility *is* the cause of, and condition for, change, growth, evolution, progress. The Shannon and Weaver model, for instance, represents communication as transport, as moving information from one place to another, but it also and at the same time represents communication as the transformation of messages into signals, of 'letters and spaces' into 'electrical pulses'.

The arrows in the 'system networks' of systemic-functional grammar (our diagram in figure 2.12 is such a 'system network') are usually transcoded by 'choose' or 'select' (e.g. ' "Conceptual" selects "Classificational", "Analytical" or "Symbolical" '). But visually the process is, again, a combination of transport and transformation. And when such networks are turned into computer programs, as indeed they have been, the visual metaphor becomes a reality in which there are not people 'choosing' between 'options', but pulses transported to points at which a change of state occurs. At that point the schematic reduction of one semiotic reality has turned into a blueprint for another, new semiotic reality, and people will have been reduced to the role of 'source' and 'destination' in an autonomized and exteriorized semiotic process, just as they are in Shannon and Weaver's communication model.

Different kinds of narrative process can be distinguished on the basis of the kinds of vector and the number and kind of participants involved.

1 Action processes

The Actor is the participant from which the vector emanates, or which itself, in whole or in part, forms the vector (as with the triangle in figure 2.10). In images they are often also the most salient participants, through size, place in the composition, contrast against background, colour saturation or conspicuousness, sharpness of focus, and through the 'psychological salience' which certain participants (e.g. the human figure and, even more so, the human face) have for viewers. In figure 2.1, for instance, the British are larger than the Aborigines, and placed in the foreground. In the Shannon and Weaver communication model (figure 2.2), the 'information source' and the 'noise source' are Actors (we will comment on their different position in the diagram, and on the different directionality of their arrows, in chapter 6):

When images or diagrams have only one participant, this participant is usually an Actor. The resulting structure we call *non-transactional*. The action in a non-transactional process has no 'Goal', is not 'done to' or 'aimed at' anyone or anything. The non-transactional action process is therefore analogous to the intransitive verb in language (the verb that does not take an object). The processes in figure 2.13 are non-transactional: the water of the Gulf Stream does not move *something*, it just moves; and the wind of the Mistral does not blow *something*, it just blows. This visual representation is akin to the way meteorological processes are represented in English; *it rains*, or *it snows*. As Halliday has pointed out (1985: 102), other languages do not necessarily do this. In one Chinese dialect, for instance, one has to say something like 'the sky is dropping water'; in other words, raining has to be represented as a transactive process. In figure 2.15, the gesture of the old man forms a vector, but he does not gesture towards anyone or anything, at least not so far as we can see in this picture. As a result, the viewer is left to imagine who or what he may be communicating with. Is he already in touch with what lies beyond life? Is that why the young boy looks at him with such concentrated fascination?

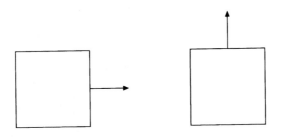

● **Fig 2.14 Actors**

 Fig 2.15 New York, 1955 (Robert Frank)

At other times, there is only a vector and a *Goal* (figure 2.16). The Goal is the participant at whom or which the vector is directed, hence it is also the participant *to whom* or which the action is done, or *at whom* or which the action is aimed.

Representations of actions which include only the Goal we will call *Events*: something is happening to someone, but we cannot see who or what makes it happen. Figure 2.17 shows a diagram which appeared in the *Sydney Morning Herald* during the first Gulf War. A vector represents the action of moving towards the town of Khafji, and the Goal is the town of Khafji itself, represented by a black dot. But nothing represents the war planes which are moving towards Khafji. Closely related is the case in which just a small part of the Actor is visible, a hand, or a foot, so that the Actor becomes anonymous. In both cases there *is* in fact an Actor, as in figure 2.17, but the Actor is either deleted from the representation or made anonymous, a visual analogue, perhaps, of 'passive agent deletion', a linguistic form of representation that plays an important role in critical linguistics and critical discourse analysis, as when a newspaper headline says, 'Fifteen Demonstrators Shot in Riots', thereby omitting to mention that they were shot by police (Trew, 1979: 97ff).

When a narrative visual proposition has two participants, one is the Actor, the other the *Goal*. The Actor in such a *transactional* process is not so much the participant which moves (as in the non-transactional process) as the participant which instigates the movement, and if we had to give a verbal paraphrase of a transactional process we would probably use

 Fig 2.16 Goal

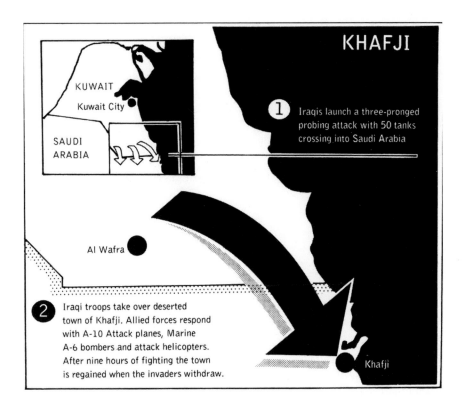

KHAFJI

KUWAIT

Kuwait City

SAUDI
ARABIA

Al Wafra

① Iraqis launch a three-pronged probing attack with 50 tanks crossing into Saudi Arabia

② Iraqi troops take over deserted town of Khafji. Allied forces respond with A-10 Attack planes, Marine A-6 bombers and attack helicopters. After nine hours of fighting the town is regained when the invaders withdraw.

Khafji

Fig 2.17 Gulf War Diagram (*Sydney Morning Herald*, 14 February 1991)

a transitive verb, a verb that takes an object (e.g. 'transport' or 'send' instead of [intransitive] 'move').

In 'The British used guns' (figure 2.1), the two men are the Actor, the Aborigines are the Goal. There is, in fact, a second transactional process: there are also vectors formed by lines that can be drawn from the heads of the Aborigines to the fire, and so constitute a process in which the Aborigines are the Actor and the fire the Goal. 'The Aborigines surround the fire', one could transcode. But the point is not to find a verbal equivalent; the point is to establish that the Aborigines are represented as Actor and the fire as Goal. Because of its smaller size and placement further towards the background, this process is a 'minor process', embedded in the major process. The whole could be transcoded as 'The British stalk the Aborigines, who surround the fire'.

It is possible to argue that structures such as the Shannon and Weaver diagram (figure 2.2) have been affected by the fact that Western culture gives such centrality to language that the structure of English, with its lexical distinction of verbs/processes and nouns/objects, may have acted as a model for a semiotic schema. So arrows as vectors/processes and boxes as participants/nouns may be a more or less unconscious translation from language into the visual. However, it is important here to insist on the distinct organization of the two modes. The visual structure of arrows and boxes conveys a strong sense of 'impacting' or 'targeting', which is quite absent in the verbal translations which come most immediately to mind. The visual structure foregrounds procedure over substantive content, the act of 'impacting' over what makes the impact, more or less in the way that, for instance, marketing experts are often more concerned about strategies for reaching consumers than about the goods and services that should reach them, or that pedagogic experts are more concerned about the format of classroom interaction than about the content of lessons.

● **Fig 2.18 Speech circuit (de Saussure 1974 [1916])**

Some transactional structures are bidirectional, each participant playing now the role of Actor, now the role of Goal, as for instance in de Saussure's well-known 'speech circuit' diagram (figure 2.18) in which 'A' and 'B' are now speaker, now listener. It is not always clear whether bidirectional transactions are represented as occurring simultaneously or in succession, although there is a tendency to use one arrow with two heads to signify simultaneity, and two arrows pointing in different directions to signify sequentiality. In figure 2.18, for instance, sequentiality is realized by two separate dotted lines (line and arrowhead, connection and directionality, are separate elements in this diagram).

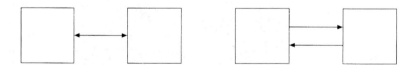

● **Fig 2.19 Simultaneous and sequential bidirectionality**

We will refer to the participants in such structures as Interactors, to indicate their double role.

2 Reactional processes

When the vector is formed by an eyeline, by the direction of the glance of one or more of the represented participants, the process is *reactional*, and we will speak not of Actors, but of Reacters, and not of Goals, but of *Phenomena*. The Reacter, the participant who does the looking, must necessarily be human, or a human-like animal – a creature with visible eyes that have distinct pupils, and capable of facial expression. The Phenomenon may be formed either by another participant, the participant at whom or which the Reacter is looking, or by a whole visual proposition, for example, a transactional structure. In figure 2.15, for instance, the old man *and* his gesture form the Phenomenon, while the young boy is the Reacter. In figure 2.20, an advertisement for mineral water, the man is Actor in a transactional action process in which the water is Goal ('The man drinks water', one might transcode): the whole angle of his body forms a strong vector between the two represented participants. This process ('Man drinks water') then becomes the Phenomenon of a reactional structure in which the woman is Reacter – a vector, formed by the direction of her glance and the angle of her left arm, leads from her to the drinking man. She reacts to his action with a smile of approval (the precise nature of reactions is coloured in by facial expression). The man as doer, the woman as faithful admirer of his actions, is a distribution of roles which, as Goffman has shown in his *Gender Advertisements* (1976), is very common in advertisements (but not only in advertisements): 'When a man and a woman

Fig 2.20 Vittel advertisement (*New Idea, 5 December 1987*)

collaborate in an undertaking, the man is likely to perform the executive role' (Goffman, 1976: 32).

Like actions, reactions can be transactional or non-transactional. In the latter case there is no Phenomenon, as is the case with the look of the old man in figure 2.15. It is then left to the viewer to imagine what he or she is thinking about or looking at, and this can create a powerful sense of empathy or identification with the represented participants. Sometimes photographers or picture editors crop photos back to close-ups of non-transactional Reacters who look bored, or animated, or puzzled, at something we cannot see. This can become a source of representational manipulation. A caption may, for instance, suggest what the Reacter is looking at, but, needless to say, it need not be what the Reacter was actually looking at when the picture was taken. Stuart Hall (1982) has described how this kind of manipulation is used in press photographs of politicians.

3 Speech process and mental process

A special kind of vector can be observed in comic strips: the oblique protrusions of the thought balloons and dialogue balloons that connect drawings of speakers or thinkers to their speech or thought. Until recently they were confined to the comic strips, although there have, of course, also been speech processes in medieval art, for instance in the form of ribbons emanating from the speaker's mouth. Today they increasingly crop up in other contexts, too; for instance, in connection with quotes in school textbooks or on the screens of automatic bank tellers. Like transactional reactions, these processes connect a human (or animate) being with 'content', but where in transactional reactions it is the content of a perception, in the case of thought bubbles and similar devices it is the content of an inner mental process (thought, fear, etc.), and in the case of speech vectors the content of the speech. Halliday (1985: 227ff.) calls this kind of structure 'projective'. The Phenomenon of the transactional Reaction, and the content of the dialogue balloon or thought balloon are not represented directly, but mediated through a Reacter, a 'Senser' (in the case of a thought balloon) or a 'Speaker' (in the case of the dialogue balloon).

4 Conversion processes

The Shannon and Weaver communication model (figure 2.2) forms a *chain* of transactional processes. This chaining results in a third kind of participant, a participant which is the Goal with respect to one participant and the Actor with respect to another. Shannon and Weaver's 'transmitter' is such a participant, acting as Goal with respect to the 'information source' and as Actor with respect to the 'receiver'. We will call this kind of participant a *Relay* (our use of this term obviously differs from that of Barthes [1977], who uses it to denote an image–text relation in which the text extends, rather than elaborates ['anchors'], the visual information). Relays do not just pass on, in unchanged form, what they receive; they always also transform it – for instance, in the case of communication models, from 'letters and spaces' into 'electrical pulses', or, as in figure 2.23, from 'grasses, sedges and flowers' into 'urine, droppings and dead carcasses'.

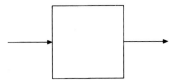

Fig 2.21 Relay

While the Shannon and Weaver model represents communication as a chained process with a beginning and an end, hence as an agentive process, a process set into motion by an Actor, other models, such as that shown in figure 2.22, represent communication as a cycle, and in that case all the participants are Relays, and agency is more weakly signified. This kind of process, which we will call a *Conversion* process, is especially common in representations of natural events; for instance, food chain diagrams or diagrammatic representations of the hydrological cycle. But, as figure 2.22 shows, it can also be applied to human (inter)action, and when this happens human (inter)action is represented as though it was a natural process.

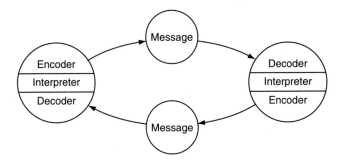

Fig 2.22 Communication model (from Watson and Hill, 1980: 147)

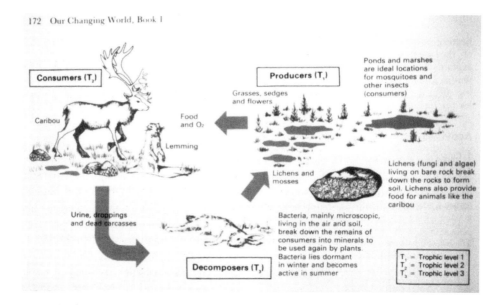

172   Our Changing World, Book 1

○ **Fig 2.23 Arctic tundra system (Sale *et al.*, 1980)**

5 Geometrical symbolism

Figure 2.24, another 'communication model', does not include any participants. There is only a vector, indicating directionality by means of an 'infinity' sign, rather than by means of an arrowhead. Dance's diagram is in fact not so much a communication model as a 'metadiagram' which shows us a process in isolation, in order to discuss why *helical* vectors are more suitable for the representation of communication than, for instance, straight or

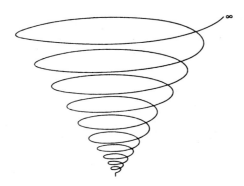

○ **Fig 2.24 Communication model (from Dance, 1967)**

curved arrows. Dance does this by pointing at the symbolic meanings of intrinsic properties of the helix. According to Dance, the shape of the helix:

> combines the desirable features of the straight line and of the circle, while avoiding the weakness of either. . . . It gives testimony to the concept that communication, while moving forward, is at the same time coming back upon itself and being affected by its past behaviour, for the coming curve of the helix is fundamentally affected by the curve from which it emerges.
>
> (Dance, 1967)

Images of this kind use pictorial or abstract patterns as processes whose meanings are constituted by their symbolic values, and so extend the vectorial vocabulary by drawing our attention to possibilities beyond the diagonal action line or the simple arrow: coils, spirals, helixes.

Variants of the arrow may affect the meaning of the process in narrative diagrams. A curved arrow, for instance, partakes of the symbolic value of the circle, so that the process is represented as 'natural' and 'organic' (see figure 2.22). Vectors may also be *attenuated*, by the use of dotted lines, by making the arrowhead smaller or less conspicuous in other ways, or by placing it in the middle, rather than at the front of the line, which diminishes the sense of 'impacting' and 'targeting', and causes the meaning of the vector to move in the direction of mere connectivity (see figure 2.25).

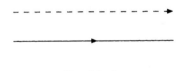

Attenuated vectors

⬤ **Fig 2.25 Attenuated vectors**

The vectorial relation may also be *amplified*, by means of bolder arrows (see figure 2.26), which perhaps suggest a certain density of 'traffic', as in figure 2.17, the diagram of

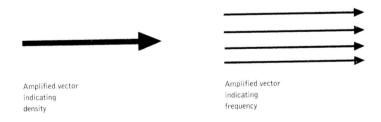

Amplified vector
indicating
density

Amplified vector
indicating
frequency

⬤ **Fig 2.26 Amplified vectors indicating density and frequency**

the attack on Khafji, or by the use of a number of arrows, which may suggest the frequency or multiplicity with which the process occurs.

In images a similar effect can be achieved by making the diagonal action lines more or less conspicuous, more or less dominant in the composition as a whole.

6 Circumstances

As we indicated in our discussion of 'The British used guns' (figure 2.1), narrative images may contain secondary participants, participants related to the main participants, not by means of vectors, but in other ways. We will refer to these participants, following Halliday (1985), as *Circumstances*. They are participants which could be left out without affecting the basic proposition realized by the narrative pattern, even though their deletion would of course entail a loss of information.

Locative Circumstances relate other participants to a specific participant we will call *Setting*. This requires a contrast between foreground and background, which can be realized in one or more of the following ways: (1) the participants in the foreground overlap, and hence partially obscure the Setting; (2) the Setting is drawn or painted in less detail (or, in the case of photography, has softer focus); (3) the Setting is more muted and desaturated in colour, with the various colours all tending towards the same hue, usually the blue of distance; (4) the Setting is darker than the foreground, or lighter, so that it acquires an 'overexposed', ethereal look. These formal features can occur in various combinations, and they are all gradients – 'more-or-less', rather than 'either–or', features.

As we will discuss in more detail in chapter 5, settings have importance for the realization of visual modality. The Settings themselves can of course be read as embedded analytical processes ('The landscape consists of grass, trees and rocks').

The tools used in action processes are often represented as *Circumstances of Means*. If this is the case, there is no clear vector between the tool and its user. The tools themselves may, of course, constitute the vectors which realize the action processes, as with the guns in 'The British used guns' (in figure 2.1), and they need not be objects. For instance, we would interpret the gesture of the old man in figure 2.15 as a non-transactional action ('The old man addresses an unseen participant'), and his hands as a Circumstance of Means ('The old man addresses an unseen participant *with* his hands').

Figure 2.27 shows a penguin with her baby. There is again no vector to relate the two. Yet the penguin and her baby clearly form two distinct participants: this is a picture of a penguin *with* a baby. In such a case we will interpret the relation as a Circumstance of Accompaniment. As the picture contains no vector and displays the penguin more or less frontally, against a de-emphasized background, we interpret it as 'analytical', as the kind of picture more likely to illustrate a text giving descriptive information about penguins than a story about what penguins do.

● Fig 2.27 Penguin with baby (Oakley *et al.*, 1985)

SUMMARY

Figure 2.28 summarizes the distinctions we have introduced in this section.[2] Following Halliday (1985), we have called processes that can take a whole visual (or verbal) proposition as their 'object' *projective*, and the others *non-projective*. The square brackets indicate a single choice; for instance, 'a transactional action is either unidirectional or bidirectional'. Our claim is that the 'choices' in figure 2.28 chart the principal ways in which images can represent the world 'narratively' – that is, in terms of 'doing' and 'happening'.

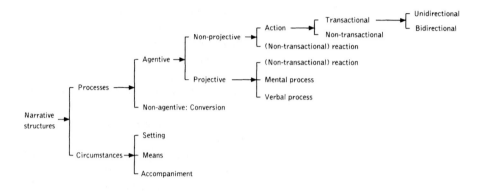

Fig 2.28 Narrative structures in visual communication

REALIZATIONS

Unidirectional transactional action	A vector, formed by a (usually diagonal) depicted element, or an arrow, connects two participants, an Actor and a Goal.
Bidirectional transactional action	A vector, formed by a (usually diagonal) depicted element, or a double-headed arrow, connects two Interactors.
Non-transactional action	A vector, formed by a (usually diagonal) depicted element, or an arrow, emanates from a participant, the Actor, but does not point at any other participant.
Actor	The active participant in an action process is the participant from which the vector emanates or which is fused with the vector.
Goal	The passive participant in an action process is the participant at which the vector is directed.
Interactors	The participants in a transactional action process where the vector could be said to emanate from, *and* be directed at, both participants.
Transactional reaction	An eyeline vector connects two participants, a Reacter and a Phenomenon.
Non-transactional reaction	An eyeline vector emanates from a participant, the Reacter, but does not point at another participant.

Reacter	The active participant in a reaction process is the participant whose look creates the eyeline.
Phenomenon	The passive participant in a (transactional) reaction is the participant at which the eyeline is directed; in other words, the participant which forms the object of the Reacter's look. The same term is used for the participant (verbal or non-verbal) enclosed by a 'thought bubble'.
Conversion	A process in which a participant, the Relay, is the Goal of one action and the Actor of another. This involves a change of state in the participant.
Mental process	A vector formed by a 'thought bubble' or a similar conventional device connects two participants, the Senser and the Phenomenon.
Senser	The participant from whom the 'thought bubble' vector emanates.
Verbal process	A vector formed by the arrow-like protrusion of a 'dialogue balloon' or similar device connects two participants, a Sayer and an Utterance.
Sayer	The participant in a verbal process from whom the 'dialogue balloon' emanates.
Utterance	The (verbal) participant enclosed in the 'dialogue balloon'.
Setting	The Setting of a process is recognizable because the participants in the foreground overlap and hence partially obscure it; because it is often drawn or painted in less detail, or, in the case of photography, has a softer focus; and because of contrasts in colour saturation and overall darkness or lightness between foreground and background.
Means	The Means of a process is formed by the tool with which the action is executed. It usually also forms the vector.
Accompaniment	An Accompaniment is a participant in a narrative structure which has no vectorial relation with other participants and cannot be interpreted as a Symbolic Attribute (see chapter 3).

VISUAL STRUCTURES AND LINGUISTIC STRUCTURES

We have drawn attention to the fact that, while both visual structures and verbal structures can be used to express meanings drawn from a common cultural source, the two modes are not simply alternative means of representing 'the same thing'. It is easy to overemphasize either the similarity or the difference between the two modes. Only a detailed comparison can bring out how in some respects they realize similar types of meaning, though in different ways, while in other, perhaps most respects they represent the world quite differently, allowing the development of the different epistemologies we discussed in the previous chapter. In this brief final section we wish to explore this in some detail with respect to narrative visual structures.

By comparison to the structures we will discuss in chapter 3, narrative visual structures are comparatively easy to 'translate'; though, as we will see, there certainly is no one-to-one correspondence. Like 'non-transactional actions', 'one-participant material processes' (Halliday, 1985: 103ff.) represent events as though they bear no relation to, and have no consequences for, participants other than the Actor. In *Many people migrated* one cannot add a second participant to this clause and say, for instance, *Many people migrated their relatives*, although one can of course add circumstances: *Many people migrated to Australia*. And, like 'transactional actions', 'two-participant material processes' (Halliday, 1985: 103ff.) involve two participants (e.g. *Migrants invaded Australia*). But linguistic 'Events' and visual 'Events' are quite different. Linguistic Events have processes that are 'happenings' which cannot have an Actor, as in *Many of my relatives died*. In the case of visual Events, the Actor is left out, but could have been used. They are the equivalent of passives with agent deletion, of clauses like *Many of my relatives were killed*, rather than of clauses like *Many of my relatives died*. To show someone dying it is necessary to show someone being killed, or to show someone performing an *action* that represents his or her death. Also, while in English many processes can take a third participant, the 'Beneficiary' (traditionally 'indirect object' in, e.g., *Mary gave him the book*), in images the possibility of such a third participant does not exist. What is a Beneficiary in English becomes a Goal in images ('she message-sends him' instead of 'she sends him a message').

On the other hand, English lacks the visual mode's structural devices to represent events as cyclical (although linguistic participants can have a double role in English – for instance, in examples like *He made them do it*, where *them* is Goal of *make do* as well as Actor of *do*; cf. Halliday, 1985: 153). Nor is there an 'interactional' process. To realize what we have called 'Interactors', English would have to make use of reflexive pronouns. Consider, for instance, the problem of trying to 'translate' figure 2.18, de Saussure's 'speech circuit' diagram, into English. A single visual process indicates something for which, in English, we need at least four clauses: 'A speaks to B', 'B speaks to A', 'A listens to B', 'B listens to A'. How can one render this in one clause? 'A and B communicate with each other'? But that causes 'A' and 'B' to lose their separate identity, transforming a reciprocal, bidirectional transaction into a jointly authored *non-transactional* action.

What we have called the 'non-transactional reaction' is in some ways akin to what Halliday calls the *behavioural* process (1985: 128), a process type which can take only one participant (who must be human) and serves to realize a restricted field of action, the field of 'physiological and psychological behaving' (1985: 128). But the meanings of visual 'non-transactional reactions' form a more restricted field, tied up as they are with one kind of behaviour – looking.

Projective processes – that is, mental and verbal processes – play an important part in English, and it is possible to distinguish a number of different types of each on the basis of formal grammatical criteria (Halliday, 1985: 106ff., 129). Mental processes, for instance, include processes of perception ('see', 'hear', etc.), processes of affection ('like', 'fear', 'wish', etc.) and processes of cognition ('know', 'think', 'believe', etc.). Each has a Senser, the person who does the seeing, or liking, or knowing (this has to be a person, or a participant represented as human), and a Phenomenon, someone or something seen, or liked, or known, by the Senser. Phenomena may be realized by participants or whole structures, just as in the case of images. In *Many people want to migrate to Australia,* the clause *to migrate to Australia* is Phenomenon; this sets mental processes apart from actions and transactions, which cannot have a clause as Goal. But what we have called the 'transactional reaction' can, if one wishes or needs to, be related to only a subset of the perception process, because non-visual Phenomena cannot directly be realized in the visual semiotic. Mental processes form, as we have shown, only a minor category in the visual semiotic; as far as we can see, there are no structural visual devices for making the strong distinction between 'cognition' and 'affection' processes that has come to characterize the ideational resources of English. The cinema, however, has developed a fairly extensive set of projective conventions for realizing different kinds of mental processes such as memories, dreams, hallucinations, and so on.

In English, verbal processes differ from mental processes in that they do not need a human 'Sayer' (one can say *The document said that . . .,* but not *The document thought that . . .*). On the other hand, like mental processes, they can take whole clauses as their object, and this in two different ways – in the form of Reported Speech (as in *He said [that] he had no idea*) and in the form of Quoted Speech (as in *He said 'I have no idea'*). There seems to be no direct, structural way of expressing this kind of difference visually. 'Dialogue balloons' always quote.

We have identified only three different types of circumstance in images: location, means and accompaniment. All three exist in English (Halliday, 1985: 137ff.), but there they are by no means the only types. English allows all kinds of information to be added to the basic narrative proposition conveyed by the process ('What happened?') and the participants ('Who or what was involved?'); information about time ('When did it happen?'; 'How long did it last?'); about purpose ('What did it happen for?'); cause ('Why did it happen?') and so on.

The following table gives an overview of some of the correspondences between linguistic and visual narrative processes:

Table 2.1 **Narrative process in language and visual communication**

Visual narrative processes	Linguistic narrative clauses
Non-transactional action	One-participant (Actor) material process ('action')
Unidirectional transactional action	Two-participant material process
Event	Passive transactional clause with agent deletion
Bidirectional transactional action	–
Non-transactional reaction	Behavioural process (field of looking)
Transactional reaction	Mental process: perception (visual only)
Mental process	Mental process (cognition and affection)
Verbal process	Verbal process (quotation)
–	Verbal process (affection)
Conversion	–

Comparisons such as these can highlight which ways of representing the world can be realized linguistically, which visually and which (more or less) in both ways. This, in turn, is useful as a background for analysing representation in multimodal texts: photographs and their captions, diagrams and their verbal glosses, stories and their illustrations. If, for instance, a diagram shows an arrow emanating from a participant labelled 'environment' and directed at another participant labelled 'message', then a 'literal' translation would be 'the environment acts upon the message'. If the accompanying text says that the 'communication process' is 'interacting with factors (or stimuli) from the environment' (Watson and Hill, 1980: 14), it 'mistranslates', and the mistranslation is not due to the limitations of either English or visual communication. A literal 'translation' of 'the source sends a message to the receiver', on the other hand, is not possible: the spatial representation of verbally conceived ideas changes the ideas themselves, and vice versa. In the next chapter we will show further examples of this problem.

Notes

1 We are grateful to the Danish art historian Lise Mark for pointing out that, in the previous edition of this book, this painting was reproduced 'on its side', i.e. tilted by 90 degrees.
2 We would like to thank Bente Foged Madsen for some useful comments that have led to improvements of this diagram.

3 Conceptual representations: designing social constructs

CLASSIFICATIONAL PROCESSES

In the previous chapter we noted that visual structures of representation can either be narrative, presenting unfolding actions and events, processes of change, transitory spatial arrangements, or conceptual, representing participants in terms of their more generalized and more or less stable and timeless essence, in terms of class, or structure or meaning.

It is to the latter category of representational structures that we now turn, beginning with *classificational processes*. Classificational processes relate participants to each other in terms of a 'kind of' relation, a taxonomy: at least one set of participants will play the role of *Subordinates* with respect to at least one other participant, the *Superordinate*. We have already come across an example in the left-hand picture of figure 2.1, where the three participants – the axe, the basket and the wooden sword – were represented as 'species' of the same 'genus', as all belonging to the same overarching category. In this example the overarching category was not shown or named. The structure was a *Covert Taxonomy*, a taxonomy in which the Superordinate is inferred from such similarities as the viewer may perceive to exist between the Subordinates, or only indicated in the accompanying text, as in figure 3.1.

One visual characteristic is crucial in the realization of covert taxonomies: the proposed equivalence between the Subordinates is visually realized by a symmetrical composition. The Subordinates are placed at equal distance from each other, given the same size and the same orientation towards the horizontal and vertical axes. To realize the stable, timeless nature of the classification, the participants are often shown in a more or less objective, decontextualized way. The background is plain and neutral. Depth is reduced or absent. The angle is frontal and objective. And frequently there are words inside the picture space. These features will be discussed in a later chapter under the heading 'modality'.

Classification processes do not, of course, simply reflect 'real', 'natural' classifications. For participants to be put together in a syntagm which establishes the classification *means* that they were judged to be members of the same class, and to be read as such. 'Naturalization' is not natural, whether in images or in language. The ordering in the image itself produces the relations. This makes it possible for the producer of an image to classify baskets and weapons (figure 2.1), or zoologists, wildlife photographers and Aboriginal storytellers (figure 3.1) as being of the same order.

Covert taxonomies are often used in advertisements, where the photographs may, for instance, show arrangements of bottles that represent the variety of products marketed under a brand name, or arrangements of different people who all use the same product. Figure 3.2 is a page from *Cosmopolitan* magazine. What do these watches have in common? They all belong to the same Xpose range.

⬥ Fig 3.1 Guide interface (Microsoft, 1994)

Other taxonomies show a higher degree of (explicit) ordering include a Superordinate. They represent and name the Superordinate within some kind of tree structure. In that structure the orientation is vertical, and the Superordinate is placed above or below the Subordinates, as in figure 3.2. The participants may be realized verbally, visually, or both verbally and visually, but the process is always visual.

Taxonomies do not have to be represented by formal diagrams with simple lines; they may be realized in more realist fashion, for instance, by an actual tree in a 'family tree'. Overt taxonomies are usually 'chained', so that the 'intermediate' participants (e.g. the 'inorganic substances' and 'organic substances' of figure 3.3) will be Superordinate with respect to some of the other participants, and Subordinate with respect to others. To indicate this we will coin the term *Interordinate*. In other words, overt taxonomies have levels, and participants at the same level are represented as being, in some sense, 'of the same kind'.

Tree structures, however, are not only used to realize 'kind of' relations. 'Reporting diagrams', showing the hierarchical structure of companies and other organizations, and genealogical or evolutionary trees, use the same structure. This means that visual grammar conflates, or at least represents as very closely related, what would, in language, be expressed by different means. Conceptual classification is represented by the same

○ Fig 3.2 Xpose range (*Cosmopolitan*, November 2001: 84)

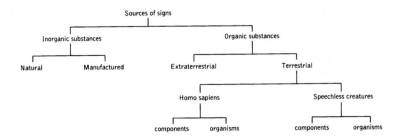

● Fig 3.3 Sources of signs (Eco, 1976b: 177)

structure as social hierarchy; that is, the more general *idea* is represented as similar to greater *power*. As Virginia Woolf has said, 'General ideas are always also Generals' ideas.' Further, hierarchies of concepts and hierarchies of social power are represented as similar to genealogies. In other words, the identity of an individual (or a species) is represented as being 'subordinate' to its 'origins' or 'ancestors' in the same way as specific concepts are subordinated to more general and abstract concepts, and lower employees or local bodies to managers or central organs.

Diagrammatic tree structures can take different forms. The branches of the tree may be parallel or oblique, straight or curved, and so on (see figure 3.4). Oblique branches

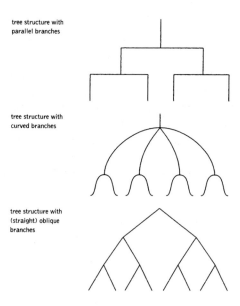

● Fig 3.4 Tree structures with parallel (straight) oblique and curved branches

abstract somewhat less from the shape of the tree than parallel branches, so that more of the symbolic meaning of the tree can be preserved. Hence they are common in contexts where a sense of 'generation' and 'growth' is connoted, as for instance in genealogies or in the diagrams used in 'generative grammar', a form of linguistics which posits that 'surface structures' are generated from (possibly innate and maybe universal) 'deep structures'. The contrast between straight and curved branches is perhaps similar to that between participants represented as boxes and participants represented as circles or ovals (see chapter 2), a contrast between the 'mechanical' and 'technological' and the 'natural' and 'organic'.

Many tree diagrams are inverted ('bottom–up'), and when the branches are oblique the overall shape will tend towards that of a pyramid. Such structures are concerned with hierarchy and hierarchical difference rather than with clarity about levels: a reading of levels is possible, but not readily facilitated. Not all trees, however, are inverted. Sometimes the specific or, in the case of genealogies and evolutionary trees, the present, is placed on the top, depicting, for instance, humankind as the pinnacle of evolution rather than as being forever dominated by its lowly origins.

Although classificational structures represent participants in terms of their place in a static order, the verbal labels and explanations which may accompany them do not always do so. The term 'reporting diagram', for instance, uses an active process ('report') rather than a static one such as 'is subordinate to'. Genealogies and evolutionary trees, similarly, may be glossed by verbs like 'generates', 'evolves into', 'begets', and so on. *Visually*, however, a hierarchical order is signified, a system. Thus the visual representation can blur the boundaries between the dynamic and the static. Is the dynamic in reality the instantiation or enactment of an underlying system? Or is the static the systemization and objectification of a dynamic and ever-changing reality? Such questions become difficult to answer in a mode which has erased the boundaries between the schema and the blueprint.

A similar blurring may occur between analytical ('part of') and classificational ('kind of') processes. The 'stack diagram' in figure 3.5 could be called classificational, and is in fact so rendered in the accompanying text: 'to the Latin word /mus/ correspond two different things which we shall call x_1 and x_2' (Eco, 1976b: 78). In other words, a 'mouse' is a kind of 'mus'. But it can also be seen as analytical. One can also say that the meaning 'mouse' is part of the meaning of 'mus'. And, most importantly, Eco has chosen the form of the *analytical* diagram.

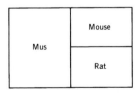

⬤ **Fig 3.5 Semantic field diagram (Eco, 1976b: 78)**

Finally, classificational diagrams may be rotated through ninety degrees so that their main *orientation* is along the horizontal axis. They have then the orientation typical of narrative diagrams, and hence a dynamic connotation. But they retain the structure of the classificational diagram. They still represent the relation between the participants as a system. Features from different types of structure are abstracted and recombined to create patterns that are ambiguously in between the dynamic and the conceptual. When such diagrams acquire arrows – as, for example, in system networks (see figure 3.8) – they become in fact dynamic and narrative. Yet they still move from the general to the specific, in contrast (for example) to flowcharts.

Taxonomies and flowcharts clearly provide two different kinds of knowledge. The one represents the world in terms of a hierarchical order. Its main concern is the ranking of phenomena from the perspective of a single unifying term, be it that of the origin of things, the most generalizing generalization, or that of the highest power. The other describes the world in terms of an actively pursued process with a clear beginning and an end (or 'input' and 'output', 'source' and 'destination', 'raw materials' and 'finished product'). It has a sequential progression and is goal-oriented. And, as we have noted already, system networks such as we use in this book attempt to combine the two perspectives.

Recently another kind of diagram has begun to gain ascendance – the 'network'. Networks seek to show the multiple interconnections between participants. Any participant in a network ('node') can form an entry-point from which its environment can be explored, and the vectors or lines ('links') between these participants can take on many different values, the value of signification ('a means b'), of combination ('a goes with b'), of composition ('a contains b'): the essence of the link between two participants is that they are, in some sense, next to each other, or close to each other, associated with each other. To demonstrate the difference with a linguistic example, a taxonomy would show, for instance, a hierarchy of words, a 'flowchart', for instance, a way of generating a clause by following a precise sequence of 'instructions', and a network might show the *collocation* of words – the other words with which any given word typically combines, regardless of the *structural* relations between the words (see figure 3.6).

Figure 3.7 shows a 'linear' (flowchart) and 'non-linear' (network) representation from an article on a 'writer's assistant' computer program. The network, its authors say, allows the writer 'to form ideas into an associative network' (Sharples and Pemberton, 1992: 22). The principle behind such networks clearly relates to the idea of the 'non-linear' text to which we have alluded in our discussion of Dick Bruna's *On My Walk* (figure 1.2) and to which we will return in greater detail in chapter 6. In discussing a page from Bruna we stressed that such pages on the one hand provide the reader with many choices, many paths to follow, but on the other hand tend to obscure the fact that the range of choices is ultimately pre-designed and limited. As such, networks are, in the end, just as much modelled on forms of social organization as taxonomies and flowcharts. The taxonomy is modelled on a static, hierarchical organization in which everything has its pre-ordained place in a grand scheme unified by a single source of authority. The flowchart is modelled on the principle of authoritatively prescribed, structured, goal-oriented activity. The network is modelled on a form of social organization which is a vast labyrinth of intersecting

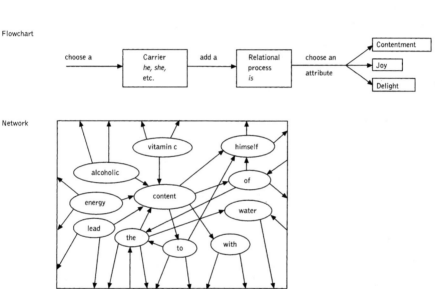

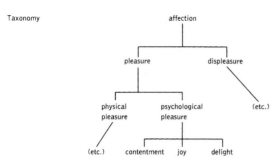

Taxonomy

Flowchart

Network

▲ Fig 3.6 Taxonomy, flowchart and network

local relations in which each node is related in many different ways to other nodes in its immediate environment, but in which it is difficult, if not impossible, to form a coherent view of the whole. Perhaps it is not accidental that this kind of network is coming to the fore in an age of increasing social fragmentation and regionalization. But regions are nevertheless connected to the whole and the network model may obscure the globalizing tendencies, which are also and simultaneously at work in contemporary society. This is recognized by those who pioneer the application of this mode of representation, for instance in connection with hypertexts, which are also networks:

> Readers who browse hypertext networks become 'lost', unaware of where they are in relation to the document, and thus unable to achieve a sense of text, i.e. an

⬤ Fig 3.7 Network (from Sharples and Pemberton, 1992)

intellectual feel for the substance of the document. This is analogous to starting at a particular word in a thesaurus and passing from one similar associative word to another. Soon it is likely that the reader would be examining a word that is completely different from the original word, with no notion of any meaning to the derivation that has just taken place.

(Ghaoui *et al.*, 1992: 110)

In the pronouncements of network guru Kevin Kelly, as reported by Jim McClellan in the *Observer*, the political implications of the network become even clearer:

The image of the atom . . . stood for power and knowledge. Its sure, regular orbits and defined spaces represented 'law-abiding solar systems of energy' under central direction. In contrast the Net – a tangle of apparent disorder – was an icon of no beginning, no centre, no end (or all beginning, all centre, all end). It was the emblem of our new understanding of the complex logic of nature and computers; the banner of systems which, in some senses, organized themselves. The atom had been the icon of the 20th century (the Atom Age), he concluded, but the Net would be the archetype of the coming network culture of the 21st.

(McClellan, *Observer* Life Magazine, 21 September 1994, p. 62)

In figure 3.8 we summarize the distinctions we have made in this section. Networks are not included in the summary as they are 'analytical' rather than 'classificational'. The difference between 'single-' and 'multi-levelled' is marked by the absence or presence of 'Interordinates'. Our discussion above has, we hope, made it clear that we see these distinctions as tools with which to describe visual structures rather than that specific, concrete visuals can necessarily always be described exhaustively and uniquely in terms of any one of our categories.

○ **Fig 3.8 Classificational image structures**

REALIZATIONS

Covert taxonomy	A set of participants ('Subordinates') is distributed symmetrically across the picture space, at equal distance from each other, equal in size, and oriented towards the vertical and horizontal axes in the same way.
Single-levelled overt taxonomy	A participant ('Superordinate') is connected to two or more other participants ('Subordinates') through a tree structure with two levels only.
Multi-levelled overt taxonomy	A participant ('Superordinate') is connected to other participants through a tree structure with more than two levels. The participants which occupy intermediate levels are Interordinates, while those which occupy the lowest level (if the Superordinate is on top) or the highest level (if the Superordinate is at the bottom) are Subordinates.

ANALYTICAL PROCESSES

Analytical processes relate participants in terms of a part–whole structure. They involve two kinds of participants: one *Carrier* (the whole) and any number of *Possessive Attributes* (the parts). We have already given an example of an analytical structure, the picture of the Antarctic explorer (figure 2.4), which analysed the explorer in terms of his 'outfit'. Fashion shots, too, are analytical. Like the picture of the Antarctic explorer, they clearly display the parts of an 'outfit', and label both the Carrier ('easy-wearing, inexpensive cottons teamed with the right accessories' – see figure 3.9) and the Possessive Attributes ('Laura Ashley trenchcoat, Stuart Membery sweater, Benetton jodhpurs'), albeit in a caption, rather than inside the picture space, and in the flowery language of fashion writing which has been described so well by Barthes (1967b).

Fig 3.9 Easy-wearing Cottons (*Vogue*, November 1987)

Different as they may seem at first sight, maps have the same structure: there is a Carrier, for instance 'Australia', and there are Possessive Attributes, for instance 'the states of Australia', and both are labelled, either inside the picture space or in a legend or caption. Maps may provide quite distinct analyses of what seems to be the same Carrier. Some maps focus on geographical features such as waterways, altitude, etc., while others concentrate on social and political boundaries. Analysis always involves selection. Some attributes or characteristics of the Carrier are singled out as criterial in the given context or, generally, while others are ignored, treated as non-essential and irrelevant.

The difference between the map and the fashion shot lies not in their ideational but in their interpersonal structures – for instance, in their modality (see chapter 5). Many analytical visuals have low modality, from the naturalistic point of view. Too much life-likeness, too much detail, would distract from their analytical purpose. Only the essential features of the Possessive Attributes are shown, and for this reason drawings of various degrees of schematization are often preferred over photographs or highly detailed artwork. The representation of depth is reduced or absent, as is the detailed representation of light and shadow, and of subtle tonal distinctions. Colour, if it is used at all, is restricted to a reduced palette, or used conventionally – for instance, to distinguish participants, such as different socioeconomic groups, or landforms. Background is left out, or only sketched in lightly. And the Possessive Attributes are labelled. Note that the arrows in figure 2.4 do not realize narrative processes but a relation of identity between a verbal and a visual realization of the same Possessive Attribute. Yet photographs, particularly posed photographs, can also be analytical, as in the case of fashion shots, or of advertisements which give a detailed depiction of the advertised product, or of press 'mugshots' of politicians and other newsworthy persons. The school social studies textbook from which we took figure 2.4 shows – on the page opposite to that showing the drawing in figure 2.4 – the picture reproduced in figure 3.10.

It is an analytical picture; there is neither a vector (narrative process) nor compositional symmetry and/or a tree structure (classificational process). It serves to identify a Carrier and to allow viewers to scrutinize this Carrier's Possessive Attributes. Some minor degree of lowered modality is also present: the background is plain, and the fact that the picture is posed adds further artificiality. Yet, although it is analytical, its purpose is more interactional and emotive than representational. The interactional system of the gaze dominates: the gaze of represented participants directly addresses the viewers and so establishes an imaginary relation with them, while more schematic analytical pictures invite impersonal, detached scrutiny. A similar argument can be made about advertisements showing the advertised product – the overall impression of an abundance of parts (or ingredients, or varieties of the product), or the alluring sensory quality of the advertised product as a whole (the streamlined sheen of the car, the vivid colour and

⬣ **Fig 3.10 Sir Douglas Mawson (Oakley *et al.*, 1985)**

texture of the ingredients of a canned soup) take precedence over more dispassionate scrutiny of the Possessive Attributes. Persuasion is foregrounded, instruction and exposition are backgrounded. The textbook includes both figure 2.4 and figure 3.10 because it seeks not only to teach children objective facts about Antarctic exploration but also to make them emotionally identify with an adventurous hero. Until recently, this then decreased in the later years of education. Advanced textbooks addressed their readers as 'no longer needing pictures', as having been weaned off everyday naturalism, and as having acquired the abstract and impersonal attitude that characterized higher learning and higher art appreciation in Western culture. However, the tendency is now for the interpersonal to enter the textbooks of later years, as well – through image and through writing. In the language of the senior secondary school textbook, as in the language of science and bureaucracy, the passive voice had been normal, realizing a more impersonal and detached form of address:

These outlines may be abstracted from topographic maps and street directories.

In the language of the primary-school textbook, as also in advertising language, 'you' was a keyword, and the reader was always directly addressed:

Here is a picture of Antarctica. If you landed here in a spaceship, how would you describe this place?

Today, the personal and the informal enter increasingly many domains which formerly were characterized by impersonal and formal modes of address, verbally as well as visually. Of course, some photographs remain almost as objective and detached as traditional diagrams and maps. This is still true of many scientific photographs and, for instance, of aerial photographs: their top–down angle ensures the absence of depth and background and, depending on the height from which they are taken, detail is more or less removed. But, as in our primary-school textbook example, they will now often be combined with less formal pictures, even in the PowerPoint conference presentations of scientists (Rowley-Jolivet, 2004).

Abstract art may also be analytical. The structure of Theo van Doesburg's *Pure Painting*, for instance (figure 3.11), is like the structure of a map. It analyses reality in terms of Possessive Attributes, highly abstract ones: rectangles of different size and colour. But it does not label either the Carrier or the Possessive Attributes. It leaves it up to the viewer to do so, and as a result the painting can be read in many different ways. We could see it, quite concretely, as the map of the modern city (green for recreational areas, yellow for housing, red for industrial areas, and so on) – figure 3.12 *is* in fact a map of a city, and looks quite similar, if we ignore the writing. We could also see it, more abstractly, as a map of desirable human qualities or activities (green for contemplation, red for passion, etc.), and of the space they should occupy in our lives. The point is, the painting represents both these things, and many more. It is open to many readings, and that constitutes its power to shape reality, a power which, however, cannot be unleashed

⬥ Fig 3.11 *Pure Painting* (Theo van Doesburg, 1920) (from Jaffé, 1967)

until the boxes are given concrete reference, so that the schema can be turned into a blueprint.

Lowered naturalistic modality, however, is not a defining characteristic of analytic visuals. Modality forms a separate (interactional) system which is present in visuals simultaneously with the kinds of structure we are describing in this chapter. At most we can say that, in specific social contexts (cartography, education at different levels, advertising fashion), there is a tendency for certain modality choices to go together with certain representational choices, certain kinds of processes. The defining characteristic of the analytical process is in fact a 'default' one. It lies in the absence of vectors and the absence of compositional symmetry and/or tree structures, and also in the absence of the features that mark the symbolic processes we will describe in the next section. There are more positive and specific characteristics, but these pertain to specific kinds of analytical process. As a whole, the analytical process is the usual, the 'unmarked', and therefore also the most elementary option in the visual system of representation – a visual 'this is'.

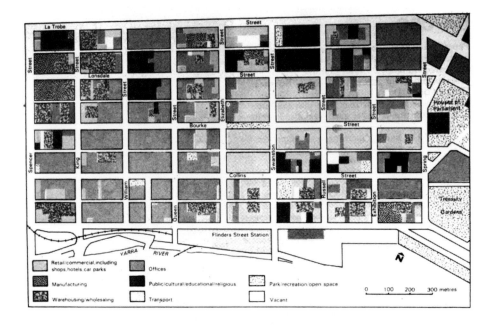

⬤ **Fig 3.12 Map of the central business district of Melbourne (Pask and Bryant, 1982)**

Experimental studies of the production of drawings would seem to bear this out: the principal task that drawers must master is the representation of objects in terms of their minimal defining characteristics, and the principal purpose for which non-specialists actually use drawing in everyday life is the production of pragmatically motivated 'descriptions', sketches of localities, clothes and hairstyles, mechanical devices, and so on, as well as the production of doodles, which often are also analytical (van Sommers, 1984: 234ff.).

1 Unstructured analytical processes

Some analytical processes are *unstructured*; that is, they show us the Possessive Attributes of the Carrier, but not the Carrier itself, they show us the parts, but not the way the parts fit together to make up a whole. The page reproduced in figure 3.13, for instance, is a kind of unstructured map, accurate in scale, but without any visual indication of the location of the Possessive Attributes relative to each other. We see the parts of the garment, but not the way they are to be assembled — although verbal labels ('coat front', 'bikini top back', etc.) provide an indication. The page does also include a photograph of the finished garment. This photograph, however, would have to be seen as a separate analytical structure, with higher naturalistic modality than the pattern itself. The magazine uses the

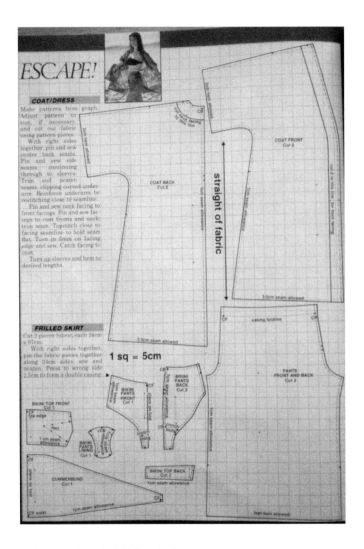

● Fig 3.13 Escape (*Australian Women's Weekly*, December 1987)

same strategy as the social studies textbook: one picture to entice you, and another to give you a more objective analysis of the Carrier.

Especially when the Carrier is abstract, there may not be a single principle for the way in which Possessive Attributes should be assembled. The Carrier cannot be visualized in an assembled state, and any arrangement of the Possessive Attributes is therefore possible: an unstructured analytical process is like a more or less unordered list. This can be seen, for instance, in advertisements which display all the parts that make up the engine of a car, or the full range of products manufactured by an advertiser, in order to impress the viewer with their sheer abundance.

2 Temporal analytical processes

The examples we have discussed so far represent the things they represent as objects. They focus on spatiality. But there is also the category of the *timeline*, a process which seems to occupy an intermediate position between the narrative and the analytical. Timelines involve the temporal dimension, and this suggests narrative. Yet these lines are not vectorial and, rather than representing history as a gradual unfolding of events, they analyse it into successive stages with fixed and stable characteristics, stages which can then be treated as though they were things. The typical evolution timeline, showing a series of figures starting with an ape on the left and ending with *homo sapiens* on the right, would be analytical in this sense, 'saying': 'the evolution of humankind *consists* of the "Ape" stage, the "Apeman" stage, the "Australopithecus" stage (etc.)', with 'the evolution of humankind' as Carrier, and the stages as Possessive Attributes.

The essential characteristic of temporal analytical processes is that they are realized by timelines: the participants (sometimes whole structures, 'scenes') are arranged on an actual or imaginary line, usually horizontal, sometimes vertical. The timeline may be topographical, drawn to scale, or topological, assembling the participants in the right sequence, but not drawing the time intervals 'to scale'.

Timelines need not be straight, and they may involve all kinds of geometrical symbolism. Figure 3.14, taken from a Swedish junior high-school history textbook, is a particularly interesting example. Here time does not progress linearly, but takes turns, goes downhill, moves towards the viewer, and changes colour, from a crystalline blue to a drab brown (the colour code employed by the series of four books of which the book containing this illustration is part, has blue as the colour of history and brown as the colour of social studies). The result is a rather ethnocentric and patriarchal story which could be said to reveal, behind the surface of Sweden's modern and egalitarian welfare state, a deep longing for the primitive uncertain life of the nomadic hunter. When 'Man' first appeared on the horizon of time, so this story goes, he was a hunter and a maker of tools. He then acquired a wife, but she, the woman of 'homo erectus', was not yet 'erectus' herself and, where her man fixed his gaze upon the future, she looked back towards the past. Then 'Man' invented fire – a male achievement, for woman is not shown to be part of it, not even as an admiring onlooker. Next, he began to cover his body and begot a child. But at this point, the point where history takes a backward turn, a curious inversion occurred. It was now *he* who crouched and *she* who was 'erectus', *he* who looked backwards and *she* who fixed her gaze upon a future which, however, was no longer there, as time had already turned backwards. But all was not lost. The union of the two provided a very 'erect', very male and very Nordic *homo sapiens* as the outcome of evolution, as 'our' ancestor, here placed in the centre of the composition and close to the viewer. This story about Swedish identity is told by visual means only, and it illustrates a text which is told, not as Swedish history, but as a history of the world. The twisting and turning of the timeline in figure 3.14 does, of course, give it a

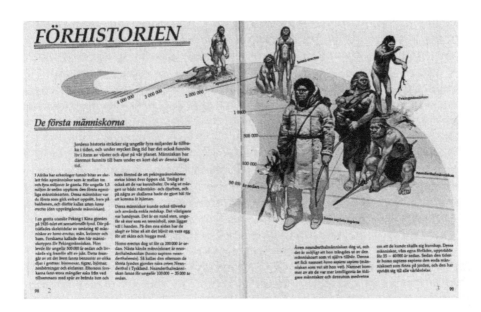

⬥ Fig 3.14 Evolution (Ohman, 1989)

dynamic quality and reminds of the helix in figure 2.24. The categories of visual grammar do not have clear-cut edges, and specific representations can merge two or more structures – for instance, the narrative and the analytical.

3 Exhaustive and inclusive analytical processes

(Spatial) structured analytical processes can be *exhaustive*, that is, they can exhaustively represent the Possessive Attributes of a Carrier, so that all of the Carrier is accounted for, all of its space taken up by Possessive Attributes. To put it in another way, in an exhaustive analytical structure there is assembly: the Possessive Attributes are joined together to make up a complex shape. Structured analytical processes can also be *inclusive*, that is, they can show us only some of the Possessive Attributes of a Carrier, leaving much of the Carrier unaccounted for, as blank space not taken up by Possessive Attributes. The circles on the left and right of Schramm's third communication model (figure 2.22) form exhaustive analytical structures, embedded in the larger narrative structure: the 'Sender' and the 'Receiver' are here analysed as being made up out of the same three components ('Encoder', 'Interpreter' and 'Decoder'), assembled in different ways, and every part of the space of the circles is covered by Possessive Attributes. The point is not, of course, that the analysis is in fact exhaustive. 'Senders' and 'Receivers' may well have other components beside these three. The point is that in the analysis the world is treated as *though* it is exhaustively represented, as though the Carriers have these major components and no others. Just as we have to assume that a map showing the states of Australia shows us *all* the states of Australia, and a picture of the outfit of an Antarctic explorer *all* the parts of this outfit, so we have to assume that this diagram shows us all the components of the 'Sender' and the 'Receiver'. Of course, 'encoding', 'interpreting' and 'decoding' might be seen as activities rather than as components. However, Schramm has *represented* them here as though they were parts of a machine, as though 'Senders' and 'Receivers' *have* these elements, or *consist* of these elements. As so often in diagrams, doings have been turned into things, spatialized and objectified.

In inclusive analytical structures, the Possessive Attributes do not exhaustively divide up the space of the Carrier. They are contained *within* the Carrier, and so take up part of its space, but not all – other parts are left blank, unanalysed. This structure also entails the possibility of *partial inclusion* and *exclusion*. In figure 3.15, A and B are Possessive Attributes of the Carrier formed by the largest circle, C is a *Partial Possessive Attribute* (in part belonging to the Carrier, in part outside it), and D is excluded, hence not a Possessive Attribute. In other words, where exhaustive structures are formed by the welding together of Possessive Attributes, inclusive structures are formed by the full or partial overlapping of the participants. And the structure is *recursive*: a Possessive Attribute can become the Carrier of other Possessive Attributes, as in the case with B in figure 3.15: it is a Possessive Attribute with respect to the larger circle, but a Carrier with respect to E. We can see this structure at work in Riley and Riley's communication model (figure 2.5). It does not tell us that 'over-all social systems' exhaustively consist of two 'larger social structures' and 'larger social structures' of two and not more than two 'primary groups', but that 'over-all social systems' contain (beside the many other things they may also contain) at least two 'larger social structures', and that 'larger social structures' contain at least two 'primary groups'. Individuals such as 'C' and 'R' are partial Possessive Attributes of the Carrier/Attribute 'larger social structure' and fully Possessive Attributes of the Carrier 'over-all social system'. To give a gloss on this structure, according to Riley and Riley, individuals cannot escape the 'over-all social

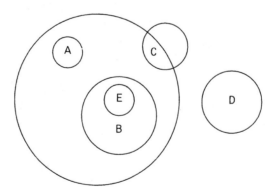

Fig 3.15 Inclusive analytical structures

system', but they can, at least in part, free themselves from the constraints of 'larger social structures'.

Many maps have a similar structure. A map of a state or nation which shows cities and towns, for instance, is not read as meaning that every city and every town has been included, or that the state or nation contains no Possessive Attributes other than cities and towns. It is read as meaning that these are some (the major) cities and towns of that state or nation or, rather, that these are the cities and towns of interest and relevance to you, the reader of this particular map. Inclusive structures are here embedded within exhaustive structures: the map as a whole may be primarily concerned with the boundaries that exhaustively divide the Carrier into Possessive Attributes (Europe into nations, Australia into states, etc.), but these Possessive Attributes themselves are Carriers in embedded inclusive structures with Possessive Attributes such as major cities, rivers, lakes, etc.

4 Conjoined and compounded exhaustive structures

In *conjoined* exhaustive structures, Possessive Attributes are either *connected*, by a line lacking a feature of directionality, or *disengaged*, by a layout of the Possessive Attributes which separates them, yet clearly shows how they fit together. The latter is the case, for instance, of the 'pie chart' in figure 3.16, where the disengagement of the Possessive Attributes acquires symbolic value, showing, literally and figuratively, the rifts that divide the nation. The former is the case in the communication model on top of figure 2.6, where all the participants are connected by lines. Such connecting lines may be purely abstract connectors, as in figure 2.6, or have a feature of *conductivity*:

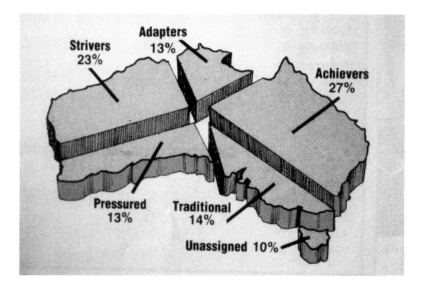

⬤ Fig 3.16 Australia: the segments (*Bulletin*, 10 January 1989)

Conductors are connectors that also represent a Possessive Attribute, a physical entity – for instance, wiring, a pipeline, a road, a railway track – and they may also be abstract, as in some communication models. Realized by a double line, conductors indicate a *potential* for dynamic interaction between the Possessive Attributes they connect. As such, they are both participant and process, connected element and connector, compounded and conjoining.

In compounded structures the Possessive Attributes are welded together, while at the same time retaining their distinct identities. This is as much the case in simple pie charts as in a technical drawing, for instance, the drawing of a machine for crushing ore, in figure 3.18.

5 Topographical and topological processes

When analytical structures are *topographical* they are read as accurately representing the physical spatial relations and the relative location of the Possessive Attributes. All of

connector ——————————————   conductor ————————————

⬥ **Fig 3.17 Connectors and conductors**

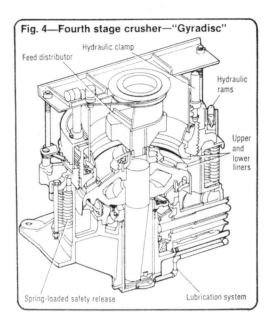

⬥ **Fig 3.18 Fourth-stage crusher (Merritt, 1984)**

the types of structured analytical processes we have discussed so far may be topographical: we read the picture of the ore crusher in figure 3.18 as accurately scaling down the dimensions and relative location of the parts of the machine, just as we read topographical maps as accurately scaling down, for example, the dimensions of a lake, and its distance from other Possessive Attributes (mountains, rivers) and from the boundaries of the Carrier.

When analytical structures are *topological*, they are read as accurately representing the 'logical' relations between participants, the way in which participants are connected to each other (whether they have common boundaries, or are partially or wholly included in each other, in which sequence they are connected, etc.), but not the actual physical size of the participants or their distance from each other or, in the case of inclusive structures, from the boundaries of the Carrier. An electrical circuit diagram, for instance, is topological (figure 3.19). It does not signify, say, that lamps a and b are 'above' and 'at the right of' the battery, and it does not accurately scale down the distance between the battery and a lamp a, or between the two lamps. But it does signify that they are connected in this particular sequence, just as evolution timelines signify that 'Ape', 'Apeman', 'Australopithecus', etc. made their first appearance in history in the order shown.

Maps, too, may either be topographical or topological, as, for instance, in maps of urban transport systems. The digital networks we discussed in the previous section are also topological diagrams, abstract maps, as they are based on adjacency, co-*location*. In other words, abstract diagrams, too, can be either topological or topographical. Schramm's communication model (figure 2.6), for instance, is topological. It does not tell us that the 'Source' is on the left, or to the west, of the 'Encoder'; it tells us only that the participants are connected in this sequence. This is not to say that the placement of the 'Source' to the left of the 'Encoder' is not significant, only that its significance derives, not from the ideational, but from the textual structure of the diagram (see chapter 6). Halliday's diagram of the 'nature of linguistic structures and their relations to other fields of scholarship' (1978: 10), on the other hand, is an intricate piece of abstract topography (see figure 3.20). The diagram uses distance to indicate how close the various kinds of language study are from what is here seen as the central and most important form of language study, the study of 'language as system'. It uses distance in a figurative, yet finely calibrated, way: 'phonetics', for example, is closer to 'language as system' than the study of dialects and registers. And it uses relative size in the same way: the study of language takes up a much greater area than all the other 'fields of scholarship' together. As in medieval

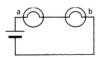

Fig 3.19 Electric circuit diagram (Hill, 1980)

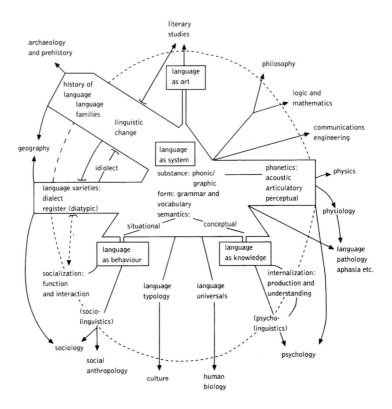

Fig 3.20 The place of linguistics on the map of knowledge (Halliday, 1978)

maps, the cartographer's 'home town' is both exaggerated in size and represented internally more accurately and with more detail than the surrounding 'countryside'.

6 Dimensional and quantitative topography

Like topographical visuals, charts are drawn to scale. The scale, however, is based, not on the physical dimensions of the participants, but on the quantity or frequency of aggregates of participants that are taken to be identical. Pie charts, for instance (see e.g. figure 3.16), divide a Carrier (the population of Australia) into components, Possessive Attributes that are in fact *aggregates* of participants analysed as being the same in some respect, and it tells us, not that 'Achievers' are found next to, and to the southeast of, 'Adapters', but that the *number* of 'Achievers' stands to the number of 'Adapters' as the size of the Possessive Attribute labelled 'Achievers' stands to the size of the Possessive Attribute labelled 'Adapters'. Quantity is translated into relative size – although it is, of course, also possible to represent quantity with quantity, as in figure 3.21, a now perhaps rather old-fashioned

Fig 3.21 Women at work (Modley and Lowenstein, 1952)

example which uses Otto von Neurath's 'picture language' Isotype (see e.g. Lupton, 1989).

Pie charts and bar charts (see figure 3.23) are *one-dimensional*: they show us one (abstract) Carrier (in the case of figure 3.16, the concrete Carrier 'Australia' is a metonym for the abstract Carrier 'the population of Australia') and its Possessive Attributes. Their structure is quite similar to that of stack diagrams (see figure 3.5). They are exhaustive, compounded analytical structures. The difference lies only in their peculiar kind of abstraction and peculiar kind of topographical accuracy, both of which are *quantitative*.

7 Spatio-temporal analytical structures

Two-dimensional charts create a conjunction between a *set* of such (exhaustive, compounded, quantitatively abstract and topographical) analytical structures and a timeline, for the sake of comparative analysis along an ordered timescale. In the case of line graphs this can result in the quasi-vectorial, quasi-narrative structure typified by temperature charts, profit charts, company growth charts, etc. (see figure 3.22). In other words, the substitution of a line for discrete entities creates something like a dynamic process (with meanings such as 'change', 'grow', 'decrease', etc.), and backgrounds or even erases the analytical structures that underlie the graph, so that the graph no longer suggests that 'In 1988 the Carrier ("incidence of AIDS") consisted of 500,000 Possessive Attributes ("AIDS cases") *and* in 1990 the Carrier consisted of 800,000 Possessive Attributes *and* . . . (etc.)', but that 'The Actor ("the epidemic") *acts* ("spreads rapidly")'. To complicate matters, one-dimensional structures can be represented as though they were two-dimensional, and so produce a sense of progress or decline, depending on the order in which the Possessive Attributes are plotted along the horizontal axis – an order not given by relations of conjoinedness or compoundness, or of inclusion or exclusion, but solely by quantity. The bar chart in figure 3.23 can easily be (mis)taken as suggesting, not that more people live in flats than in large houses, but that people, as time progresses, increasingly live in flats.

Something quite similar can happen in language. Hodge and Kress (1978, 1993) drew attention to the effects of the transformation of nominalization, which turns clauses (reports of events) such as *people learned* into nominals (names of objects) such as *people's learning* which may then become actors in new events (*the new learning spread*). Martin *et al.* described this process in history textbooks. They commented that such transformations favour the 'anthropomorphic metaphor of birth, growth and death' (1988: 157) and allow historians to analyse history in successive periods in which similar things go on. In other words, despite their apparent status as active, dynamic processes, these structures still serve to establish stable, conceptual orders.

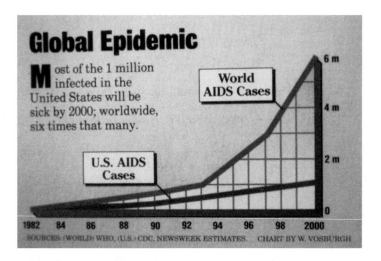

● Fig 3.22 Global epidemic (*Bulletin*, 26 June 1990)

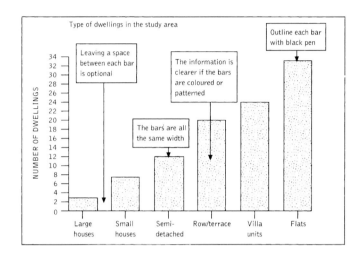

Fig 3.23 Types of dwelling (Bindon and Williams, 1988)

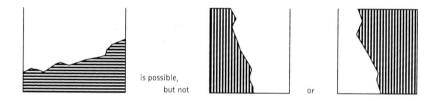

Fig 3.24 Dynamization of analytical processes

This dynamization of two-dimensional analytical processes cannot occur when the arrangement is vertical (see figure 3.24). The Possessive Attributes then remain discrete, and the graphs as a whole suggest a stable order rather than a dynamic process. This is borne out, for instance, by the fact that one cannot 'fill in' the space of the Carrier.

It is our impression that there has been, in Western cultures, a shift from a focus on the vertical to a focus on the horizontal, a change from a concern with 'What is the state of affairs?' and 'Where are we?' to 'Where are we going?' and 'Have we progressed or are we in decline?' This is borne out also by the fact that scripts which were traditionally written top–down are now beginning to be written from left to right.

In figure 3.25, we summarize the distinctions introduced in this section. Note that the superscript 'I' means 'if' and the superscript 'T' means 'then'. In other words, if there is a topographical timeline, then the topography must be quantitative.

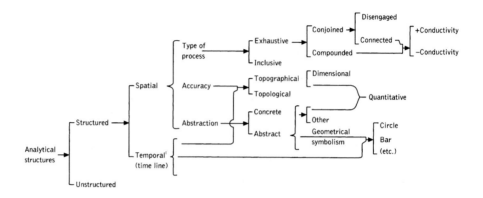

🔺 **Fig 3.25 Analytic image structures**

REALIZATIONS

Unstructured analytical process	An unordered set of participants ('Possessive Attributes') is interpreted as the set of parts of a whole which itself is not represented.
Temporal analytical process	A set of participants ('Possessive Attributes') is ordered linearly on a (horizontal or vertical) timeline and interpreted as the set of successive stages of a temporally unfolding process.
Exhaustive analytical process	A participant ('Carrier') is depicted as made up of a number of parts ('Possessive Attributes') and the structure is interpreted as showing all the parts from which the whole is made up.
Dimensional topographical accuracy	The Carrier and the Possessive Attributes of an analytical process are drawn to scale.
Quantitative topographical accuracy	The size of the Possessive Attributes in an analytical process accurately represents the number or some other quantitative attribute of the Possessive Attributes.
Topological accuracy	The Carrier and the Possessive Attributes of an analytical process are not drawn to scale, but the way they are interconnected is drawn accurately.
Abstraction	The participants in an analytical process may be concrete.

SYMBOLIC PROCESSES

Symbolic processes are about what a participant *means* or *is*. Either there are two participants – the participant whose meaning or identity is established in the relation, the *Carrier*,
and the participant which represents the meaning or identity itself, *the Symbolic Attribute*
– or there is only one participant, the *Carrier*, and in that case the symbolic meaning is
established in another way, to be described below. The former type of process we will call
Symbolic Attributive; the latter, *Symbolic Suggestive*.

Art historians have charted the formal pictorial characteristics which can realize the
Symbolic Attribute relation (see especially Hermeren, 1969). Symbolic attributes are
objects with one or more of the following characteristics.

(1) They are made salient in the representation in one way or another; for instance, by
    being placed in the foreground, through exaggerated size, through being especially well
    lit, through being represented in especially fine detail or sharp focus, or through their
    conspicuous colour or tone.
(2) They are pointed at by means of a gesture which cannot be interpreted as an action
    other than the action of 'pointing out the symbolic attribute to the viewer' – here we
    can include also the arrows which can connect visual realizations of participants with
    verbal realizations of the same participant, or vice versa, as in figure 2.4, for these
    also establish a relation of identity through 'pointing'.
(3) They look out of place in the whole, in some way.
(4) They are conventionally associated with symbolic values.

Such conventional symbols were very common in the Middle Ages and the Renaissance:
see, for instance, figure 3.27, where the apple, looking somewhat out of place in St
Jerome's study, symbolizes the Fall, Temptation, Original Sin, and so brings these
immediately to mind for the viewer of the painting. To take a modern example, the scientist
depicted in figure 3.28 is clearly not doing anything with, or to, the fungi which are
displayed in the foreground and of which he is holding one in his right hand. His position in
relation to the fungi seems contrived and posed. The fungi function here as the Attributes
that establish his identity as an expert on fungi.

Human participants in Symbolic Attributive processes usually pose for the viewer,
rather than being shown as involved in some action. This does not mean that they are
necessarily portrayed front-on and at eye level, or that they necessarily look at the viewer,

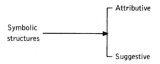

Fig 3.26 Types of symbolic image structure

⬤ Fig 3.27 *St Jerome in his Study* (Jan van Eyck, 1434) (from Hermeren, 1969)

even though all of these will often be the case. It means that they take up a posture which cannot be interpreted as narrative: they just sit or stand there, for no reason other than to display themselves to the viewer.

Symbolic Suggestive Processes have only one participant, the Carrier. They cannot be interpreted as analytical, because in this kind of image detail tends to be de-emphasized in favour of what could be called 'mood' or 'atmosphere'. This can be realized in a number of ways: the colours may all blend together, into a hazy blue, for instance, or a soft golden glow; the focus may be soft; or the lighting may be extreme, rendering the participants as outlines or silhouettes. It is this which lends Symbolic Suggestive pictures their genericity, their quality of depicting not a specific moment but a generalized essence. The *way in which* the blurring of detail occurs then lends symbolic value to the Carrier – a soft golden glow, for instance, would confer on the Carrier all the values associated with softness, and with gold, as in the Bushells advertisement reproduced in plate 2. As a result Symbolic Suggestive processes represent meaning and identity as coming from within, as deriving from qualities of the Carrier themselves, whereas Symbolic Attributive processes represent meaning and identity as being conferred to the Carrier.

Expressionist landscapes (e.g. Nolde's Tropical Sun, see plate 1) also diminish the detail of the representation, in favour of overall colour effects evolving a strong mood, and imbuing the Carrier ('autumn evening') with symbolic meanings.

● Fig 3.28 Fun with fungi (*Sydney Morning Herald*, 18 June 1992)

EMBEDDING

In language, sentences can be simple (consisting of only one clause/process) or complex (containing several clauses, each with their own process, coordinated with or subordinated to each other). Pictures, too, can be simple or complex. We have already discussed how in figure 2.1 the relation between the Aborigines and the fire constitutes a second, minor, transactional process, subordinated to the 'major' process, which is constituted by the relation between the British and the Aborigines; and how participants such as the British or the landscape can themselves be read as analytical structures, with a Carrier (e.g. the landscape) and Possessive Attributes (e.g. rocks and trees). Which of these structures are major and which are minor is, in visuals, determined by the relative size and conspicuousness of the elements. The cover of the book from which we took 'The British used guns' provides an example of this kind of complexity (figure 3.29). We can recognize four different processes in this picture:

(1) A classificational process in which the five children are Subordinates of the class of 'young Australians', in what we have called a Covert Taxonomy. They are shown against a neutral background and arranged in a symmetrical fashion, in a circle which

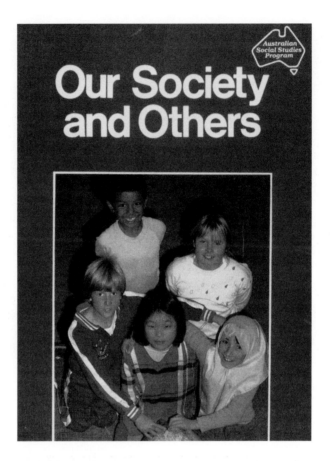

▲ Fig 3.29 *Our Society and Others* (Oakley *et al.*, 1985)

is closed (and reiterated) by the globe. (We will discuss the meaning of circularity more fully in chapter 6.)

(2) A number of analytical processes in which each child is Carrier in relation to a number of (prototypical, 'essential') Possessive Attributes (skin colour, colour and kind of hair, colour of eyes, items of clothing) – attributes which create visual concepts of their different ethnicities.

(3) A symbolic attributive process in which the globe is a conventional symbol with strong associations. It is placed in the foreground of the picture, and two of the children touch it with a gesture which cannot easily be interpreted as an action other than one that draws the viewer's attention to the globe. The children are thus shown to be part of the world, a microcosm of the world in Australia.

(4) Transactional processes in which three of the children have put their arms round other children. The boy on the left would seem to be the major Actor here, while the two girls

are Goal with respect to his action. The two girls, who have their arms round each other, on the other hand, relate in a more reciprocal way. They are what we have called Interactors.

From this multiple analysis we can see that the picture (even when we disregard the interactive and compositional structures which are also present, and which will be discussed in the next three chapters) forms a powerful, multidimensional structure.

Turning to the relation between these processes, we might say that because of its sheer size and conspicuousness the circular arrangement of the children is dominant, while the analytical processes are embedded in it: five children are co-classified, and each of them can be further analysed in terms of Possessive Attributes. In other words, the major message is that these children belong to the same category, despite the difference in gender and ethnicity; the minor message is that they are, nevertheless, different. As far as the transactional and symbolic processes are concerned, we would argue that the white lines on the boy's tracksuit form strong and dominant vectors.

Perhaps the 'transactional' process of which this boy is Actor and the symbolic process of which he is Carrier weigh as heavily in the scale as the classificational process, and also form major processes. The transactional processes of which the girls in the foreground are both Actor and Goal, and the symbolic process of which the girl on the right is the Carrier, however, are considerably less conspicuous and might be interpreted as minor processes. In other words, as Actors of the gesture of solidarity, and as Carriers of the symbolic value of 'representing the world', the 'ethnic' girls have, in this representation, a much less significant role to play than the white Australian boy in his tracksuit.

CONCEPTUAL STRUCTURES IN LANGUAGE

There are some points of contact between the way conceptual structures are realized in language and in images. The comparison would have to be made with the kinds of linguistic structures Halliday calls 'relational' and 'existential' processes (see Halliday, 1985: 112ff.). These have at least this in common with conceptual images that they represent the world in terms of more or less permanent states of affairs or general truths, rather than in terms of actions or mental processes. Halliday recognizes two main categories of relational process, the *Attributive* and the *Identifying* process. The meaning of an Attributive process clause can be schematically described as 'a is an attribute of x'. The *attribute* 'a' is then simply called Attribute, and the participant whose attribute it is, is the *Carrier* – we have borrowed these terms in our analysis of images. In *Some people are racist*, for instance, *some people* is Carrier, *are* is the Relational (Attributive) process, and *racist* is the Attribute. Attributive processes can be *Intensive* – that is, they can be about what a Carrier *is*, as in the example just given; they can be *Circumstantial* – that is, they can be about 'where' or 'when' or 'what with' a Carrier is (e.g. in *Their home was in Ho Chi Minh City, their home* is Carrier, *was* an Attributive [Circumstantial] Relational process, and *in Ho Chi Minh City* an Attribute); and they can be *Possessive* – that is, they can be about what a Carrier has (e.g. in *I didn't own a thing in the world, I* is Carrier, *own* the Attributive [Possessive] Relational process, and *a thing in the world,* the Attribute).

The meaning of an *Identifying Relational process* clause can be schematically described as 'a is the identity of x'. The identity 'a' is then termed the Value and the participant 'x' whose identity it is, is called the Token. In *Rev Peter Nyangingu is the Minister of the Uniting Church at Ernabella, Rev Peter Nyangingu* is Token, *is* is the Identifying Relational process, and *the Minister of the Uniting Church at Ernabella* is the Value. The Value, then, tends to be a 'status' or 'function' or 'meaning' which serves to identify the Token, and the Token is the name or some description of the holder of the status, or of the occupant of the function, or of the sign which has the meaning. Picture captions are often identifying clauses, with a reference to the picture as Token and the meaning of the Picture as Value (for instance, *This is oyster farming in Palm Island*). Identifying and Attributive clauses can be distinguished from each other by means of the reversibility test: in Identifying clauses the order of the participants can be reversed (e.g. *The Minister of the Uniting Church at Ernabella is Rev Peter Nyangingu* is just as acceptable as *Rev Peter Nyangingu is the Minister of the Uniting Church at Ernabella*), whereas in Attributive clauses this is not the case (*Racist are some people* is much more unusual than *Some people are racist*).

Existential clauses, finally, simply state that 'something exists'. They have only one participant, the Existent – that is, the participant whose existence the structure affirms. Existents may either be Events (e.g. in *It's terrible weather*) or Entities (e.g. in *There was a public library*). The presence of a 'dummy subject' (*there* or referentless *it*) is the principal identifying characteristic of existential clauses (see Halliday, 1985: 130).

Visual Classificational and Analytical structures could therefore be said to be akin to, respectively, Intensive and Possessive Attributive clauses, and Symbolic Attributive structures could be seen as akin to Identifying clauses, and there is perhaps also some affinity between Symbolic Suggestive structures and Existential clauses. But the differences are greater than the similarities and, especially in the area of Classificational and Analytical images, the visual semiotic has a range of structural devices which have no equivalent in language: the difference between visual conceptualization and linguistic conceptualization is evidently quite large. All the more important to have a vocabulary for expressing what can be done and is done with each in concrete texts that combine the two semiotics, texts such as 'The Overland' (figure 3.30), a school project by an eight-year-old boy. Looking first at the words, the structure of the verbal text on the left page is Possessive Attribute throughout. There is a Carrier ('The Overland'), and there are six Possessive Attributes ('five first class carriages', 'three second class carriages', 'two dining car's', 'two engines' and 'one club car', 'one motor rail cart'). The process itself is elided.

The picture, too, is concerned with the relation of parts to a whole. It has all the hallmarks of an exhaustive, structured analytical process: the picture is front-on and eye level, there is no Setting, and the different Possessive Attributes (signs, windows, wheels, suspension and rails) are shown clearly, but without unnecessary detail: it is relatively 'abstract'. The relation between picture and text is not one of illustration. The picture does not duplicate the text, it does not represent visually what has already been represented

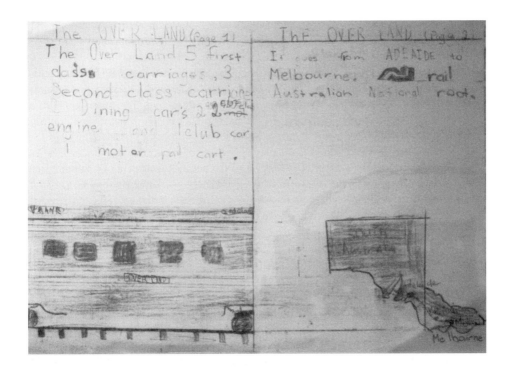

Fig 3.30 'The Overland'

linguistically. Nor is there a relation of 'anchorage' (Barthes, 1977) in which the text elaborates the information given in the picture without providing new information. It is true that both text and picture are about part–whole relations but this does not mean they duplicate each other, because in the text the Carrier is the train as a whole, whereas in the picture the Carrier is one *of* the carriages *of* the train. The child has taken a topic, the 'Overland Express', and treated it verbally and visually in such a way that each part of the text supplements the other part.

Let us analyse the second page. The words are as follows:

It goes from ADELAIDE to Melbourne rail Australian National root.

Here we have first of all a non-transactional action, with an Actor ('it') and an Action ('goes'), as well as two Circumstances of place ('from Adelaide' and 'to Melbourne'), There follows an identification of the route, with the Token and the Process elided ('rail Australian National root'): the child objectifies the action 'going', turns it into a thing, a 'route', by means of an identifying relational process in which the 'root' is Value. Finally the route is described in more detail, through a visual analytical process in which the relevant section of Australia is the Carrier, and Adelaide, Melbourne and the 'route' the

Possessive Attributes, in a process which uses many of the structural devices of the analytical visual to show precisely how the Possessive Attributes are spatially related, how they 'fit together'.

'My Adventure' (figure 3.31) is another school project, written by a child from the same school and year as the author of 'The Overland'. Most of the verbal processes are transactional and non-transactional actions in which the narrator is Actor: he walks, finds a cave, finds some nails, and so on. He is not describing something but telling a story, narrating a particular event:

> Not long ago I went for a journey down to the beach. I walked all along the beach until I found a cave. That cave was big. Then there was some wood but I couldn't make a raft without nails. Just then I found some nails in the cave. I said to myself 'Somebody must have been here'. So I got a piece of wood and started making the raft. I used a piece of wood for a. . . .

Still, there is also a conceptual element. In this part of the story the writer is preoccupied with the materials needed for building a raft. There is a hidden attributive process, something like 'the materials for a raft are wood and nails', but it is transformed into the story of the finding of these materials (which emerge mysteriously in a big cave). As in the story

▲ **Fig 3.31 'My Adventure'**

that opens the book of Genesis, which is also a narrative concerned with conceptualizing the elements that make up a whole, the world, the writer alternates actional and trans-actional processes ('I found some nails') with more conceptual existential processes ('then there was some wood').

The verbal text stops abruptly, in the middle of the Circumstance of Purpose, and it is continued, not on the following page, but by the picture, which shows what these materials were used for: the parts of a raft. It is an Unstructured Analytical process, with the sail, and the raft itself (already complete with mast and rudder), as Possessive Attributes. These are, in the child's conceptualization, the parts from which a raft is made. However, there is also a strong narrative element in this picture: it has a Setting (the shoreline, the cave) and it does not use the frontal, eye-level perspective typical of most analytical images (and already successfully used by the author of 'The Overland') but a high and oblique angle. In both the picture and the words, the writer blends the conceptual and the narrative or, rather, narrativizes the conceptual. In the verbal text he does this through conjunctions ('then', 'just then', etc.), through the use of the past tense and through the use of transactional and non-transactional Action processes with the narrator as a (first-person) Actor. In the picture he does it through the use of a Setting and a narrative perspective. Finally, the words and the picture again complement each other. The picture does not illustrate the story but continues it.

It is clear, we hope, that children actively experiment with the representational resources of word and image, and with the ways in which they can be combined. Their drawings are not just illustrations of a verbal text, not just 'creative embellishment'; they are part of a 'multimodally' conceived text, a semiotic interplay in which each mode, the verbal and the visual, is given a defined and equal role to play.

4 Representation and interaction: designing the position of the viewer

In the previous chapter we discussed visual resources for the representation of interactions and conceptual relations between the people, places and things depicted in images. But visual communication also has resources for constituting and maintaining another kind of interaction, the interaction between the producer and the viewer of the image. Another way of saying this is that images (and other kinds of visual) involve two kinds of participants, *represented participants* (the people, the places and things depicted in images) and *interactive participants* (the people who communicate with each other *through* images, the producers and viewers of images), and three kinds of relations: (1) relations between represented participants; (2) relations between interactive and represented participants (the interactive participants' attitudes towards the represented participants); and (3) relations between interactive participants (the things interactive participants do to or for each other through images).

Interactive participants are therefore real people who produce and make sense of images in the context of social institutions which, to different degrees and in different ways, regulate what may be 'said' with images, how it should be said, and how it should be interpreted. In some cases the interaction is direct and immediate. Producer and viewer know each other and are involved in face-to-face interaction, as when we make photographs of each other to keep in wallets or pin on pinboards, or draw maps to give each other directions, or diagrams to explain ideas to each other. But in many cases there is no immediate and direct involvement. The producer is absent for the viewer, and the viewer is absent for the producer. Think of photographs in magazines. Who is the producer? The photographer who took the shot? The assistant who processed and printed it? The agency who selected and distributed it? The picture editor who chose it? The layout artist who cropped it and determined its size and position on the page? Most viewers will not only never meet all these contributors to the production process face to face, but also have only a hazy, and perhaps distorted and glamorized, idea of the production processes behind the image. All they have is the picture itself, as it appears in the magazine. And producers, similarly, can never really know their vast and absent audiences, and must, instead, create a mental image of 'the' viewers and 'the' way viewers make sense of their pictures. In everyday face-to-face communication it is easy enough to distinguish interactive participants from represented participants: there is always an image-producer and a viewer (who, depending on the situation, may swap roles with the producer, add to the scribbled floorplan or diagram, for instance), and then there are the represented participants (for instance, the people on the quick sketch of the dinner table arrangement, or the landmarks on the hand-drawn map), and these may, of course, include the producer and/or the viewer themselves. Producer and viewer are physically present. The participants they represent need not be. But when there is a disjunction between the context of production and the context of reception, the producer is not physically present, and the viewer is alone with the image and cannot reciprocate – an illuminating exception is the case of the 'defacement' of billboard advertisements, when graffiti artists 'respond' to the initial 'turn' or statement of the image.

Something similar occurs in writing. Writers, too, are not usually physically present when their words are read, and must address their readers in the guise of represented participants, even when they write in the first person. Readers, too, are alone with the written word, and cannot usually become writers in turn. Literary theorists (e.g. Booth, 1961; Chatman, 1978) have addressed this problem by distinguishing between 'real' and 'implied' authors, and between 'real' and 'implied' readers. The 'implied author' is a disembodied voice, or even 'a set of implicit norms rather than a speaker or a voice' (Rimmon-Kenan, 1983: 87): 'he, or better, it has no voice, no direct means of communicating, but instructs us silently, through the design of the whole, with all the voices, by all the means it has chosen to let us learn' (Chatman, 1978: 148). The 'implied reader', 'preferred reading position', etc., similarly, is 'an image of a certain competence brought to the text and a structuring of such competence within the text' (Rimmon-Kenan, 1983: 118): the text selects a 'model reader' through its 'choice of a specific linguistic code, a certain literary style' and by presupposing 'a specific encyclopedic competence' on the part of the reader (Eco, 1979: 7). This we can know. Of this we have evidence in the text itself. Real authors and real readers we cannot ultimately know. This bracketing out of real authors and real readers carries the risk of forgetting that texts, literary and artistic texts as much as mass media texts, are produced in the context of real social institutions, in order to play a very real role in social life – in order to do certain things to or for their readers, and in order to communicate attitudes towards aspects of social life and towards people who participate in them, whether authors and readers are consciously aware of this or not. Producers, if they want to see their work disseminated, must work within more or less rigidly defined conventions, and adhere to the more or less rigidly defined values and beliefs of the social institution within which their work is produced and circulated. Readers will at least recognize these communicative intentions and these values and attitudes for what they are, even if they do not ultimately accept them as their own values and beliefs. They can 'recognize the substance of what is meant while refusing the speaker's interpretations and assessments' (Scannell, 1994: 11).

However important and real this disjunction between the context of production and the context of reception, the two do have elements in common: the image itself, and a knowledge of the communicative resources that allow its articulation and understanding, a knowledge of the way social interactions and social relations can be encoded in images. It is often said that the knowledge of the producer and the knowledge of the viewer differ in a fundamental respect: the former is active, allowing the 'sending' as well as the 'receiving' of 'messages'; the latter is passive, allowing only the 'receiving' of 'messages'. Producers are able to 'write' as well as 'read', viewers are able only to 'read'. Up to a point this is true, at least in the sense that the production of images is still a specialized activity, so that producers 'write' more fluently and eloquently, and more frequently, than viewers. But we hope our attempts to make that knowledge explicit will show that the interactive meanings are visually encoded in ways that rest on competencies shared by producers and viewers.

The articulation and understanding of social meanings in images derives from the visual articulation of social meanings in face-to-face interaction, the spatial positions allocated to different kinds of social actors in interaction (whether they are seated or standing, side by side or facing each other frontally, etc.). In this sense the interactive dimension of images is the 'writing' of what is usually called 'non-verbal communication', a 'language' shared by producers and viewers alike.

The disjunction between the context of production and the context of reception has yet another effect: it causes social relations to be *represented rather than enacted*. Because the producers are absent from the place where the actual communicative transaction is completed, from the locus of reception, they cannot say 'I' other than through a substitute 'I'. Even when the viewer receives an image of the 'real author' or a contributor to the production process – the presenter in a television programme, the painter in a self-portrait, the owner of the company (or the worker in the centuries-old distillery) in an advertise-ment – that image is only an image, a double of the 'real author', a representation, detached from his or her actual body. And the 'real authors' may also speak in the guise of someone else, of a 'character', as when, instead of the owner of a company, it is Uncle Sam, or a larger-than-life walking and talking teddy bear, who addresses us in an advertisement. This dimension of representation is another one which has been studied extensively in literary theory (e.g. Genette, 1972). The relation between producer and viewer, too, is represented rather than enacted. In face-to-face communication we must respond to a friendly smile with a friendly smile, to an arrogant stare with a deferential lowering of the eyes, and such obligations cannot easily be avoided without appearing impolite, unfriendly or impudent. When images confront us with friendly smiles or arrogant stares, we are not obliged to respond, even though we do recognize how we are addressed. The relation is only represented. We are *imaginarily* rather than really put in the position of the friend, the customer, the lay person who must defer to the expert. And whether or not we identify with that position will depend other factors – on our real relation to the producer or the institution he or she represents, and on our real relation to the others who form part of the context of reception. All the same, whether or not we identify with the way we are addressed, we do understand how we are addressed, because we do understand the way images represent social interactions and social relations. It is the business of this chapter to try and make those understandings explicit.

THE IMAGE ACT AND THE GAZE

In the previous chapters we showed two pictures of an Antarctic explorer, taken from the Australian primary-school social studies textbook *Our Society and Others* (Oakley *et al.*, 1985). Figure 3.10 was a photograph in which the Australian Antarctic explorer Sir Douglas Mawson looked directly at the viewer. The schematic and 'generalized' explorer in figure 2.4, on the other hand, did not look at the viewer. The two images are in fact positioned side by side, the photo on the left page, the drawing on the right. Together, they combine two different communicative functions. The photo seeks above all to bring about an imaginary relation between the represented explorer and the children for whom the book is written, a relation perhaps of admiration for, and identification with, a national hero. And this means also that the image-producer (the institution of educational publishing) addresses the children in the voice of the national hero and makes that national hero an 'educational' voice. The drawing, on the other hand, seeks, first of all, to be read as a piece of objective, factual information, and in this way aims to set into motion the actual process of learning.

There is, then, a fundamental difference between pictures from which represented participants look directly at the viewer's eyes, and pictures in which this is not the case. When represented participants look at the viewer, vectors, formed by participants' eyelines, connect the participants with the viewer. Contact is established, even if it is only on an imaginary level. In addition there may be a further vector, formed by a gesture in the same direction, as in figure 4.1.

This visual configuration has two related functions. In the first place it creates a visual form of direct address. It acknowledges the viewers explicitly, addressing them with a visual 'you'. In the second place it constitutes an 'image act'. The producer uses the image

Fig 4.1 Recruitment poster (Alfred Leete, 1914) (Imperial War Museum)

to do something to the viewer. It is for this reason that we have called this kind of image a 'demand', following Halliday (1985): the participant's gaze (and the gesture, if present) demands something from the viewer, demands that the viewer enter into some kind of imaginary relation with him or her. Exactly what kind of relation is then signified by other means, for instance by the facial expression of the represented participants. They may smile, in which case the viewer is asked to enter into a relation of social affinity with them; they may stare at the viewer with cold disdain, in which case the viewer is asked to relate to them, perhaps, as an inferior relates to a superior; they may seductively pout at the viewer, in which case the viewer is asked to desire them. The same applies to gestures. A hand can point at the viewer, in a visual 'Hey, you there, I mean you', or invite the viewer to come closer, or hold the viewer at bay with a defensive gesture, as if to say, 'Stay away from me'. In each case the image wants something from the viewers – wants them to do something (come closer, stay at a distance) or to form a pseudo-social bond of a particular kind with the represented participant. And in doing this, images define to some extent who the viewer is (e.g. male, inferior to the represented participant, etc.), and in that way exclude other viewers.

In the history of art, this look was a significant innovation. Although in Italian painting small figures among the bystanders of the Crucifixion and other biblical scenes can be seen to look at the viewer from the fourteenth century onwards, the 'demand' picture comes into its own in the fifteenth century. According to Panofsky (1953: 190), it originated in self-portraits, and Jan van Eyck was the first to use it in *Man in a Red Turban* (1433), which is regarded by most art historians as a self-portrait.

> In 1433 Jan van Eyck made one of the great discoveries in portraiture. In the portrait of a 'Man in a Red Turban', completed in October 21 of that year, the glance of the sitter is turned out of the picture and sharply focused on the beholder with an air of skepticism intensified by the expression of the thin mouth with its slightly compressed corners. For the first time the sitter seeks to establish direct contact with the spectator. . . . We feel observed and scrutinized by a wakeful intelligence.
>
> (Panofsky, 1953: 198)

Others trace it back further. According to Belting (1990: 57), 'the suggestion of reciprocity between the viewer and the person depicted in the image' had a devotional purpose. By the thirteenth century, monks in their cells 'had before their eyes images of the Virgin and her crucified son, so that while reading, praying and sleeping, they could look upon them and be *looked upon* with the eyes of compassion' (our italics).

Represented participants who look at the viewer are usually human (or animal), but not always: the headlights of a car can be drawn as eyes looking at the viewer, for instance, and on the screen of one automatic bank teller, a creature whose combined head and body has the box-like shape of a machine, smiles at the viewer, holding out his hand in an inviting gesture, thus 'demanding' a friendly relation between the machine and its user (figure 4.2). The point is, whether they are human or not, by being represented as looking at the viewer, they are represented as human, anthropomorphized to some degree.

Fig 4.2 ATM screen

Other pictures address us indirectly. Here the viewer is not object, but subject of the look, and the represented participant is the object of the viewer's dispassionate scrutiny. No contact is made. The viewer's role is that of an invisible onlooker. All images which do not contain human or quasi-human participants looking directly at the viewer are of this kind. For this reason we have, again following Halliday (1985), called this kind of image an 'offer' – it 'offers' the represented participants to the viewer as items of information, objects of contemplation, impersonally, as though they were specimens in a display case.

It is always interesting to study which kinds of represented participants are, in a given context, depicted as demanding an imaginary social response of some kind from the viewer, and which are not. In *Our Society and Others* (Oakley *et al.*, 1985), the Australian primary-school textbook from which we drew many of our key examples in the first version of this book, immigrant families smile at the viewer. However, the human participants in pictures from these immigrants' countries of origin do not look at the viewer, not even in close-up portraits, as, for instance, in the portrait of an Italian grandmother who stayed behind. In the chapter on Aborigines, by contrast, hardly any of the Aboriginal participants look at the viewer. The Aboriginal poet Oodgeroo Noonuccal, referred to in the book as 'Kath Walker', and depicted in close-up in the last illustration of that chapter, is the only exception (see figure 4.3 below). Her expression, her make-up, her hairstyle and dress hardly distinguish her from non-Aboriginal women of her age. At most her skin is somewhat darker, but even that is not very pronounced in the black-and-white shot. Other Aboriginal people in the chapter are much more clearly depicted as 'other', and even if they do, occasionally, look directly at the viewer, they do so from a long distance, which greatly diminishes the impact of their look, or are figures in the background, looking blankly and more or less

Fig 4.3 Oodgeroo Noonuccal (Oakley *et al.*, 1985)

accidentally in the direction of the camera. Aboriginal people, in this primary-school text-book, are depicted as objects of contemplation, not as subjects for the pupil to enter into an imaginary social relation with. Immigrants, by contrast, at least once they are in Australia, are portrayed as people with whom the pupils should engage more directly, and in a friendly way, as equals.

The choice between 'offer' and 'demand', which must be made whenever people are depicted, is not only used to suggest different relations with different 'others', to make viewers engage with some and remain detached from others; it can also characterize pictorial genres. In some contexts – for instance, television newsreading and the posed magazine photograph – the 'demand' picture is preferred: these contexts require a sense of connection between the viewers and the authority figures, celebrities and role models they depict. In other contexts – for example, feature film and television drama and scientific illustration – the 'offer' is preferred: here a real or imaginary barrier is erected between the represented participants and the viewers, a sense of disengagement, in which the viewer must have the illusion that the represented participants do not know they are being looked at, and in which the represented participants must pretend that they are not being watched. And what in one context is accepted convention may in another be a startling mistake or an innovative experiment. Film theorists (e.g. Allen, 1977; Wollen, 1982) have hailed the look at the camera as a daring, Brechtian, 'self-reflexive'-style figure, but in television newsreading the look at the camera is commonplace and, we would think, not exactly 'self-reflexive' – at least for the presenters: an interviewee who looks at the camera in a television news programme breaks the rules in an unacceptable way. Not everyone may address the viewer directly. Some may only be looked at, others may themselves be the bearers of the look. There is an issue of communicative power or 'entitlement' (Sacks, 1992) involved in this, not only in pictures, but also in everyday face-to-face communication, for instance in interactions between men and women:

> As he answers the girl's last statement he begins talking and reaches the point where normally he would look away, but instead he is still staring at her. This makes her uncomfortable, because she is forced either to lock eyes with him, or to look away from him while he is talking. If he continues to talk and stare while she deflects her eyes, it puts her into the 'shy' category, which she resents. If she boldly locks eyes with him, he has forced her into a 'lover's gaze', which she also resents.
>
> (Morris, 1977: 76)

Diagrams, maps and charts are most often found in contexts that offer a kind of knowledge which, in Western culture, has traditionally been valued highly – objective, dispassionate knowledge, ostensibly free of emotive involvement and subjectivity. Hence the 'demand' has been rare in these visual genres. But there were contexts in which the two forms of address were combined. School textbooks of the kind we used as data when we wrote the first edition of this book, for instance, constructed a progression from 'demand' to 'offer' pictures, and this not only in the course of a chapter, as in the chapter on Antarctic exploration, but also in the course of a whole book or series of books and, indeed, in the course of education as a whole – illustrations that served to involve students emotively in the subject matter then gradually dropped out as higher levels of education were reached. In senior high-school textbooks we found 'demand' pictures at most in the cartoons which, in almost apologetic fashion, sought to alleviate the seriousness of the text from time to time, as in a cartoon in a geography textbook (Bindon and Williams, 1988) where a girl looked despondently at the viewer, with the words 'What does hypothesis mean?' in a dialogue balloon emanating from her mouth. In the context of education, the 'demand' picture played an ambivalent role. On the one hand, it was not a highly valued form, but a form deemed suitable only for beginners, a form one grew out of as one climbed the educational ladder; on the other hand, it played an indispensable role in educational strategy: objective knowledge had to be built, apparently, upon a foundation of emotive involvement, of identification with celebratory mythologies, for instance. This foundation was then, gradually, repressed, for if it was not repressed, the knowledge built on it could not be seen to be objective. Outside the sphere of education, the value of the 'demand' picture depended on the assumed educational level of the reader. When, for instance, the mass media (or automatic teller machines) began to use 'demand' pictures, those educated in the linguistic and visual genres of objective knowledge and impersonal address would have felt patronized, 'addressed below their class'. Those not so educated (or those who contested the value of such an education) would have felt that communication had become more effective (and more fun) than was the case in the era of more formal and impersonal public communication. As we already discussed in the previous chapters, this situation is now changing and, with the gradual disappearance of the semiotic distinction, the class and age distinctions it supported (and the different values and attitudes that were associated with these distinctions) also began to erode.

It is possible to relate the meanings conveyed by 'demands' and 'offers' to the linguistic system of person. As we have seen, 'demand' pictures address the viewer directly, realizing a visual 'you'. But this is not matched by a visual 'I'. The 'I' is absent in pictures or, rather, objectified, hiding behind a he/she/they. The 'demand' picture therefore reminds more of the language of, for instance, advertisements and instructions, where 'you's' abound but 'I's' are rare, than, say, of the language of personal letters, where 'I's' and 'you's' are likely to be equally common. 'Real producers' cannot refer to themselves directly. They must speak impersonally, as traditionally in bureaucratic and scientific language, where 'I's' were, and in many cases still are, also repressed. The public, on the other hand, is addressed directly. And yet, as we have seen, the distinction between 'offers' and 'demands' derives historically from attempts of Renaissance painters to find ways of saying 'I' in the self-portraits which expressed their new-found self-confidence and status of independent artists rather than humble craftsmen.

But the concepts of 'offer' and 'demand' can also be related to another key concept in linguistics, that of the 'speech act'. As mentioned, we have taken the terms from Halliday's description of four basic speech acts (or 'speech functions' as he calls them in his *Introduction to Functional Grammar,* 1985). Each of these speech acts, says Halliday, is part of an interactional dyad, and has its 'expected' and its 'discretionary' (alternative) social response. Thus speech acts can (1) 'offer information', that is, form a statement, in which case the response sought is 'agreement', although the statement may of course also be contradicted; they can (2) 'offer goods-and-services' (e.g. *Would you like a drink?*), in which case the expected response is 'acceptance', although the offer may also be rejected; they can (3) 'demand information', that is, form a question, in which case the expected response is an answer, although the listener may also disclaim the question, for instance by saying *I don't know* or *I can't tell you that*; and (4), they can 'demand goods-and-services', that is, constitute some kind of command, in which case the expected response is for the listener to undertake what he or she has been asked to do, although listeners may of course also refuse to do so.

These speech acts are realized by the linguistic system of 'mood', that is, by syntactic permutations, permutations of the order of the subject and the finite element of the verbal group (i.e. the element of the verbal group that expresses tense and modality). The 'offer of information' (statement), for instance, is realized by the indicative mood, in which the finite element follows the subject, as in this sentence from *Vogue*:

Women (subject) *cannot* (finite) *live by diamonds alone.*

'Demanding information', the question, is realized by the interrogative mood, which has the subject following the finite in the case of the 'polar question' (the kind of question to which one can just answer 'yes' or 'no'), and, in the case of a 'WH-question' a WH-subject followed by the finite, or the finite element followed by the subject:

Can (finite) *women* (subject) *live by diamonds alone?*

Who (WH-subject) *could* (finite) *live by diamonds alone?*

What could (finite) *women* (subject) *live by?*

The imperative mood, the 'command', has no subject at all and, when the polarity is positive, no finite either:

Don't (finite) *live by diamonds alone*

Live by diamonds alone

The speech act of 'offering goods-and-services', finally, is not realized by a permutation of subject and finite, but by various idioms (e.g. *Here you are*), by questions, in conjunction with specific mental process verbs (e.g. *Do you want a drink?*) or by commands (*Have a drink*) and, indeed, in various other ways.

There are many subtypes of these four basic kinds of speech act. They are realized through specific combinations of additional linguistic features. A 'prediction', for example, is an 'offer of information' with future tense and either second- or third-person subject, or first-person subject with a 'non-volitional' verb (e.g. *You will live by diamonds alone,* or *I will die young*). A 'promise' is an 'offer of information' with future tense, a first-person subject and a volitional verb (e.g. *I will buy you diamonds*). It would take us too far to discuss these in detail. The point to remember is that in language there are a few 'core' types and a very large number of further types which are constructed out of the core types. The same is true in the case of images. A visual 'invitation' is a 'demand' picture with a beckoning hand and a smiling expression; a visual 'summons', a 'demand' picture with a beckoning hand and an unsmiling expression; a visual 'warning', a 'demand' picture with a raised forefinger and a stern expression; and so on.

Despite these broad similarities, it would seem that 'image acts' do not work in the same way as speech acts. When images 'offer', they primarily offer information. Of course, an image, say an advertising image, may show someone offering something to the viewer, and this offer may in fact be a real offer, which can be obtained by writing to an address specified in the advertisement. But if there is such an 'offer of goods-and-services' in images, it must take the *form* of an 'offer of information'. It must be *represented*. It cannot be enacted directly.

When images 'demand', they demand, one could say, the 'goods-and-services' that realize a particular social relation. Of course, an image could show a gesture of puzzlement, a 'silent' question, but the example is somewhat contrived and would need verbal reinforcement, or reinforcement by a conventional visual sign, for instance, a question mark. There is no image act for every speech act. But this need not be so forever. Although language and image do have their specific affordances, what can be 'said' and 'done' with images (and with language) does not only depend on the intrinsic and universal characteristics of these modes of communication, but also on historically and culturally specific social needs. It is quite possible to extend the semantic reach and use of images into domains which formerly were the exclusive province of language, as is already done, on a small scale, in places where people are unlikely to have any given language in common (for example, international airports).

SIZE OF FRAME AND SOCIAL DISTANCE

There is a second dimension to the interactive meanings of images, related to the 'size of frame', to the choice between close-up, medium shot and long shot, and so on. Just as image-producers, in depicting human or quasi-human participants, must choose to make them look at the viewer or not, so they must also, and at the same time, choose to depict them as close to or far away from the viewer – and this applies to the depiction of objects also. And, like the choice between the 'offer' and the 'demand', the choice of distance can suggest different relations between represented participants and viewers. In handbooks about film and television production, size of frame is invariably defined in relation to the human body. Even though distance is, strictly speaking, a continuum, the 'language of film and television' has imposed a set of distinct cut-off points on this continuum, in the same way as languages impose cut-off points on the continuum of vowels we can produce. Thus the close shot (or 'close-up') shows head and shoulders of the subject, and the very close shot ('extreme close-up', 'big close-up') anything less than that. The medium close shot cuts off the subject approximately at the waist, the medium shot approximately at the knees. The medium long shot shows the full figure. In the long shot the human figure occupies about half the height of the frame, and the very long shot is anything 'wider' than that. Stylistic variants are possible, but they are always seen and talked about in terms of this system, as when film and television people talk of 'tight close shots' or 'tight framing', or about the amount of 'headroom' in a picture (i.e. space between the top of the head and the upper frame line).

In everyday interaction, social relations determine the distance (literally and figuratively) we keep from one another. Edward Hall (e.g. 1966: 110–20) has shown that we carry with us a set of invisible boundaries beyond which we allow only certain kinds of people to come. The location of these invisible boundaries is determined by configurations of sensory potentialities – by whether or not a certain distance allows us to smell or touch the other person, for instance, and by how much of the other person we can see with our peripheral (sixty-degree) vision. 'Close personal distance' is the distance at which 'one can hold or grasp the other person' and therefore also the distance between people who have an intimate relation with each other. Non-intimates cannot come this close and, if they do so, it will be experienced as an act of aggression. 'Far personal distance' is the distance that 'extends from a point that is just outside easy touching distance by one person to a point where two people can touch fingers if they both extend their arms', the distance at which 'subjects of personal interests and involvements are discussed'. 'Close social distance' begins just outside this range and is the distance at which 'impersonal business occurs'. 'Far social distance' is 'the distance to which people move when somebody says "Stand away so I can look at you" ' – 'business and social interaction conducted at this distance has a more formal and impersonal character than in the close phase'. 'Public distance', finally, is anything further than that, 'the distance between people who are and are to remain strangers'. These judgements apply, of course, within a particular culture, and Hall cites many examples of the misunderstandings which can arise from intercultural differences in the interpretation of distance.

With these differences correspond different fields of vision. At intimate distance, says Hall (1964), we see the face or head only. At close personal distance we take in the head and the shoulders. At far personal distance we see the other person from the waist up. At close social distance we see the whole figure. At far social distance we see the whole figure 'with space around it'. And at public distance we can see the torso of at least four or five people. It is clear that these fields of vision correspond closely to the traditional definitions of size of frame in film and television; in other words, that the visual system of size of frame derives from the 'proxemics', as Hall calls it, of everyday face-to-face interaction. Hall is aware of this and in fact acknowledges the influence of the work of Grosser, a portrait painter, on his ideas. According to Grosser (quoted in Hall, 1966: 71–2), at a distance of more than 13 feet (4m), people are seen 'as having little connection with ourselves', and hence 'the painter can look at his model as if he were a tree in a landscape or an apple in a still life'. Four to eight feet (1.25–2.5m), on the other hand, is the 'portrait distance':

> the painter is near enough so that his eyes have no trouble in understanding the sitter's solid forms, yet he is far enough away so that the foreshortening of the forms presents no real problem. Here at the normal distance of social intimacy and easy conversation, the sitter's soul begins to appear. . . . Nearer than three feet [90cm], within touching distance, the soul is far too much in evidence for any sort of disinterested observation.

The distances people keep, then, depend on their social relation – whether this is the more permanent kind of social relation on which Hall mainly concentrates (the distinction between intimates, friends, acquaintances, strangers, etc.) or the kind of social relation that lasts for the duration of a social interaction and is determined by the context (someone in the audience of a speech given by an acquaintance or relative would nevertheless stay at public distance, the distance of the 'stranger'). But these distances also, and at the same time, determine how much of the other person is in our field of vision – just as does the framing of a person in a portrait or film shot.

Like the 'demand' picture, the close-up came to the fore in the Renaissance. Ringbom (1965: 48) argues that it has its origin in devotional pictures, where it served to provide 'the "near-ness" so dear to the God-seeking devout'. In Italian and Dutch paintings of the early sixteenth century it acquired a 'dramatic' function, allowing 'the subtlest of emotional relationships with a minimum of dramatic scenery' (p. 48).

The people we see in images are for the most part strangers. It is true that we see some of them (politicians, film and television stars, sports heroes, etc.) a good deal more than others, but this kind of familiarity does not of itself determine whether they will be shown in close shot or medium shot or long shot. The relation between the human participants represented in images and the viewer is once again an imaginary relation. People are portrayed *as though* they are friends, or *as though* they are strangers. Images allow us to imaginarily come as close to public figures as if they were our friends and neighbours – or to look at people like ourselves as strangers, 'others'. In the primary-school social studies textbook from which we have quoted several examples, three Aboriginal boys are shown in long shot, occupying only about a quarter of the height of the 'portrait' format frame. The caption reads, 'These people live at Redfern, a suburb of Sydney.' They are shown impersonally, as strangers with whom we do not need to become acquaintances, as 'trees in a landscape'. Although they do look at the viewer, they do so from such a distance that it barely affects us. Indeed, they are so small that we can hardly distinguish their facial features. 'Their soul does not yet begin to appear', to use Grosser's words. The caption, significantly, gives them no name; in fact, where the more friendly 'boys' could have been, the quite formal 'people' has been used.

The portrait of the Aboriginal poet Oodgeroo Noonuccal (figure 4.3), already mentioned in the previous section of this chapter, is a tight close shot. *She* is depicted in a personal way. If this was all we could see of her in reality, we would be close enough to touch her. As mentioned, the section in which the photo occurs concludes a chapter on Aborigines in which no other Aborigine smiles at the viewer in this way. One of her poems is quoted: 'Dark and white upon common ground! In club and office and social round! Yours the feel of a friendly land! The grip of the hand' (Oakley *et al.*, 1985: 164). But Noonuccal's message is not borne out by the way 'dark and white' are portrayed in the chapter.

Patterns of distance can become conventional in visual genres. In current affairs television, for example, 'voices' of different status are habitually framed differently: the camera 'moves in for bigger close-ups of subjects who are revealing their feelings, whereas the set-up for the "expert" is usually the same as that for the interviewer – the breast pocket shot'. Both kinds of 'statused participants' tend to be 'nominated' (their names appear on the screen in superimposed captions) and 'have their contributions framed and summed up' (Brunsdon and Morley, 1978: 65). In other words, distance is used to signify respect for authorities of various kinds, on television as in face-to-face interaction.

In diagrams the human figure is almost always shown in medium long or long shot – objectively, 'as if he were a tree in a landscape'. The pictures in figure 4.4 illustrated a front-page newspaper story about a murder case in Sydney. The diagrams show exactly what happened, from an objectifying and impersonal distance (and from a high angle). The close-up photos accompany testimonies by former patients of the victim, but are represented as also 'friends' of we readers of the *Sydney Morning Herald,* and therefore as people whose relation with the victim we should identify with. As in the chapter on Antarctic exploration, the personal and the impersonal, the emotive and the detached, are combined.

So far we have discussed social distance in relation to human-represented participants,

HIS PATIENTS

Fig 4.4 The murder of Dr Chang (*Sydney Morning Herald*, 5 July 1991)

but unlike the system of 'offer' and 'demand', the system of social distance can apply also to the representation of objects and of the environment. As size of frame is traditionally defined in terms of specific sections of the human body, beginning students of film and television are often at a loss as to which terms to use for describing shots of objects and landscapes. The scale of seven sizes of frame seems too fine-grained. There are no clear-cut equivalents for the shoulder, the waist, the knees. And objects come in many different shapes and sizes. We would nevertheless suggest that at least three significant distances can be distinguished, and that there are correspondences between these distances and our everyday experience of objects and the environment; in other words, that size of frame can also suggest social relations between the viewer and objects, buildings and landscapes. At close distance, we would suggest, the object is shown as if the viewer is engaged with it as if he or she is using the machine, reading the book or the map, preparing or eating the food. Unless the object is very small, it is shown only in part, and often the picture includes the user's hand, or a tool – for instance, a knife scraping the soft margarine in an advertisement. Film and television 'cutaways' ('overshoulders') of objects, in which the objects shown are integrated into an action through the editing, use this distance. At middle distance, the object is shown in full, but without much space around it. It is represented as within the viewer's reach, but not as actually used. This type of picture is common in advertising: the advertised product is shown in full, but from a fairly close range, and a steep angle, as if the viewer stands just in front of the table on which it is displayed. At long distance there is an invisible barrier between the viewer and the object. The object is there for our contemplation only, out of reach, as if on display in a shop window or museum exhibit. The screenshot of the European PlayStation website, in figure 4.5, uses both middle distance and close distance, significantly putting the close shot on the right, as the 'New' (see chapter 6).

The same kind of distinctions can be made with respect to representations of buildings and landscapes. We can see a building from the distance of someone about to enter it, in which case we will not see the whole of the building, as is (again) often the case in film shots in which the building is related to some action. We can also see it from the distance of someone who just identified it as his or her destination, and is surveying it for a moment, before moving towards it. In that case the frame will include only the building and leave out the surrounding environment. Or we can see it, so to speak, from behind the gates that keep the public at a respectful distance from the palace, or the fortress, or the nuclear reactor, and in that case the representation will include also the space around the building. Land-scapes, too, can be seen from within; from a kind of middle distance, with a foreground object suggesting, perhaps, that the viewer is imaginarily located within the landscape, but stopping for a moment, as if to take stock of what is ahead; or from a long distance, from the air, perhaps, or from a 'lookout' position, a place not itself in the landscape but affording an overview of it, as, for instance, in many of the photographic illustrations in geography textbooks.

▲ Fig 4.5 PlayStation website (http://eu.playstation.com/europe_select.jhtml)

We will end with some brief comments on the very different way in which social distance is realized in the English language mainly through permutations in the formality of style (see Joos, 1967). Intimate language is a kind of personal language, spoken perhaps only by the members of a couple or family, or by a group of school friends. The speakers of such a 'language of intimates' often have special names for each other, names which outsiders do not get to use. And the language itself is minimally articulated: a half-word is enough to understand each other. Facial expressions, eye contact, intonation, voice quality, etc. carry most of the meaning, and people who are in an intimate relation with each other become finely attuned to the reading of meanings conveyed in this way. 'Personal' language is casual, with a good deal of colloquialism and slang. Non-verbal expression still carries much of the meaning but not so much that 'half a word is enough'. 'Social language', though still colloquial, already begins to introduce a hint of formality. And there is, in this kind of situation, less sharing of information and assumptions. The language needs to be more articulate, more verbally explicit, so that non-verbal expression is no longer as important as in intimate and personal style. Public language, finally, is the language used in more or less formal address. Here language becomes monologic: listeners no longer participate as they do in the other styles of speech. Speech is no longer improvised, but thought out in advance, perhaps even fully or partially written out. Intonation and other forms of non-verbal expression become as formal, as much subjected to control as syntax and word usage. Speech must be fully explicit, meanings fully articulated verbally. Colloquialisms are out of place and a more formal vocabulary must be employed. Writers can of course use these styles to address us as friends or even intimates, even when we are not, just as pictures can give us close-ups of people who, in reality, are and will remain strangers to us – think of the colloquial, chummy informality with which we are addressed in many advertisements.

PERSPECTIVE AND THE SUBJECTIVE IMAGE

There is yet another way in which images bring about relations between represented participants and the viewer: perspective. Producing an image involves not only the choice between 'offer' and 'demand' and the selection of a certain size of frame, but also, and at the same time, the selection of an angle, a 'point of view', and this implies the possibility of expressing subjective attitudes towards represented participants, human or otherwise. By saying 'subjective attitudes', we do not mean that these attitudes are always individual and unique. We will see that they are often socially determined attitudes. But they are always encoded as though they were subjective, individual and unique. The system of perspective which realizes 'attitude' was developed in the Renaissance, a period in which individuality and subjectivity became important social values, and it developed precisely to allow images to become informed by subjective points of view. Paradoxically, while these were the meanings encoded, perspective rests on an impersonal, geometric foundation, a construction which is a quasi-mechanical way of 'recording' images of reality. Socially determined viewpoints could, in this way, be naturalized, and presented as 'studies of nature', faithful copies of empirical reality. Only recently has it become possible again to see that perspective is also 'a daring abstraction' (Hauser, 1962: 69), and to discuss its semiotic effects, for instance, in film theory (e.g. Comolli, 1971).

Pre-Renaissance forms, frescoes on the wall of a church nave, for example, or mosaics in the domed roof of a church, did not have perspective to position the viewer. Viewers of such works were positioned, not by the internal structure of the work, but by the structure of its environments, both the immediate environment of the church, its proximity to the altar, for instance, and the wider social environments. In other words, the syntax of the object depended for its completion, its closure, not on a particular relation with the viewer but on a particular relation with its surroundings, and the point of view was the position the viewer actually took up in relation to the image: 'The world in the picture was experienced as a direct continuation of the observer's own space' (Arnheim, 1974: 274). As a result, the viewer had a certain freedom in relation to the object, a degree of what, today, we would call 'interactive use' of the text, albeit in the context of a highly constrained social order. From the Renaissance onwards, visual composition became dominated by the system of perspective, with its single, centralized viewpoint. The work became an autonomous object, detached from its surroundings, movable, produced for an impersonal market, rather than for specific locations. A frame began to separate the represented world from the physical space in which the image was viewed: at the time perspective was developed, pictures began to be framed precisely to create this division, to mark off the image from its environment, and turn it into a kind of 'window on the world'. At the same time, images became more dependent on the viewer for their completion, their closure, and viewers became more distanced from the concrete social order in which the world had formerly been embedded: they now had to learn to internalize the social order. This yielded greater freedom with respect to the immediate, concrete social context, but diminished freedom in relation to the work. A parallel can be made with the developments which, more or less simultaneously, took place in music (see Shepherd, 1977). In medieval modes, based as they were on the pentatonic, any note of the scale could stand in only intervallic relation to any other note. Hence any note could provide a sense of resolution, of closure. In the new diatonic music a strict hierarchy was established between the fundamentals, so that any melody, whatever the harmonic progressions it traversed, had to return, ultimately, to the same predetermined note, the 'tonic', in the key of which the piece was scripted. The notes in music thus relate to the key centre in the same fixed way in which viewers relate to the perspectival centre of the visual work.

There are, then, since the Renaissance, two kinds of images in Western cultures: subjective and objective images, images *with* (central) perspective (and hence with a 'built-in' point of view) and images *without* (central) perspective (and hence without a 'built-in' point of view). In subjective images the viewer can see what there is to see only from a particular point of view. In objective images, the image reveals everything there is to know (or that the image produced has judged to be so) about the represented participants, even if, to do so, it is necessary to violate the laws of naturalistic depiction or, indeed, the laws of nature. The history of art has many striking examples of this – for example, the sculptures of winged bulls and lions which flanked the doors of Assyrian temples: from the side these had four moving legs, and from the front two stationary legs, five altogether, so as to provide, from every side, a view from which no essential parts were missing. Modern technical drawings may still show what we know about the participants they represent, what is objectively there, rather than what we would see if we were looking at them in reality, rather than what is subjectively there. If we were, in reality, to see the front of the cube in figure 4.6 the way we know it 'objectively' is (a square), we would not at the same time be able to see the top and the side. It is an impossible picture (or a possible picture of a highly irregular hexahedron, rather than a cube) from the point of view of what we can see in reality. Yet in many contexts (for instance, assembly instructions for a piece of furniture) an 'objective' picture like this is entirely acceptable. Objective images, then, disregard the viewer. They say, as it were, 'I am this way, regardless of who or where or when you are.'

By contrast, the point of view of the subjective, perspectival image has been selected *for* the viewer. As a result there is a kind of symmetry between the way the image-producer relates to the represented participants, and the way the viewer must, willy-nilly, also relate to them. The point of view is imposed not only on the represented participants, but also on the viewer, and the viewer's 'subjectivity' is therefore subjective in the original sense of the word, the sense of 'being subjected to something or someone'. In a short essay on Chinese art, Bertolt Brecht has commented on this:

> As we know, the Chinese do not use the art of perspective. They do not like to see everything from a single point of view. Chinese composition thus lacks the compulsion to which we have become altogether accustomed ... and rejects the subjugation of the observer.
>
> (Brecht, 1967: 278–9)

The system of perspective is fundamentally naturalistic. It developed in a period in which the world of nature was no longer seen as manifesting a divine order (which was also, and at the same time, a social order), but as an autonomous and ultimately meaningless order

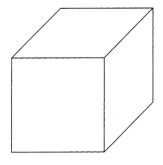

🔺 **Fig 4.6 Frontal-isometric cube**

whose laws also governed the conduct of people. It was explicitly grounded in the new scientific spirit, legitimized by the authority of scientific observation and the physical laws of nature. The new music, similarly, was constructed as congruent, not with a (divine and) social order, but with the physical laws of sound.

In the late nineteenth century, after centuries of hegemony, both systems came into crisis, in the high arts (Cubism, twelve-tone music) as well as in the popular arts. Film, for example, still uses perspectival images, but, in a near-Cubist fashion, provides multiple and constantly shifting viewpoints in its editing. Modern television, especially in programmes not based on the model of film, such as news programmes, has gone a step further, and challenges perspective also within the image. A newsreader may have, behind him or her, on the left a verbal text, and on the right a chroma-keyed moving picture on the wall (a wall which is in fact a kind of two-dimensional screen on which to project a 'layout', and in front of which to position the newsreader). Modern magazine and website layouts form another category of visual works which are no longer based solely on the compositional principles of perspective. Of course, they still contain many perspectival images but these have been subordinated to a structure that can no longer be said to be perspectival. Two examples may illustrate this.

The picture on the Ford Mondeo website (figure 4.7) is naturalistic. What we observe here could also be observed in reality. There could be a car positioned in this way, in front of this particular couple and this particular building. As a result of the angle and the social distance (a low-angle 'long shot', with the car in the foreground), viewers are then made to relate to the represented participants in a certain way. They are made to 'look up to' them, and they are made to see them as if they notice the car and the stylish couple from across the street, with envy. In the picture on the Ford Fiesta page (figure 4.8), on the other hand, the viewer, rather than being positioned in the natural world, is confronted with a world

🔺 Fig 4.7 New-look Ford Mondeo (www.ford.co.uk/ie/mondeo)

● Fig 4.8 Ford Fiesta Rock Solid (http://www.ford.co.uk)

which openly presents itself as a semiotic construct, mixing perspectival and non-perspectival elements in such a way as to give the appearance of a continuum of forms from the representational to the significational, while the visual as a whole remains non-naturalistic: the car, on this page, cannot be said to be 'behind' the Las Vegas road sign or 'behind' the word 'rock solid' in the way that the couple and the building in figure 4.7 can be said to be behind the Ford Mondeo. 'In front of' and 'behind' lose their ideational dimension, and become textual principles only. The two pages thus exemplify a shift from the dominance of nature to the dominance of signification, and from the dominance of the perceptual to the dominance of the conceptual – in a way very similar to that which we observed in chapter 1 when we compared *Baby's First Book* (figure 1.1) to Dick Bruna's *On My Walk* and *On The Farm* (figure 1.2).

INVOLVEMENT AND THE HORIZONTAL ANGLE

When we prolong the converging parallels formed by the walls of the houses in figure 4.9, they come together in two vanishing points. Both points are located outside the vertical

● Fig 4.9 Aborigines (Oakley *et al.*, 1985)

boundaries of the image, as shown in figure 4.10. These vanishing points allow us to reconstruct what we can see even without the aid of geometrical projection: the scene has been photographed from an oblique angle. The photographer has not situated himself or herself in front of the Aborigines, but has photographed them from the side.

Figure 4.10 shows how the position from which the photo was taken can be reconstructed by dropping lines from the vanishing points in such a way that they meet to form a 90° angle on the line drawn through the closest corner of the cottages. Figure 4.11 shows the scene from above. The line (ab) represents the frontal plane of the subject of the photograph: the line formed by the front of the cottages, which, as it happens, is also the line along which the Aborigines are lined up. The line (cd) represents the frontal plane of the photographer (and hence of the viewer). Had these two lines been parallel to one another, the horizontal angle would have been frontal – in other words, the photographer would have been positioned in front of the Aborigines and their cottages, facing them. Instead, the two lines diverge: the angle is oblique. The photographer has not aligned himself or herself with the subject, not faced the Aborigines, but viewed them 'from the sidelines'.

Horizontal angle, then, is a function of the relation between the frontal plane of the image-producer and the frontal plane of the represented participants. The two can either be parallel, aligned with one another, or form an angle, diverge from one another.

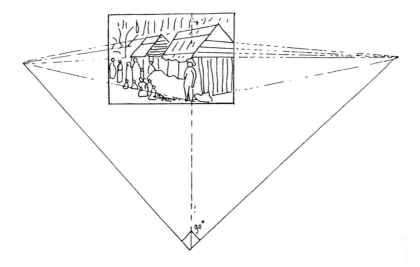

○ **Fig 4.10 Schematic drawing: vanishing points of 'Aborigines' (figure 4.9)**

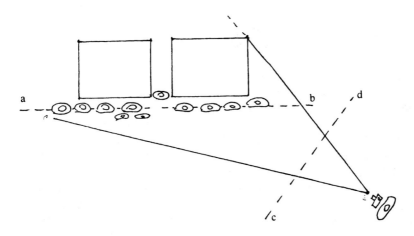

○ **Fig 4.11 Schematic drawing: top view of 'Aborigines' (figure 4.9)**

The image can have either a frontal or an oblique point of view. It should be noted that this is not strictly an either/or distinction. There are degrees of obliqueness, and we will, in fact, speak of a frontal angle so long as the vanishing point(s) still fall(s) within the vertical boundaries of the image (they may fall outside the horizontal boundaries).

Figure 4.12 has a frontal angle. As shown in figure 4.13, there is only one major vanishing point, and it lies inside the vertical boundaries of the image. Figure 4.14 shows how the frontal plane of the photographer (line ab) and the frontal plane of the represented participants (line cd) run parallel – that is, *if one only considers one set of represented participants,* the teachers, the blackboard and the reading chart. The frontal plane of the Aboriginal children (line ef) makes an angle of ninety degrees with the frontal plane of the teachers and with the frontal plane of the photographer. The Aboriginal children have been photographed from a very oblique angle.

The difference between the oblique and the frontal angle is the difference between detachment and involvement. The horizontal angle encodes whether the image-producer (and hence, willy-nilly, the viewer) is 'involved' with the represented participants or not. The frontal angle says, as it were, 'What you see here is part of our world, something we are involved with.' The oblique angle says, 'What you see here is *not* part of our world; it is *their* world, something *we* are not involved with.' The producers of these two photographs have, perhaps unconsciously, aligned themselves with the white teachers and their teaching tools, but *not* with the Aborigines. The teachers are shown as 'part of our world', the Aborigines as 'other'. And as viewers we have no choice but to see these represented

Fig 4.12 Aboriginal children at school (Oakley *et al.*, 1985)

⬥ **Fig 4.13 Schematic drawing: vanishing point of 'Aboriginal children at school' (figure 4.12)**

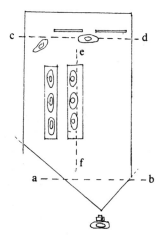

⬥ **Fig 4.14 Schematic drawing: top view of 'Aboriginal children at school' (figure 4.12)**

participants as they have been depicted. We are addressed as viewers for whom 'involvement' takes these particular values. In reality, they might not – we might be Aboriginal viewers, for example. It is one thing for the viewer to be limited by what the photograph shows (and to understand what this means, for example exclusion, in the case of an Aboriginal viewer); it is another thing to actually identify with the viewpoint encoded in the photo. We can accept or reject, but either way we first need to understand what is meant.

The primary-school social studies textbook *Our Society and Others* provides a further illustration. A shot of the New South Wales Parliament House in Sydney is frontal, and taken from a low angle. A shot of the church is taken from an oblique and somewhat higher angle. The former illustrates a section about Sydney in the chapter 'What is a City?'; the latter, a section about a Maori family in the chapter on immigrants. Religion is depicted as something which, in the context of primary-school social studies, does not belong to 'our society' – the book contains statements like, 'The British believed in one God' (note the past tense) and questions like, 'Do you think a church or a cemetery is like a sacred site?' It fosters a detached, outsider's attitude towards the Christian religion.

In the depiction of humans (and animals), 'involvement' and 'detachment' can interact with 'demand' and 'offer' in complex ways. The body of a represented participant may be angled away from the plane of the viewer, while his or her head and/or gaze may be turned towards it (see e.g. figure 4.24 below) – or vice versa. The result is a double message: 'although I am not part of your world, I nevertheless make contact with you, from my own, different world'; or 'although this person is part of our world, someone like you and me, we nevertheless offer his or her image to you as an object for dispassionate reflection.' The latter is the case, for example, in an illustration from a Dutch junior high-school geography textbook (Bols *et al.*, 1986: 21). In a section entitled 'De Derde Wereld in onze straat' ('The Third World in our Street'), two pictures are shown side by side. On the left we see three older women, their headscarves an emblem of their status as immigrants. They are photographed from an oblique angle, hence as 'not part of our world' and in long shot, hence as 'others', 'strangers'. On the right we see, left in the foreground, a blonde girl, clearly meant to be taken as Dutch, with a black friend, who has his arm around her. The angle is a good deal more frontal than that of the shot of the three women, and the shot is a close-up: she is shown as like 'us', Dutch high-school students, and from 'close personal' distance. But she does not make contact with the viewers. She does not invite the viewers to identify with her, and with her relationship to a black man. Instead, the viewer is invited to contemplate her relationship detachedly, to ponder the fact that some people like 'us' have relationships with black people, but not, it is implicitly suggested, 'we' viewers ourselves. She is a phenomenon to be observed, not a person addressing the viewer.

Equally complex and ambivalent is the back view. One of the authors, at age 21, photographed his parents in a snow-covered park, just outside Brussels (figure 4.15) and, perhaps more importantly, it was this picture he chose to pin on the pinboard of his student room in Amsterdam, rather than one of the other, more frontal pictures he had taken on the same day. At the time, his feelings for his parents were complex. Deep attachment mixed with only half-understood desire to distance himself from the world in which he was brought up. Perhaps the picture crystallized these confused emotions for him. On the one hand, it showed his parents turning their back on him, walking away from him (a reversal, of course, of the actual situation); on the other hand, it showed this gesture of 'turning one's back', in a sense, 'frontally', in a maximally 'confronting' way. But to expose one's back to someone is also to make oneself vulnerable, and this implies a measure of trust, despite the abandonment which the gesture also signifies. Perhaps the picture reminded him of a passage from a Dutch novel he liked at the time:

● Fig 4.15 Photograph of author's parents, 1968

Through the window he sees them walk away. 'How much I love that man', he thinks, and how impossible he has made it for me to express that. . . . His mother has linked arms with him. With hesitant steps she walks beside him on the frozen pavement. He keeps looking at them until they turn the corner, near the tall feathered poplars.

(Wolkers, 1965: 61)

How is 'involvement' realized in language? Perhaps the system of possessive pronouns comes closest to realizing the kinds of meanings we have discussed here. But the two systems, the visual system of horizontal angle and the linguistic system of possessive pronouns, differ in many ways. Involvement, as we have seen, is always plural, a matter of 'mine' and 'his/her/its'; a matter of distinguishing between what belongs to 'us' and what to 'them'. And, while in language one cannot easily have *degrees* of 'ourness' and 'theirness', in images such gradation is an intrinsic part of the system of involvement. Finally, there is no 'yours' in the system of horizontal angle. The visual 'you-relation' is, as we have seen, realized by the system of 'offer' and 'demand'. Perspective puts a barrier between the viewer and the represented participants, even in the case of a frontal angle: the viewer looks at the represented participants and has an attitude towards them, but does not imaginarily engage with them.

POWER AND VERTICAL ANGLE

Textbooks of film appreciation never fail to mention camera height as an important means of expression in cinematography. A high angle, it is said, makes the subject look small and insignificant, a low angle makes it look imposing and awesome: 'Low angles generally give an impression of superiority, exaltation and triumph . . . high angles tend to diminish the individual, to flatten him morally by reducing him to ground level, to render him as caught in an insurmountable determinism' (Martin, 1968: 37–8). But this leaves the viewer out of the picture. We would rather say it in a somewhat different way: if a represented participant is seen from a high angle, then the relation between the interactive participants (the producer of the image, and hence also the viewer) and the represented participants is depicted as one in which the interactive participant has power over the represented participant – the represented participant is seen from the point of view of power. If the represented participant is seen from a low angle, then the relation between the interactive and represented participants is depicted as one in which the represented participant has power over the interactive participant. If, finally, the picture is at eye level, then the point of view is one of equality and there is no power difference involved.

This is, again, a matter of degree. A represented participant can tower high above us or look down on us ever so slightly. In many of the illustrations in school textbooks we look down rather steeply on people – workers in the hall; children in a school yard. In such books the social world lies at the feet of the viewer, so to speak: knowledge is power. The models in magazine advertisements and features, and newsworthy people and celebrities in magazine articles, on the other hand, generally look down on the viewer: these models are depicted as exercising symbolic power over us. As shown in figure 4.5, products advertised in the advertisements may be photographed both from a low angle, as having symbolic power over us, and from a high angle, as being within reach and at the command of the viewer. The photograph reproduced in figure 4.16 shows a guard in the 'death row' section of a prison in Texas. The angle is low, to make him look powerful. But what makes this picture extraordinary is that not the guard, but the horse is closest to the viewer, and that it is not the guard, but the horse, whose every movement is commanded by this guard, who is looking at the viewer. What can this horse 'demand' from us? Therein lies the mystery and the force of this picture. Empathy with a fate of being subjugated to the power represented by the guard? Or with a fate of suffering?

How is power realized in language? Here we need, again, to remember the difference between face-to-face communication and mediated communication. In the classroom, for example, power will manifest itself first of all in the relation between teacher and pupil. This, as Cate Poynton has shown (1985: ch. 6), is in the main realized through the *difference* between the linguistic forms that may be used by the teachers and the linguistic

Fig 4.16 Prison guard (Danny Lyon, 1969)

forms that may be used by the pupils; in other words, through a lack of reciprocity between the choices available to each party in the interaction. The teacher may use first names in addressing the pupils; the pupils may not use first names in addressing teachers. The teacher may use imperatives to 'demand goods-and-services'; the pupils would have to use polite forms, for instance, questions. This lack of reciprocity has its effect on every level of language: phonology, grammar, vocabulary, discourse, and on ideational, interpersonal, as well as textual meanings. If there is, in face-to-face communication, any question of power relations between represented participants and the pupils, then this results from the power relation between the teacher and the pupils.

To some extent this is the case in writing also, and not just because in writing – as in mediated communication generally – the absence of the writer causes, from the start, a fundamental lack of reciprocity (you cannot talk back to the writer), but also because the writer and the reader are often unequal in a number of other ways. The reader may be addressed directly, by means of the second-person pronoun *you*, while the writer hides behind impersonal forms. Mental processes may be attributed to the reader while the writer's mental processes are never referred to. Imperatives may be used, as modulated processes predicated of the reader (*you can, you should, you need,* etc.), while such forms are not used of the writer. Here are some examples of texts in which power is encoded in this way – the first from a Revlon advertisement, the second from *Our Society and Others* (Oakley *et al.*, 1985):

> Wrinkles. They don't start where you think they do. They start underneath your skin. That's why Anti-Aging Daily Moisturizer goes beyond mere surface treatment.

> When you study places and people you need to have a way of keeping the information you collect. One way of doing this is to take notes from the books which you read. You cannot write down all the things you read as this would mean writing out the whole book. Notes are a short way of recording the most important information.

In the first text the writer does not directly refer to himself or herself, but writes as an impersonal authority, in terms of relational processes ('They start underneath your skin'). The reader is referred to directly ('you'), and the writer not only knows what the reader thinks ('where you think they do'), but also that the reader's thoughts are misguided: the authority of the writer is firmly based on the reader's ignorance. In the second text, too, the writer does not directly refer to himself or herself, but writes impersonally, in terms of relational processes ('Notes are a short way of recording the most important infor-mation'), while the reader is addressed directly ('you'). The processes with which the reader is associated are modulated in various ways ('you need', 'you cannot'). In both cases the lack of reciprocity which realizes power is encoded in the text itself.

But this omniscient knowledge of the reader's mind, this direct postulation of what the reader needs (must do, should think, will feel, and so on) and this lack of reciprocity between the writer and the reader or the speaker and hearer, cannot be realized in the same way in images. In images, the power of an image-producer must, as it were, be transferred on to one or more represented participants – the power of the advertiser on the model, the power of the producer of the textbook on the ordinary people represented in the textbook. The nearest equivalent in speech would be the use of evaluative adjectives. We might, for example, transcode a picture in which we look down on factory workers or refugees as '*the humble workers*' or '*the downtrodden refugees*'. In the issue of the *Australian Women's Weekly* from which we took many of our original examples, this kind of transcoding occurs a number of times. The magazine contains photographs of a bejewelled Queen Elizabeth, and the actor Michael Douglas – both taken from a low angle. On the cover the relevant articles are announced by the following lines: 'DAZZLING – The Queen's jewels'; 'FASCINATING – Michael Douglas' "Fatal Attraction" '. But there remains a very big difference. What in the image is an attitude towards the represented participants becomes in language a characteristic of the represented participants: it objectifies the attitude.

NARRATIVIZATION OF THE SUBJECTIVE IMAGE

In many cases there is no immediately apparent motivation for point of view (and for size of frame). The angle may be high and frontal, and so convey power over and involvement with the represented participants, but the precise nature of the relation of power and involvement is not given. Thus a high-angle picture of workers in a factory could be said to be taken from the viewpoint of a supervisor in an elevated office, with a window overlooking the factory, but this remains a metaphor. We do not see the office in the picture. Other possibilities might also serve to make concrete the relation of power and involvement. In other cases the (imaginary) viewer intrudes in the picture to a greater or lesser degree. In an advertising campaign that ran at the time we worked on the first version of this book, this was done by including the hands of the imaginary viewer in the foreground of the picture. These could then be male or female, and groomed in different ways – they could wear driving gloves, expensive rings, and so on. In figure 4.17 they created the viewpoint of a couple.

In films the sequencing of images can fulfil this function. The shot of the factory, showing the workers from a high angle, can be preceded by a low-angle shot of the elevated office, with a supervisor behind the window looking down at the workers. In such cases the text narrativizes the point of view and imposes a fictional viewer between the represented and the interactive participants. But even when their origins are not shown, viewpoints can always be related to concrete situations. One can, and perhaps should, always ask, 'Who could see this scene in this way?', 'Where would one have to be to see this scene in this way, and what sort of person would one have to be to occupy that space?'

OBJECTIVE IMAGES

Scientific and technical pictures, such as diagrams, maps and charts, usually encode an objective attitude. This tends to be done in one of two ways: by a directly frontal or

⬧ Fig 4.17 Sterling advertisement (*New Idea*, November 1987)

perpendicular top–down angle. Such angles do suggest viewer positions, but special and privileged ones, which neutralize the distortions that usually come with perspective, because they neutralize perspective itself. To illustrate this with a simple example, when a cube is drawn perspectivally its sides are not of equal length, and the degree of distortion depends on the angle, on the encoded viewer position. The cube does not look 'as we know it is', with all its sides of equal length, but 'as we see it', from a particular position. But from directly in front the third dimension disappears, and the cube appears flat, with all its sides of equal length. From above, exactly the same effect occurs. Perspective and its attitudinizing effect have been neutralized:

⬧ Fig 4.18 Cube seen from an angle, frontally and from above

Plate 1 *Tropical Sun* (Emil Nolde, 1914)

"Love a cup"

For the times you want the rich full flavour of a truly satisfying granulated coffee... love a cup of Bushells Master Roast Coffee.

Bushells **MASTER ROAST**
GRANULATED INSTANT COFFEE
RICH, FULL FLAVOUR
NET 150g

⬥ Plate 2 Bushells advertisement (*Woman's Weekly*, 1987)

● Plate 3 *Joshua Smith* (William Dobell, 1943) (Art Gallery of New South Wales)

Plate 4 *Patrick White* (Louis Kahan, 1963) (Art Gallery of New South Wales)

Plate 5 *Cossacks 1910–11* (Vassily Kandinsky) (Tate Gallery)

LIFE & STYLE

Left and below: Hamish and Vanessa's love of earthy colours shows in their sitting room. Inset: Vanessa transformed a bowl from a junk shop bowl using decoupage

Hamish: 'It's funny now when we go to visit them and see our stuff in their homes.'

Plate 7 Palgrave colour scheme

Plate 8 Colourful thoughts (transparency)

Frontal and top–down angles, however, are not objective in entirely the same way. The frontal angle is the angle of maximum involvement. It is oriented towards action. The pictures of the Antarctic explorer (figure 2.4) could be transcoded as 'These are the clothes you should wear and this is the way you should wear them if you want to explore the Antarctic.' The frontal angle is the angle of 'this is how it works', 'this is how you use it', 'this is how you do it'. The top–down angle, on the other hand, is the angle of maximum power. It is orientated towards 'theoretical', objective knowledge. It contemplates the world from a god-like point of view, puts it at your feet, rather than within reach of your hands. Abstract diagrams can sometimes be read in both ways. A communication model, for instance (e.g. figure 2.2), can be read as a map ('top–down', a schema, a 'theory of communication': 'this is what communication looks like, from the point of view of a disinterested observer'), or as a frontal view, a blueprint, a 'practical manual of communication' ('this is what you do when you communicate') – and this is perhaps one of the sources of its social power.

A third objective viewpoint, the cross-section, and the 'X-ray' view, should also be considered: its objectivity derives from the fact that it does not stop at appearances, but probes beyond the surface, to deeper, more hidden levels. In Western culture it is almost exclusively used in diagrams, although one can sometimes also observe experiments with it in children's drawings.

Not all diagrams, maps and charts, however, are completely objective. The vertical angle of the Gulf War map in figure 4.19, is high, but not completely top–down, and its horizontal

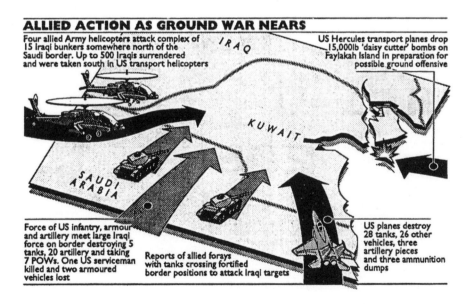

Fig 4.19 Gulf War map (*Sydney Morning Herald*, 22 January 1991)

angle is oblique, causing us to look at the theatre of war from the sidelines, in a relatively detached way. In books about science for young children we find similar angles (see figure 5.11, for example), their obliqueness perhaps suggesting that they are not (or not yet quite) meant as 'how to do it' pictures.

Elements of perspective may also be added to graphs and cross-sections, to give a sense of reality, of physical existence, to abstract, two-dimensional visuals. Having first been abstracted from the concrete, three-dimensional world of people, places and things, they are now restored to it, but in a transformed way, as new, human-made kinds of things and places. Thus we can see – for instance, in lavishly produced annual company reports – three-dimensional bar graphs, looking like skyscrapers or monoliths, against a background of clean and smooth hills in flat, primary colour. In figure 4.20 graphs become a setting for action: tourists move through the abstractly represented, but nevertheless three-dimensional, world of the international tourist business, just as may also be the case in television news graphics, where a further sense of reality may be given to such pictures by means of animation.

The addition of perspective adds nothing to the representational meaning of these diagrams, maps and charts; but it does add attitudinal meanings. In all these examples the angle is high, *explicitly* attitudinalizing the objective stance of the god-like top–down view, and often narrativizing it as the view from the satellite, that modern tool of the production of visual knowledge and symbol of informational power. The horizontal angle, on the other hand, may vary: with the 'increase in tourism' we are directly involved; the events of the Gulf War (figure 4.19), on the other hand, we watch 'from the sidelines', as bystanders. This process of attitudinalization happens, not so much in the contexts where this new

▲ Fig 4.20 An increase in tourism (*Sydney Morning Herald*, 23 January 1991)

visual knowledge is produced and this new informational power exercised, but in the contexts in which it is disseminated in popularized form, and celebrated: here conceptual and schematic images are dressed up in the clothes of visual reality, and literally and figuratively 'animated'.

To conclude this section we add some notes on different, less 'subjective' kinds of perspective. If, in central perspective, the kind of perspective we have been discussing so far, something is seen from the front and at eye level, the sides, top and bottom will be hidden from view. A cube would appear as in drawing 1 of figure 4.21. If the same cube is seen from an oblique angle, one of the sides will come into view, but the other will remain hidden. If the angle is high, so that we look down on the cube, the top will also come into view, as in drawing 4 of figure 4.21. But in this case the front will no longer be a square. It will be distorted. The horizontal parallels in an image in central perspective converge towards one or more vanishing points – and so do the vertical parallels, although this is often less obvious, as vertical distances are not so great, and as vertical distortion is often 'corrected' in drawings and paintings.

Drawing 2 in figure 4.21, on the other hand, is an example of 'frontal-isometric' perspective. Here the front of the cube is not distorted, yet we can see the side and the top. And the horizontal parallels do not converge towards a vanishing point. Frontal-isometric perspective is based on the 'objective' dimensions of the represented participants, on what we know these dimensions to be, rather than on how they *appear* to us. For this reason frontal-isometric perspective is used in technical drawings, where it is important to be able to measure the dimensions of the represented objects from the drawing. In frontal-isometric perspective, then, there is not, as yet, a choice between involvement and detachment. It is the analogy in visual terms of the 'impersonality' characteristic of scientific language.

The perspective used in drawing 3 of figure 4.21 is called angular-isometric perspective. Here the front is distorted, the square no longer represented as a square. But the horizontal and vertical parallels do not converge. There is no end to space in this kind of perspective – it stretches on indefinitely. Angular-isometric perspective was used, for example, in eighteenth-century Japanese woodcuts – Japanese artists of this period always chose an oblique point of view, as well as a relatively high angle. They looked at the world without a sense of involvement, from a detached point of view, from a meditative distance.

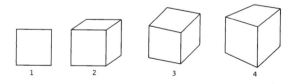

◭ **Fig 4.21 (1) Cube seen from the front; (2) cube in frontal-isometric perspective; (3) cube in angular-isometric perspective; (4) cube seen from an angle In central perspective**

Fig 4.22 Detail from a fourteenth-century Spanish nativity (from Arnheim, 1974)

This brief survey does not exhaust the possibilities. In medieval art 'inverted perspective' was sometimes used (see figure 4.22). This allows both sides of an object to be seen and causes the perspectival vectors to diverge rather than converge. It can often be found in children's drawings (young children also tend to draw the world as they know it to be, rather than as they see it) and, in recent times, has been taken up by painters such as Picasso and Braque, who looked for more objective ways of representing the world, regarding the simple viewpoint of central perspective as one-sided and restrictive, and viewing reality as multifaceted, a complex whole of often incompatible and mutually clashing viewpoints. In this way, as Arnheim notes (1974: 132), 'they make the contradictions of which Marxists speak visual'.

A SUMMARY

Figure 4.23 summarizes the main kinds of interactive meaning we have discussed in this chapter. It should be remembered that these are 'simultaneous systems' (as indicated by the curly brackets): any image must either be a 'demand' or an 'offer' *and* select a certain

REALIZATIONS

Demand	gaze at the viewer
Offer	absence of gaze at the viewer
Intimate/personal	close shot
Social	medium shot
Impersonal	long shot
Involvement	frontal angle
Detachment	oblique angle
Viewer power	high angle
Equality	eye-level angle
Represented participant power	low angle

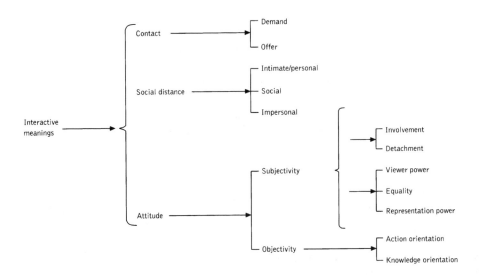

⬤ Fig 4.23 Interactive meanings in images

size of frame *and* select a certain attitude. In the next few sections we will discuss some examples at greater length, to show how the systems of 'contact', 'social distance' and 'attitude' interact to create more complex and subtle relations between represented and interactive participants.

TWO PORTRAITS AND TWO CHILDREN'S DRAWINGS

Rembrandt's famous *Self-portrait with Saskia* dates from 1634. John Berger (1972: 111) calls it 'an advertisement of the sitter's good fortune, prestige and wealth' and, he adds, 'like all such advertisements it is heartless'. Yet, from the point of view of the interactive meanings we have discussed in this chapter, the painting is perhaps a little more complex than Berger's remarks suggest. On the one hand, it is a 'demand' picture – Rembrandt and Saskia smile at the viewer, Rembrandt perhaps a little more effusively and invitingly than Saskia: he even raises his glass in a gesture directed at the viewer. On the other hand, he has shown himself and Saskia from behind, and from what Hall would call 'close social' distance, with Saskia a little further away from the viewer than Rembrandt – her head is considerably smaller than Rembrandt's even though she is sitting on his lap and should therefore, strictly speaking, be closer to the viewer than Rembrandt (the angle at which her head is turned to acknowledge the viewer also seems unnatural). Is Rembrandt distancing himself (and Saskia even more) from the viewer, excluding the viewer from involvement and intimacy with his new-found (and Saskia's already established) social status, thus contradicting the invitation? Perhaps – but the portrait is also a self-portrait. Rembrandt, the miller's son, now married into a wealthy and respectable family and living in grand style, also distances *himself* from his new self (and to some extent from Saskia), as if he cannot feel fully involved and intimate with his new environment. As a self-portrait the picture may be self-congratulatory and smug, 'heartless', but it also betrays a degree of alienation, positioning the represented Rembrandt in a complex and contradictory social class position, between the world of his origins, which is also the point of view of the picture, and the world of Saskia into which he has moved. This, we think, makes it a little less smug, and a little more touching than Berger gave it credit for.

Figure 4.25 shows a later self-portrait, painted in 1661. By this time, Saskia has died, and Rembrandt has gone bankrupt. He now lives with his former housekeeper, Hendrickje, in a more downmarket neighbourhood, and in much reduced circumstances. In this portrait

⬤ **Fig 4.24** *Self-portrait with Saskia* (Rembrandt, 1634) (Pinakotek, Dresden)

△ **Fig 4.25** *Self-portrait* (Rembrandt, 1661) (Kunsthistorisches Museum, Vienna)

he is able to come face-to-face with himself, to confront himself (and the viewer) squarely and intimately with himself: 'He is an old man now. All has gone, except a sense of the question of existence, of existence as a question' (Berger, 1972: 112).

The picture on the cover of 'My Adventure' (figure 4.26), the story by an eight-year-old boy which we have already featured in the previous chapter, constitutes a 'demand': the little boy is looking at us, and smiling. He seeks our recognition. He wants to be acknowledged. On the other hand, the angle is oblique, and high, and the boy is shown from a great distance. Not only does the writer of this story show himself in the role of being ship-wrecked, he also shows himself as 'other' (the oblique angle), as someone over whom the viewer has power (the high angle) and as socially distant, a 'stranger' (the long shot). In other words, he uses the interactive resources of the subjective image (quite precociously, we feel) to show himself as small, insignificant and alienated, yet demanding recognition from the viewer. At the same time the act of drawing himself like this affords him, as the producer of the image, some power over that image of himself, an outlet for his feelings. In support of this interpretation it can be noted that the boy does not exactly play a heroic role in the story. After creating the raft, and just as the raft 'started to be good fun', everything goes wrong for him: he loses his money and never finds it again, the raft collapses and is lost irretrievably, and the hero has to walk all the way home, wet and cold. It is an unhappy ending for a hero unable to control the unpleasant events that happen to him.

Figure 4.27 is the front cover of a 'story' on sailing boats by a child from the same class as the author of 'My Adventure'. Its subject is similar: people on a boat. But the systems of 'image act', 'social distance' and 'attitude' take on very different values. The characters do not look at us: the picture is an 'offer'. The angle is frontal and eye level, and the two figures in the boat are neither particularly distant, nor particularly close. There is no setting, no texture, no colour, no light and shade. The sailing boat is drawn with geometrical accuracy. But for the two figures – simply drawn, and more or less identical, except for their size (a father and son?) – this could be a technical drawing. As such it suits the

△ **Fig 4.26 Cover illustration of My Adventure'**

⏷ **Fig 4.27 Cover illustration of 'Sailing Boats'**

objective, generic title, 'Sailing Boats', just as the cover illustration of 'My Adventure' suits that story's subjective, specific title. In most of the illustrations inside the essay, no human figures are seen, as though the child already understands that the 'learning' of technical matters should be preceded by a 'human element' to attract non-initiates to the subject.

Clearly, children actively experiment both with the interactive resources of language and with the interactive resources of visual communication. They are active sign-makers. And the different ways in which these two children represent boats show two very different subjectivities at work.

5 Modality:
designing models of reality

MODALITY AND A SOCIAL THEORY OF THE REAL

One of the crucial issues in communication is the question of the reliability of messages. Is what we see or hear true, factual, real, or is it a lie, a fiction, something outside reality? To some extent the form of the message itself suggests an answer. We routinely attach more credibility to some kinds of messages than to others. The credibility of newspapers, for instance, rests on the 'knowledge' that photographs do not lie and that 'reports' are more reliable than 'stories', though since we wrote the first edition of this book the rise of Photoshop and 'spin' have begun to undermine both these types of knowledge.

More generally, and with particular relevance to the visual, we regard our sense of sight as more reliable than our sense of hearing, 'I saw it with my own eyes' as more reliable evidence than 'I heard it with my own ears'.

Unfortunately, we also know that, while the camera may not lie – or not much, at any rate – those who use it and its images can and do. The questions of truth and reality remain insecure, subject to doubt and uncertainty and, even more significantly, to contestation and struggle. Yet, as members of a society, we have to be able to make decisions on the basis of the information we receive, produce and exchange. And in so far as we are prepared to act, we have to trust some of the information we receive, and do so, to quite some extent, on the basis of modality markers in the message itself, on the basis of textual cues for what can be regarded as credible and what should be treated with circumspection. These modality markers have been established by the groups within which we interact as relatively reliable guides to the truth or factuality of messages, and they have developed out of the central values, beliefs and social needs of that group.

In this chapter we will discuss these modality cues. As throughout the book, we take them to be motivated signs – signs which have arisen out of the interest of social groups who interact within the structures of power that define social life, and also interact across the systems produced by various groups within a society. As we have discussed in the Introduction, the relation between the signifiers and signifieds of motivated signs is, in principle, one of transparency. Sign-makers choose what they regard as apt, plausible means for expressing the meanings they wish to express. We are therefore focusing on the range of signs from which such choices can be made – some of them specialized modality markers, others part of a much wider and more general range of means of expressing meanings of truth and falsehood, fact and fiction, certainty and doubt, credibility and unreliability.

A social semiotic theory of truth cannot claim to establish the absolute truth or untruth of representations. It can only show whether a given 'proposition' (visual, verbal or otherwise) is represented as true or not. From the point of view of social semiotics, truth is a construct of semiosis, and as such the truth of a particular social group arises from the values and beliefs of that group. As long as the message forms an apt expression of these beliefs, communication proceeds in an unremarkable, 'felicitous' fashion. This does mean, however, that our theory of modality has to account for a complex situation: people not only communicate and affirm as true the values and beliefs of their group. They also communicate and accord degrees of truth or untruth to the values and beliefs of other groups.

The term 'modality' comes from linguistics and refers to the truth value or credibility of (linguistically realized) statements about the world. The grammar of modality focuses on such modality markers as the auxiliary verbs which accord specific degrees of modality to statements, verbs like *may, will* and *must* (cf. the difference between *He may come* and *He will come*) and their related adjectives (e.g. *possible, probable, certain*) and adverbs (see Halliday, 1985: 85–9). But modality is not only conveyed through these fairly clear-cut linguistic systems (see Kress and Hodge, 1978, 1993: 127). Take this example, from *Our Society and Others* (Oakley *et al.*, 1985). Clearly, it not only contains statements such as 'Aboriginal people had no religion' and 'the whole land was a cathedral', but also indications of the truth value of these statements:

> Governor Phillip, the settlers, and the convicts could find no churches or cathedrals or works of art like those of Britain. Perhaps this made them think that Aboriginal people had no religion. In fact, the Aborigines had very complicated religious beliefs. These had been passed down from one generation to the next through Dreamtime stories for thousands of years. For the Aborigines the whole land was a cathedral. Their art was joined to their religion. Much of their art had been kept safely for thousands of years.
>
> (Oakley *et al.*, 1985: 142)

The statement 'Aboriginal people had no religion' is given low modality. The writers distance themselves from it by attributing it to 'Governor Phillip, the settlers, and the convicts' by formulating it as a subjective idea ('this made them think that . . .') and by using the past tense (after all, what was true in the past need not be true in the present). The writers' own statements (e.g. 'the Aboriginals had very complicated religious beliefs') are not qualified in this way; they are formulated as objective facts ('In fact, the Aborigines had . . .') and not attributed (it is curious, however, that they are not extended to the present time!). The statements that embody the 'beliefs' of the Aborigines, finally, are given lower modality. They are explicitly attributed to the Aborigines and therefore not subscribed to by the writers, and they are qualified by terms like 'story', 'dream' and 'belief' – terms which, in Western culture, signify low modality and are contrasted with high-modality terms such as 'reality', 'fact' and 'truth'.

The example shows that modality is 'interpersonal' rather than 'ideational'. It does not express absolute truths or falsehoods; it *produces* shared truths aligning readers or listeners with some statements and distancing them from others. It serves to create an imaginary 'we'. It says, as it were, these are the things 'we' consider true, and these are the things 'we' distance ourselves from, for instance: 'we' have no religion, but the Aborigines do, and although this religion is true for 'them', it is not true for 'us'. Nevertheless, as (for 'us') art and religion are not 'joined', 'we' can appreciate Aboriginal religion as 'art', as beautiful 'stories' and 'dreams' (art, in Western culture, has lower modality than, for instance, science – hence the greater licence given to artists). We call the 'we' the text attempts to produce 'imaginary' because many of the children who are made to read the book may in fact 'have religion'. However, we realize that the social groupings discursively instituted in this way may be very real and may have very real effects on children's lives.

The concept of modality is equally essential in accounts of visual communication. Visuals can represent people, places and things as though they are real, as though they actually exist in this way, or as though they do not – as though they are imaginings, fantasies, caricatures, etc. And, here too, modality judgements are social, dependent on what is considered real (or true, or sacred) in the social group for which the representation is primarily intended. Consider, for instance, the 'speech circuit' diagram from de Saussure's famous *Course in General Linguistics* (1974 [1916]), shown once more in figure 5.1 (see also figure 2.18). It depicts two humans, 'A' and 'B', and a process, circular and continuous, described as the 'unlocking of sound-images in the brain', followed by the 'transmitting of an impulse corresponding to the image to the organs used in producing sounds', followed by the 'travelling of the sound waves from the mouth of A to the ear of B' (1974 [1916]: 11–12). In another version (figure 5.2), de Saussure schematizes the diagram even further, making it look almost like an electrical circuit.

The photograph in figure 5.3 also represents the speech process, or rather part of it, since we see only 'A' speaking, and only 'B' 'unlocking sound-images in his brain'. It is a scene from Robert Aldridge's movie *The Big Knife* (1955), starring Rod Steiger and Jack Palance.

The three representations of the speech process differ in a number of ways. First, while the photograph restricts itself to representing what would normally be visible to the naked eye, the diagrams do not: they make visible what is normally invisible (mental processes, 'sound-images in the brain') and they do show what can normally only be heard ('sound waves'). To do so they take recourse to abstract graphic elements (dotted and continuous lines, arrows) and to language. Second, while the photograph presents us with a moment

A   B

◗ **Fig 5.1 Speech circuit (de Saussure, 1974 [1916])**

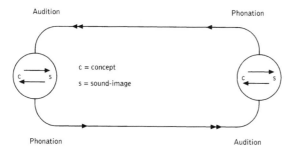

Audition   Phonation

c = concept

s = sound-image

Phonation   Audition

Fig 5.2 Schematized speech circuit (de Saussure, 1974 [1916])

Fig 5.3 Rod Steiger and Jack Palance in *The Big Knife* (Aldridge, 1955)

frozen in time, the diagrams depict a process that takes a certain amount of time to unfold: one utterance of 'A' as well as one utterance of 'B', at the very least. Third, while the photograph depicts 'A' and 'B' in great detail, showing strands of hair, wrinkles, glimmers of light in Steiger's dark glasses, the diagrams reduce the two to schematic profiles, or even circles, minimal geometric shapes, abstract elements. And, while the photograph shows depth, modelling caused by the play of light and shade, and a setting, a background, the diagrams omit all of these. They are abstract and schematic where the photograph is concrete and detailed; conventionalized and coded where the photograph presents itself as a naturalistic, unmediated, uncoded representation of reality.

Does this mean that diagrams are less 'real' than photographs, and hence lower in modality, and that photography is more true than diagrammatic representation? Not necessarily. To the viewers for whom de Saussure's diagrams are intended, they may in fact be more real than the photograph, in the sense that they reveal a truth which represents more adequately what the speech process is *really* like.

Reality is in the eye of the beholder; or rather, what is regarded as real depends on how reality is defined by a particular social group. From the point of view of naturalism reality is defined on the basis of how much correspondence there is between the visual representation of an object and what we normally see of that object with the naked eye (or, in practice, on the capacity of 35mm photography to resolve detail and render tonal or colour differentiation: images, including photographs, can be experienced as 'hyper-real', as showing 'too much detail', 'too much depth', 'too much colour' to be true). Scientific realism, on the other hand, defines reality on the basis of what things are like *generically* or *regularly*. It regards surface detail and individual difference as ephemeral, and does not stop at what can be observed with the naked eye. It probes beyond the visual appearance of things. In other words, reality may be in the eye of the beholder, but the eye has had a cultural training, and is located in a social setting and a history; for instance, in the community of linguists, or of semioticians in de Saussure's day, a community which saw reality in that form, in terms of abstractions and deeper regularities. A 'realism' is produced by a particular group, as an effect of the complex of practices which define and constitute that group. In that sense, a particular kind of realism is itself a motivated sign, in which the values, beliefs and interests of that group find their expression.

As the examples suggest, definitions of reality are also bound up with technologies of representation and reproduction. The relatively recent change from the dominance of black and white to the dominance of colour in many domains of visual communication shows how quickly these histories can develop, and how closely they are related to technological change. For us, now, as common sense viewers, everyday members of society at large, the defining technology is perhaps still that of 35mm colour photography, as we suggested above. But the shift to digital photography is already creating a new standard for naturalism, which still aims at ever higher resolution, naturalistic colour rendition, and so on, but has in fact made a decrease in resolution and contrast to become acceptable as the norm in many domains.

Each realism has its naturalism – that is, a realism is a definition of what counts as real – a set of criteria for the real, and it will find its expression in the 'right', the best, the (most) 'natural' form of representing that kind of reality, be it a photograph, digital or otherwise, or a diagram. This is not to say that all realisms are equal. Although different realisms exist side by side in our society, the dominant standard by which we judge visual realism, and hence visual modality, remains for the moment, naturalism as conventionally understood, 'photorealism'. In other words, the dominant criterion for what is real and what is not is based on the appearance of things, on how much correspondence there is between what we can 'normally' see of an object, in a concrete and specific setting, and what we can see of it in a visual representation – again, at least in theory, for in effect it is based on currently dominant conventions and technologies of visual representation. We judge an image real when, for instance, its colours are approximately as saturated as those in the standard, the most widely used photographic technology. When colour becomes more saturated, we judge it exaggerated, 'more than real', excessive. When it is less saturated we judge it 'less than real', 'ethereal', for instance, or 'ghostly'. And the same can be said about other aspects of representation, the rendition of detail, the representation of depth, and so on. Pictures which have the perspective, the degree of detail, the kind of colour rendition, etc. of the standard technology of colour photography have the highest modality, and are seen as 'naturalistic'. As detail, sharpness, colour, etc. are reduced or amplified, as the perspective flattens or deepens, so modality decreases.

Like many other advertisements, the advertisement in plate 2 is a composite text. It shows a picture of the product (the jar of instant coffee), with a verbal caption, and a picture which visualizes the pleasure the product will afford. This picture, showing two lovers sharing an intimate moment, uses soft focus and soft colours, tending towards the same golden-brown hue, and so deliberately lowering modality, representing 'what using the product will be like' as fantasy or promise, as 'what might be', rather than as reality, as 'what is'. The picture of the product itself, however, is in sharper focus and uses more saturated and differentiated colours: the product is given higher modality, higher reality value, than the promise of bliss attached to it, and the advertisement as a whole therefore accords varying degrees of 'credibility' to the different representations it contains, just like the text on 'Aboriginal religion'. The lower modality of the photo of the romantic scene, however, is not a matter of the scene itself being improbable or fantastic (although that, too, often happens in advertising photographs). Probable as well as improbable events may have high or low modality. Just as one can say *There certainly are ghosts* (high modality) and *I believe ghosts may exist* (low modality), so one can also show realistic and not-so-realistic depictions of ghosts.

What is the difference between these uses of colour? We would put it this way: the more that is taken away, abstracted from the colours of the representation, the more colour is *reduced*, the lower the modality. There is a continuum which runs from full colour saturation to the absence of colour, black and white, in which only the brightness values of the colours, their 'darkness' or 'lightness', remains. There is also a continuum which runs from full colour differentiation to a 'reduced palette' and eventually monochrome. For example, eighteenth-century landscape painting (e.g. Claude Lorrain) was often restricted to various shades of brown for the foreground and to desaturated, silvery blues for the distance. This is not the only way in which abstraction from 'naturalistic' colour is possible. The colour of many objects is not even. Pale skin, for instance, may vary in redness, may have the blue veins showing through, and so on, and such differences may either be rendered or abstracted from. In other words, colour may be idealized to a greater or lesser degree – a scale which runs from naturalistic photography via the choice of different values of a colour for the representation of light and shade, to the flat, unmodulated colour used by children in their drawings, or, for example, in the work of painters such as Matisse. Matisse was not a child, of course, when he produced the paintings we now admire. His unmodulated colours expressed a different view of what counts as real, as do the unmodulated colours in children's drawings – we will comment on this in more detail later. From the point of view of naturalism, however, modality is decreased in such images. The continuum from modulated to flat colour is at the same time a continuum from high to low modality. And in both cases the rule applies: the greater the abstraction (away from saturation, differentiation and modulation), the lower the modality.

It should be stressed that what we are talking about is not abstraction from what we actually see, from 'the real world'. The literature of other ages and cultures attests to the fact that people have marvelled at the 'lifelikeness' of works which, by our standards, are far from 'naturalistic'. What we are talking about at this point is abstraction relative to the standards of contemporary naturalistic representation.

MODALITY MARKERS

So far we have discussed the role of colour as a marker of naturalistic modality, in terms of three scales:

(1) *Colour saturation,* a scale running from full colour saturation to the absence of colour; that is, to black and white.
(2) *Colour differentiation,* a scale running from a maximally diversified range of colours to monochrome.
(3) *Colour modulation,* a scale running from fully modulated colour, with, for example, the use of many different shades of red, to plain, unmodulated colour.

At one end of these scales the particular dimension of colour is maximally reduced. At the other end it is most fully articulated, used to its maximum potential. Each point of the scale has a certain modality value in terms of the naturalistic standard. However, the point of highest modality does not coincide with either extreme of the scale: naturalistic modality increases as articulation increases, but at a certain point it reaches its highest value and thereafter it decreases again. Naturalistic modality scales could therefore be represented as in the following example:

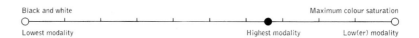

Black and white   Maximum colour saturation

Lowest modality   Highest modality   Low(er) modality

🔺 **Fig 5.4 Modality scale for colour saturation**

We will now discuss the other key markers of visual modality on which we already touched in our discussion of figure 5.3.

(4) *Contextualization*, a scale running from the absence of background to the most fully articulated and detailed background.

Within the naturalistic coding orientation, the absence of setting lowers modality. By being 'decontextualized', shown in a void, represented participants become generic, a 'typical example', rather than particular, and connected with a particular location and a specific moment in time. The scale of 'contextualization' runs from 'full contextualization', to 'plain, unmodulated background'. One step away from 'full contextualization' we find settings which are out of focus to a greater or lesser degree, or which lose detail through overexposure, resulting in a kind of ethereal brightness, or underexposure, resulting in muddy darkness, or through the loss of visual detail in the depiction. Further decontextualization can be achieved through ellipsis: a few 'props' suffice to suggest a setting, or a small, irregularly shaped patch of green under the feet of a figure with a few lines suggesting grass indicates the setting, while the rest of the paper is left blank. Or perhaps the background may merely show an irregular pattern of light and shade, or a field of unmodulated colour, or black, or white.

Again, the most fully articulated background does not have the highest naturalistic modality. The limitations imposed by the resolution of standard 35mm photographic emulsions and by the depth of field of standard lenses have accustomed us to images in which the background is less articulated than the foreground. When the background is sharper and more defined than this, a somewhat artificial, 'more than real' impression will result – as, for instance in older Hollywood movies shot in a studio with back projection (a close-up of an actor in a car, in front of a rear window behind which we see the receding landscape in sharp focus), or in much Surrealist painting, such as in the work of Salvador Dali.

(5) *Representation*, a scale running from maximum abstraction to maximum representation of pictorial detail.

An image may show every detail of the represented participants: the individual strands of hair, the pores in the skin, the creases in the clothes, the individual leaves of the tree, and so on, or it may abstract from detail to a greater or lesser degree. Again, there is a point beyond which a further increase of detail becomes 'hyper-real' and hence lower in modality from the point of view of 'photographic' naturalism. Similarly, in discussing decontextualization, above, we have pointed out that reduced representation of detail may form one of the ways in which the modality of backgrounds, of what is 'distant', is lower than the modality of the foreground (there is a parallel here with the lower modality of the past tense in language).

In photography it is not only sharpness of focus, but also exposure which can reduce detail. In artwork a variety of techniques could be ranked on a scale from maximum to minimum detail. Texture can become stylized, rendered by lines which trace the folds in the clothes, for example, and these lines may be many and fine, as in detailed engravings, or few and coarse, as in quick and ready styles of drawing. In medical drawings, for example, texture may become entirely conventional: dots to indicate the texture of one layer of skin, short, curved lines to indicate the texture of another. Texture can also be omitted altogether – the participant is then represented merely by the lines that trace its contour. Beyond this, the contour may be simplified to different degrees: a head may become a circle, the eyes two dots, the mouth a short, straight line. Diagrams and geometrical art take abstraction even further and reduce the shape of things to a small vocabulary of abstract forms, as in the paintings of Mondrian, or in figure 5.2, de Saussure's schematized 'speech circuit' diagram.

(6) *Depth*, a scale running from the absence of depth to maximally deep perspective.

By the criteria of standard naturalism, central perspective has highest modality, followed by angular-isometric perspective, followed by frontal-isometric perspective, followed by depth created by overlapping only. Again, perspective can become 'more than real', as when strong convergence of vertical lines is shown, or a 'fish-eye' perspective is used.

(7) *Illumination*, a scale running from the fullest representation of the play of light and shade to its absence.

Naturalistic depictions represent participants as they are affected by a particular source of illumination. Less naturalistic images, on the other hand, may abstract from illumination, and show shadows only in so far as they are required to model the volume, especially of round objects. They have 'shading' rather than shadow. Or they use shading to indicate receding areas and highlights to indicate protruding areas, often in ways which have no explanation in terms of the logic of illumination. This can be done to different degrees: with a fully modulated darkening of the areas of shadow; with just two degrees of brightness, one for the 'lit' areas and one for those in shadow; with more or less dense hatching or dotting of the shaded areas; and so on. At the extreme end of the scale, light and shade are abstracted from altogether, and line rather than shading is used to indicate receding contours.

(8) *Brightness*, a scale running from a maximum number of different degrees of brightness to just two degrees: black and white, or dark grey and lighter grey, or two brightness values of the same colour.

Brightness values can also contrast to a greater or lesser degree: in one picture the difference between the darkest and the lightest area may be very great (deep blacks, bright whites), in another the difference may be minimal, so that a misty, hazy effect is created. The paintings of Rembrandt are interesting from this point of view, in part because his use of illumination and brightness is so often invoked as a paradigm example of naturalism, and in part because of the way his subtle divergences from naturalism often acquire ideational functions, in a broadly allegorical sense.

The ability of photography to render black and white is limited, as is its ability to differentiate brightness values. Again, a contrast range and a range of brightness values which exceeds this ability may be experienced as 'more than real' and hence as being of lower modality.

It follows from our discussion that modality is realized by a complex interplay of visual cues. The same image may be 'abstract' in terms of one or several markers and 'naturalistic' in terms of others. Impressionist paintings, for example, often have a narrow brightness range, and abstract from light and shadow, but they have a highly naturalistic approach to colour. Yet, from this diversity of cues an overall assessment of modality is derived by the viewer.

From all this it might seem that the realization of modality in images is much more complex and finely graded than the realization of modality in language. Yet language, too, allows complex combinations of different modality cues. Take, for instance, the sentence *I absolutely don't think he could possibly have done it*. Is this 'low', 'middle' or 'high' modality? How does one 'compute' these various modality cues into one 'degree of credibility'? Frequently there are even contradictions: *It is probably definitely true that* . . . And in language, too, the value of modality cues depends on context. In academic writing, for example, qualifications such as *It may well be the case* . . . or *It is quite possible that* . . . (both low modality, strictly speaking) serve in fact to increase the credibility of the text, as indicators of the care with which the writer's judgements were made, and hence of the reliability of these judgements.

CODING ORIENTATION

So far we have described the value of modality markers in terms of the naturalistic criteria for 'what counts as real'. We have hypothesized that the ability of modern colour photography to render detail, brightness, colour, etc. constitutes for our culture today a kind of standard for visual modality. When this standard is exceeded, an image becomes 'more than real' – an effect which can be achieved not only in art (and is often the favoured modality in Surrealism), but also by means of the special techniques, materials and equipment of studio photography. A certain standard of photographic naturalism, dependent on the state of photographic technology and on current photographic practices, hence ever evolving, has become the yardstick for what is perceived as 'real' in images, even when these images are not photographs. Underpinning this is the belief in the objectivity of photographic vision, a belief in photography as capable of capturing reality as it is, unadulterated by human interpretation. Behind this, in turn, is the primacy which is accorded to visual perception in our culture generally. Seeing has, in our culture, become synonymous with understanding. We 'look' at a problem. We 'see' the point. We adopt a 'viewpoint'. We 'focus' on an issue. We 'see things in perspective'. The world 'as we see it' (rather than 'as we know it', and certainly not 'as we hear it' or 'as we feel it') has become the measure for what is 'real' and 'true'.

So visual modality rests on culturally and historically determined standards of what is real and what is not, and not on the objective correspondence of the visual image to a reality defined in some ways independently of it. At the moment holograms are probably still seen by most people as 'more than real'. In the images we are most used to, the absence of the third dimension, the flatness of the picture, does not function as an indicator of low modality, just as the absence of perspective in cultures whose art does not employ it does not function as an indicator of low modality for members of those cultures.

As we have already discussed in relation to de Saussure's 'speech circuit', however, even within our own culture the same standards for what is 'real' and what is not do not apply in every context. In technological contexts, a different concept of reality underlies visual modality, a concept we could call 'Galilean reality'. In the early seventeenth century, Galileo wrote:

> I do not find myself absolutely compelled to apprehend [objects] as necessarily accompanied by such conditions as that they must be white or red, bitter or sweet, sonorous or silent, smelling sweetly or disagreeably. . . . I think that these tastes, smells, colours, etc. with regard to the object in which they appear to reside are nothing more than mere names. . . . I do not believe that there exists anything in external bodies for exciting tastes, smells, sounds, etc., except size, shape, quantity and motion.
>
> (quoted in Mumford, 1936: 48)

Here 'real' means 'what can be known by means of the methods of science'; that is, by means of counting, weighing and measuring. By this standard of what is real, a technical line drawing, without colour or texture, without light or shade, and without perspective, can have higher modality than a photograph. Everyday common sense naturalism and realism no longer merge here. The realism (and hence the 'naturalism') of scientific-technical images is of a different kind, based, in the end, on the questions 'Can we use it?', 'Can we measure the real dimensions from it?', 'Can we find out from it how to set up the experiment?', and so on. Whatever does not contribute to this purpose merely adds a dimension of 'illusionism' to the picture, and dilutes 'Galilean realism' with common sense 'naturalism'. The latter, of course, is sometimes done for the purpose of communicating scientific ideas or technological complexities to a public of non-initiates. In his book *Writing Biology* (1990) Greg Myers compares the reporting of the 'same' research findings in specialist and popular journals such as *Scientific American,* and visual representations in the latter tend to be lavish, full-colour and 'hyper-real', while in the former sparse line drawings are the only form of visual image. Furthermore, we have to be aware that there are competing theories of reality in today's science, despite the fact that for many practical purposes Galilean reality remains of overriding importance. Alternative theories might lead to different standards for high and low modality.

In other contexts the 'hyper-real' does not have the decreased modality it has in 'photographic' naturalism. Magazine photos of food are one example. A different principle for what counts as real operates here, the converse of Galilean reality: the more a picture can create an illusion of touch and taste and smell, the higher its modality. In such images everything is done to appeal to 'sensory' qualities: reality here is constituted precisely by those sensations which Galileo branded as illusions: texture, colour, 'feel'. It is here that the affective values of colours come into their own, for example. The emotive value of colour is sometimes seen as a general characteristic of colour. But in scientific-technological contexts, colour may be conventional (more or less arbitrary 'colour codes' to facilitate the reading of complex diagrams), and in naturalism colours are there 'because they are there in reality'. From the point of view of the 'sensory' definition of reality, on the other hand, colours are there to be experienced sensually and emotively – it is for this reason that people enjoy the highly saturated and unmodulated colours of, say, Matisse, or that children enjoy the highly saturated and unmodulated colours of their plastic toys. Within naturalism these colours are 'less than real', but within a realism that takes subjective emotions and sensations as the criterion for what is real and true, they have the highest modality.

There is, finally, a third area in which the standard of 'photographic' naturalism does not apply, the area of 'abstract realism' – both in science (e.g. the 'speech circuit' diagram in figures 5.1 and 5.2) and in abstract art. Higher education in our society is, to quite some extent, an education in detachment, abstraction and decontextualization (and against naturalism), and this results in an attitude which does not equate the appearance of things with reality, but looks for a deeper truth 'behind appearances'. Just as academically trained persons may accord greater truth to abstract expository writing than to stories about concrete, individual events and people, so they may also place higher value on visual representations which reduce events and people to the 'typical', and extract from them the 'essential qualities'.

While our ideas here are drawn to a large extent from the theoretical work of Jurgen Habermas (especially his *Theory of Communicative Action*, 1984), and to some extent from that of Bourdieu (1986), we will use Bernstein's term 'coding orientation' (1981) for these different reality principles. Coding orientations are sets of abstract principles which inform the way in which texts are coded by specific social groups, or within specific institutional contexts. We distinguish the following:

(1) *Technological coding orientations*, which have, as their dominant principle, the 'effectiveness' of the visual representation as a 'blueprint'. Whenever colour, for example, is useless for the scientific or technological purpose of the image, it has, in this context, low modality.

(2) *Sensory coding orientations*, which are used in contexts in which the pleasure principle is allowed to be the dominant: certain kinds of art, advertising, fashion, food photography, interior decoration, and so on. Here colour is a source of pleasure and affective meanings, and consequently it conveys high modality: vibrant reds, soothing blues, and so on – a whole psychology of colour has evolved to support this.

(3) *Abstract coding orientations*, which are used by sociocultural elites – in 'high' art, in academic and scientific contexts, and so on. In such contexts modality is higher the more an image reduces the individual to the general, and the concrete to its essential qualities. The ability to produce and/or read texts grounded in this coding orientation is a mark of social distinction, of being an 'educated person' or a 'serious artist'.

(4) The common sense *naturalistic coding orientation*, which remains, for the time being, the dominant one in our society. It is the one coding orientation all members of the

culture share when they are being addressed as 'members of our culture', regardless of how much education or scientific-technological training they have received. Individuals with special education or group allegiance may draw on non-naturalistic coding orientations in certain contexts, but they are likely to revert to the naturalistic coding orientation when they are 'just being themselves'. They may, for example, use the abstract coding orientation when visiting a gallery, and the naturalistic coding orientation when watching television or reading a magazine. For those without such education, however, abstract and technological images will never have high modality and always remain 'unreal'. Today, however, naturalism is coming into crisis, as a result of new ways of thinking and new image technologies. In this context the role of some or all of the non-naturalistic coding orientations is likely to become of increasing importance.

The diagram in figure 5.5 shows how the same colour continuum, running from 'no abstraction' to 'full abstraction' (abstraction always being a matter of degree) can have different modality values, according to the four coding orientations. It is drawn here for colour saturation, but it could also have been drawn for any of the other modality markers we discussed in the previous section.

MODALITY IN MODERN ART

The issue of modality becomes particularly complex in modern art, because it has, to a large extent, been the project of modern art to redefine 'reality', and to do so in contradistinction to photographic naturalism. In this section we will attempt to discuss a few of the issues, beginning with some Australian examples.

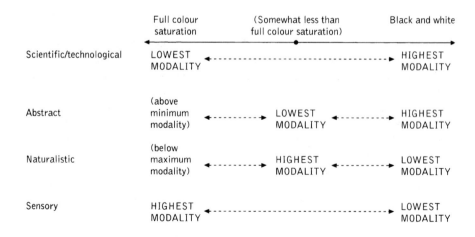

Fig 5.5 Modality values of colour saturation in four coding orientations

The picture in plate 3 shows William Dobell's portrait of Joshua Smith, a painting which won the annual Australian Archibald Prize competition for portrait painting in 1943. It was the first modern painting to do so. All previous winners had been conventional 'academic' portraitists, staying well within the bounds of naturalistic depiction. After Dobell had been awarded the prize, a number of conservative painters took the trustees of the prize to court for giving it to a painting which, they argued, was not eligible, as it was not a portrait but a caricature. The prosecutor, Garfield Barwick, interrogated Dobell about every detail of the painting, asking him whether he had faithfully represented the ears, the neck, the arms, and so on. The painter, in exasperation, answered: 'Yes, within the limits of art.' From a naturalistic point of view, the painting does of course have comparatively low modality, both in the direction of 'less than real' and in the direction of 'more than real'. Colour differentiation is greatly reduced, to a palette of orange, yellow and brown. The representation of detail, on the other hand, is amplified, exaggerated, 'more than real'. From a naturalistic point of view, the prosecutor was right. But he applied a criterion which was no longer valid in the context of modern art, a way of matching modality values to the scales of colour differentiation, representation and so on which, in the history of modern art, had been successfully contested decades earlier. In modern art, the truth of painting no longer lies in being faithful to appearances, but in being faithful to something else – for example, to some modern abstract truth, in the case of this rather 'expressionist' painting, to 'the spirit of the man', and 'the essence of what he looks like', as Dobell himself formulated it during the trial.

Attempts to alter definitions of reality are always likely to produce scandal, and therefore resisted. Whether in the trials of D.H. Lawrence's novel or Dobell's painting, the issues are far larger and more far-reaching than aesthetics or artistic convention. Changes in the definition of reality have profound cultural and social effects, and this helps to explain extreme reactions such as the proscription of 'entartete Kunst' or the burning of books.

Despite the trial, future winners of the Archibald Prize would, without exception, be modern artists rather than conventional portrait painters. The picture shown in plate 4, a portrait of the writer Patrick White by Louis Kahan, is one of them. It shows a different modality configuration, a different set of abstractions and amplifications. Unlike Dobell, Kahan does not deviate from the naturalistic representation of detail: if one disregards the strangely unseeing eyes, White's features are rendered with naturalistic faithfulness. But texture is amplified: the figure of White seems to have been carved out of some porous, chalky rock, and the rendition of its surface is so detailed that one can almost feel its cold, wet touch – a 'sensory' orientation, but in the direction of displeasure rather than pleasure. Colour, on the other hand, is greatly reduced: in what is at once a pun on White's name and a symbolic gesture, White is drained of all colour. Thus Kahan depicts him as cold, hard, almost repulsive to the touch, and the expression of this 'truth' has taken precedence over the faithful rendering of outward appearances; indeed, has become possible only by means of these 'deviations' from the naturalistic standard. The visual pun reminds us that modality is always related to the values, meanings and beliefs of a particular group, in this case an 'ordering' of the figure of Patrick White within the system of Australian high culture, and of Australian society generally.

Our second example pertains to the geometric abstractionism of the 1920s. When European painters, after studying visible reality for centuries, began to conceive of it as made up of abstract, geometrical elements (circles, cones, squares, triangles), reality was redefined as a configuration of basic elements, just as had already happened, for instance, in physics. Within this new definition of reality, painters at first still sought to produce recognizable representations, as shown in figure 5.6. Mondrian, who tried to paint trees in this way, complained that it was difficult to represent trees as arrangements of rectangular shapes. But soon these painters went a step further and abandoned the attempt to reconcile the visible surface appearance of things with their geometric inner structure (see figure 5.7). From here it was only one step to, for instance, Gerrit Rietveld's *Colour Project for the Schröder Residence* (1923–4).

Rietveld's work (figure 5.8) is no longer a reduced, abstract representation of reality, but a design for a new reality, yet to be constructed. Of course, blueprints and plans had existed alongside visual representation long before the 1920s, but in separate domains. In the twentieth century, however, they became intertwined. Art became intertwined with design, just as science had already become intertwined with technology. The boundaries between representing reality and constructing reality became blurred. And when real things were produced from designs such as these, the processes of abstraction could come full circle and yield 'naturalistic' images again (figure 5.9).

In the work of Ryman, a contemporary American artist, abstraction is perhaps taken to its limit. Many of his paintings are, at least at first glance, white surfaces. Everything is reduced, everything abstracted. There is no colour, no line, no background. And, in terms of our earlier chapters, there is neither representation of action or of social constructs, nor yet any indication of textuality, of composition. This truly is the degree zero of representation.

▲ Fig 5.6 *Card-players* (Theo van Doesburg, 1916–17) (Doesburg Archive, The Hague)

⚠ Fig 5.7 *Composition 9* (abstract version of *Card-players*) (Theo van Doesburg, 1916–17) (from Jaffé, 1967)

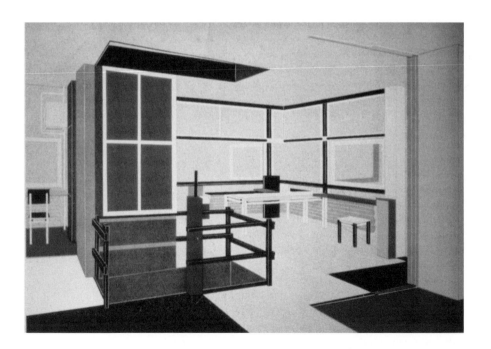

⚠ Fig 5.8 *Colour Project for the Schröder Residence* (Gerrit Rietveld, 1923–4) (Catalogue 81, Stedelijk Museum, Amsterdam)

▲ Fig 5.9 Photograph of the Schröder residence ('Rietveld House') (from Brown, 1958)

But if reduction and abstraction serve to reveal otherwise hidden, inner truths, the same might be said about Ryman's paintings. Indeed, like so many other non-naturalistic artists, he sees his work as realistic, and calls his paintings 'realistic paintings': they aspire to present the reality and the truth of the process of representation and the *process* of perception, and thereby perhaps also of the social and cultural world.

There is, however, another, much less abstract feature of Ryman's painting: his concern with texture. His work shows a constant preoccupation with the materials of representation, and with the materiality of the processes of representation. Some of the paintings leave a patch of the canvas uncovered and only thinly cover the rest. Others display a variety of brushstrokes or, by contrast, completely de-emphasize the way in which the paint is applied, resulting in totally flat, presumably sprayed surfaces. Again others emphasize the frame, or the means by which frames are attached to walls, or the flatness of the painting, by rotating it through ninety degrees, and so foregrounding its two-dimensionality.

In other words, there is a strong representational concern in these paintings, but it is a concern with representing the process of representation. Does this suggest low modality, given the enormous distance from everyday naturalism? Or does it suggest the highest modality, in which the negation of representation forms an ultimate truth, or in which the highest modality is accorded to the representation which does not represent but simply *is*?

As before, our answer is one which refers to the social. Whether a representation is judged credible or not is not necessarily a matter of absolute truth. What one social group considers credible may not be considered credible by another. This is why we see modality as interactive, rather than ideational, as social, rather than as a matter of some independently given value. Modality both realizes and produces social affinity, through aligning the viewer (or reader, or listener) with certain forms of representation, namely those with which the artist (or speaker, or writer) aligns himself or herself, and not with others. Modality realizes what 'we' consider true or untrue, real or not real. In this lies some of the power of art. To the extent that people are drawn into this 'we', new values, new modes of thinking and perceiving can establish themselves. And when enough people are drawn in, the organs of popular(izing) culture, such as advertising, will quickly move in to amplify the new forms, and move them into the mainstream of culture.

MODALITY CONFIGURATIONS

The examples in the previous section show that the modality values in art can be complex. A painting can reduce naturalism in the way it treats colour, amplify it in the way it treats texture, and yet represent its subject in a naturalistic way, as in plate 4. It can be abstract in respect of one modality marker, naturalistic in respect of another and sensory in respect of yet another, and this allows a multiplicity of possible modality configurations, and hence a multiplicity of ways in which artists can relate to the reality they are depicting and 'define' reality in general. In many other kinds of images, too, 'modality markers' do not move *en bloc* in a particular direction across the scales, say from the abstract to the sensory, but behave in relatively independent ways. Most glossy magazine food photographs, for instance, are highly sensory in their depiction of the food. The colours are intense. The texture of the food is shown in sharp detail. Lighting enhances the fresh droplets of water on a bunch of grapes, or the viscosity of a sauce, or the glazing of the ham and the cherries in a pie. But the surrounding objects tend to have lower modality. The weave of the tablecloth on which the food is displayed, for instance, may be only just be visible and often the setting is absent altogether, with the food shown against a black background. In other words, such pictures are not only sensory, they are also abstract. The 'sensorily' depicted food is taken out of its context, idealized and essentialized. And this shows that each of the modality choices in such a modality configuration is expressive of specific meanings, which then come together in the whole.

From our inventory of modality markers we could construct 'modality prints' (borrowing the metaphor of 'voice print', 'DNA print', etc.) to characterize the modality configurations, and show which modality markers are reduced, made 'less than real', and which are amplified, made 'more than real' – and this *either* in relation to an anchoring point of common sense high naturalistic modality (as one might do for an audience of 'lay' people at an art exhibition, taking the representational function of art as a common sense point of departure) *or* in relation to an anchoring point situated in some other realism. Figure 5.10 is an attempt to show what we have in mind.

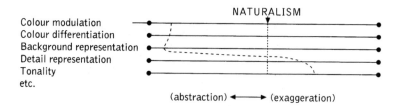

Colour modulation
Colour differentiation
Background representation
Detail representation
Tonality
etc.

NATURALISM

(abstraction) ←——→ (exaggeration)

▲ **Fig 5.10 Modality configuration**

Such modality configurations would describe what, in a specific genre or a specific work, is regarded as real, as adequate to reality. And it would also demonstrate that images are polyphonic, weaving together choices from different signifying systems, different representational modes, into one texture. In this view, a term such as 'painting' is an artificial construct which brings together and treats as a homogeneous unit what is in reality a complex configuration of different voices, different representational modes. (In the same way it can be said that 'grammar' is an artifice of theory, describing widely different representational modes – phonic substance, intonation, lexis, syntax, etc.) And it is of course from here that the interesting questions can be asked. Are there, or could there be, social and historical explanations for these modality configurations?

Here is an example, from a science textbook for the upper years of primary school, produced in Australia (figure 5.11). This is a scientific-technical picture for children. As such it forms a compromise between the naturalistic and the technological coding orientation, perhaps because a 'pure' technological picture would have been regarded by the writer as beyond the understanding of young children. On the one hand, it is a drawing and not a photograph and it lacks a Setting; on the other hand, it uses perspective (angular-isometric), colour (idealized, flat colour), and it shows at least something of light and shade (though in a rather simple and, in part, inconsistent way), and of texture (the grain of the wood, the texture of the head of the nail, the creases in the piece of cloth). The producer of this image perhaps operates with the assumption that children are familiar with the naturalistic coding orientation (that is, 'where they come from') and have to be inducted into the technological coding orientation (that is, the progression into disciplinary knowledge). The image captures this transitional phase.

Diagrams, maps and charts for lay readers may be 'naturalized' in similar ways. Newspaper diagrams and maps, for instance, may be drawn in perspective (see the Gulf War map in figure 4.19). Magazines may add colour and pictorialize pie charts. In company brochures or annual reports, the bars of bar graphs may become three-dimensional and rise, like featureless skyscrapers, from a clean landscape of undulating hills in strong, flat colour. This shows that modality is a system of social deixis which 'addresses' a particular kind of viewer, or a particular social/cultural group, and provides through its system of modality markers an image of the cultural, conceptual and cognitive position of the addressee. At the same time it shows the transition across and between such groups,

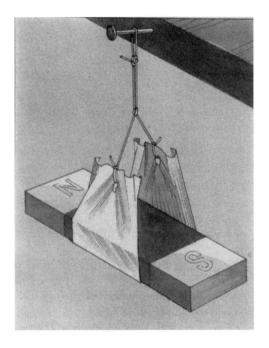

Fig 5.11 Compass (Jennings, 1986)

and in doing so demonstrates the social aspect of modality. Most crucially, it shows how modality is motivated, in the close matching of modality and the modal address (location) of specific (and assumed) aspects of the viewer's subjectivity.

Figure 5.12 shows a drawing by Newton, illustrating the set-up for one of his colour experiments. Figure 5.13 is a modern scientific illustration showing the set-up for an experiment by Stratton which caused him to see himself stretched out in space as indicated in the drawing. To modern eyes, Newton's drawing has not yet advanced very far in the direction of high technological modality: he uses (inverted) perspective, and shows the Setting. The modern drawing, by contrast, leaves out the setting and simplifies the forms, concentrating on the relation between them, rather than on the representation of the experimenter and the mirrors.

As Halliday has shown (Halliday and Martin, 1993: 54–68), Newton's writing did not yet have the objective, impersonal stance and the lexical density of modern scientific writing. At the same time he made some decisive moves towards developing the grammatical resources that would become characteristic of scientific writing. Clearly the same can be said of his scientific drawings. And that shows that, however great the differences between the verbal and the visual grammar, they derive from similar concerns and orientations.

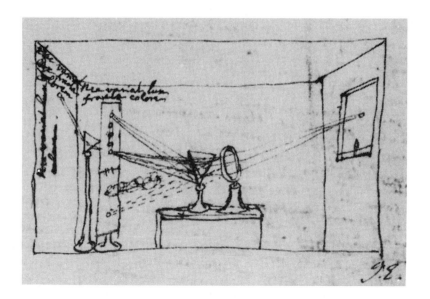

Fig 5.12 Drawing by Newton (Bodleian Library)

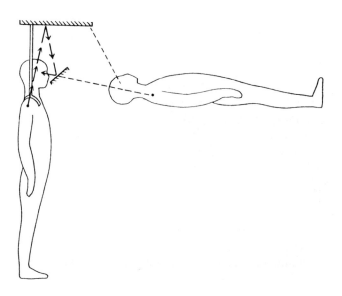

Fig 5.13 Drawing of Stratton's experiment (Gregory, 1970)

6 The meaning of composition

COMPOSITION AND THE MULTIMODAL TEXT

In previous chapters we have considered the way images represent the relations between the people, places and things they depict, and the complex set of relations that can exist between images and their viewers. Any given image contains a number of such representational and interactive relations. In figure 6.1, an image from Bergman's *Through a Glass Darkly* (1961), we see Karin (Harriet Andersson), who suffers from an incurable mental disease, and her younger brother Minus (Lars Passgard). From the point of view of representation, the shot contains what we have called a 'non-transactive reaction' (Karin looks out of the frame, at something the viewer cannot see) and a 'transactive reaction' (Minus looks up at his sister). These choices relate to the themes of the dramatic action: Karin has visions, sees things other people cannot see; Minus is caught in the here and now of his problematic relations with the other characters in the film. From the point of view of interactive meaning, the viewer is positioned closer to Karin ('medium shot') than to Minus ('long shot'); and, while Minus is seen from behind, Karin faces the viewer frontally.

◯ Fig 6.1 Harriet Andersson and Lars Passgard in *Through a Glass Darkly* (Bergman, 1960)

Clearly, the viewer is meant to be most centrally involved with Karin, and with her mental turmoil.

These patterns do not exhaust the relations set up by the image. There is a third element: the composition of the whole, the way in which the representational and interactive elements are made to relate to each other, the way they are integrated into a meaningful whole. Minus, for instance, is placed on the left, and Karin on the right. If this were turned around, the representational and interactive meanings would not be affected. Karin's reaction would still be 'non-transactive' and Minus' reaction 'transactive', and Karin would still be in medium shot, Minus still in long shot. But the meaning of the whole would no longer be the same. In other words, the placement of the elements (of the participants and of the syntagms that connect them to each other and to the viewer) endows them with specific information values relative to each other. We will discuss the value of 'left' and 'right' in the next section.

In addition, Karin is the most *salient*, the most eye-catching element in the composition, not just because she is placed in the foreground and because she forms the largest, simplest element in the picture, but also because she is in sharper focus and receives the greatest amount of light. Throughout much of the film Karin is dressed in light colours and made to bathe in light, in an almost supernatural fashion, this in contrast to the other characters. For these reasons she is also the most salient element in the shots where one of the other characters, for example her husband, is placed in the foreground. Her white clothes and the light on her pale face draw attention to her, even when she is placed in the background. To generalize, pictorial elements can receive stronger or weaker 'stress' than other elements in their immediate vicinity, and so become more or less important 'items of information' in the whole.

A vertical line formed by the left edge of the door of the shed, and continued by the dividing line between a particularly light and a darker board on the roof of the shed, runs through the middle of the picture, dividing it into two sections, literally and figuratively 'drawing a line' between the space of Karin, who can 'look into the beyond', and the space of Minus, who cannot. The world of Karin is thus separated from the world of Minus, in this pictorial composition as in the dramatic action of the film as a whole, where Minus' desire for contact and communion with his sister remains unfulfilled. There is yet another demarcation line in the picture: the horizon, which divides the picture into the zone of 'heaven' and the zone of 'earth'. In his discussion of Titian's *Noli Me Tangere*, Arnheim (1982: 112–13) describes how the staff of Christ forms a 'visual boundary' between Christ, who is already 'removed from earthly existence', and Magdalen, who is not; and how 'the lower region is separated by the horizon from the upper region of free spirituality, in which the tree and the buildings on the hill reach heavenward'. In figure 6.1, similarly, Karin straddles the two zones, half still of the earth, half already in the realm of 'free spirituality', while Minus is 'held down by the horizon into the region of the earth'. More generally, composition also involves *framing* (or its absence), through devices which connect or disconnect elements of the composition, so proposing that we see them as joined or as separate in some way, where, without framing, we would see them as continuous and complementary: there would be no visual 'directive' of this kind.

Composition, then, relates the representational and interactive meanings of the image to each other through three interrelated systems:

(1) *Information value*. The placement of elements (participants and syntagms that relate them to each other and to the viewer) endows them with the specific informational values attached to the various 'zones' of the image: left and right, top and bottom, centre and margin.

(2) *Salience*. The elements (participants as well as representational and interactive syntagms) are made to attract the viewer's attention to different degrees, as realized by such factors as placement in the foreground or background, relative size, contrasts in tonal value (or colour), differences in sharpness, etc.

(3) *Framing*. The presence or absence of framing devices (realized by elements which create dividing lines, or by actual frame lines) disconnects or connects elements of the image, signifying that they belong or do not belong together in some sense.

These three principles of composition apply not just to single pictures, as in the example we have just discussed; they apply also to composite visuals, visuals which combine text and image and, perhaps, other graphic elements, be it on a page or on a television or computer screen. In the analysis of composite or *multimodal* texts (and any text whose meanings are realized through more than one semiotic code is multimodal), the question arises whether the products of the various modes should be analysed separately or in an integrated way; whether the meanings of the whole should be treated as the sum of the meanings of the parts, or whether the parts should be looked upon as interacting with and affecting one another. It is the latter path we will pursue in this chapter. In considering, for example, the picture of the train (figure 3.30) we do no seek to see the picture as an 'illustration' of the verbal text, thereby treating the verbal text as prior and more important, nor treat visual and verbal text as entirely discrete elements. We seek to be able to look at the whole page as an *integrated* text. Our insistence on drawing comparisons between language and visual communication stems from this objective. We seek to break down the disciplinary boundaries between the study of language and the study of images, and we seek, as much as possible, to use compatible language, and compatible terminology to speak about both, for in actual communication the two, and indeed many others, come together to form integrated texts.

In our view the integration of different semiotic modes is the work of an overarching code whose rules and meanings provide the multimodal text with the logic of its integration. There are two such integration codes: the mode of spatial composition, with which we will be concerned in this chapter; and rhythm, the mode of temporal composition. The former operates in texts in which all elements are spatially co-present – for example, paintings, streetscapes, magazine pages. The latter operates in texts which unfold over time – for example, speech, music, dance (see van Leeuwen, 1999). Some types of multimodal text utilize both, for example film and television, although rhythm will usually be the dominant integrative principle in these cases.

It follows that the principles of information value, salience and framing apply, not only to pictures, but also, for example, to layouts. Plate 2, an advertisement for Bushells instant coffee, contains two photographs and a small amount of verbal text. The larger photo is a pictorial representation of the 'promise' of the product, and it is placed in the top section. The photo of the product is smaller, and placed below the larger photograph, together with the text. Reversing this would produce an entirely different effect, and probably result in a rather anomalous layout. Just what information values this arrangement accords to the two sections of the page will be discussed below. As far as salience is concerned, we can note that this page is not divided into two equal halves. The top section is the most salient, not only because of its size but also because the salience of the woman, who is positioned on the right and catches most of the golden glow of the light. Thus the advertisement gives greater stress to the promise of the product than to the product itself, or the verbal information. Finally, a sharp line creates a boundary between the photo and the verbal text, dividing the page into two separate sections, two spaces, reserved for two different kinds of meaning – one for the promise of the product, enhanced intimacy between lovers; the other for the product itself. Just as there is a dividing line between heaven and earth in Titian's *Noli Me Tangere*, and in the still from Bergman's *Through a Glass Darkly*, so there is, in this advertisement too, a dividing line between the world of 'what might be', the happiness the product might bring, and the world of 'what is', the product itself – and, just as in the two earlier examples, this product, the jar of instant coffee, straddles the two domains of meaning, forming a bridge between them. The home page of Sony's website (http://www.sony.com) has a similar structure. The top part shows the pleasure derived from using the company's products, and welcomes the user to the 'world of Sony', while the bottom part shows a range of actual products and allows the user to click on the pages from where the products can be ordered.

Early printed pages still treated text as 'visual material'. Walter Ong (1982: 119ff.) describes how sixteenth-century title pages broke up words without regard for syllable boundaries, and used different typesizes in a way that was not related to the relative importance of words, but served to create pleasing visual patterns. However, the printed page soon developed into the 'densely printed page' in which reading is linear and textual integration achieved by linguistic means (conjunctions, cohesive ties, etc.). In books of this kind it seems that the page has ceased to be a significant textual unit. The page shown in plate 2, on the other hand, is a semiotic unit, structured, not linguistically, but by principles of visual composition. In such a page verbal text becomes just one of the elements integrated by information value, salience and framing, and reading is not necessarily linear, wholly or in part, but may go from centre to margin, or in circular fashion, or vertically, etc. And this is the case, not only in contemporary magazines and websites, but also in many other contexts – for instance, in modern school textbooks, as we will show later (e.g. figure 6.6).

It should be noted, of course, that the layout of the densely printed page is still visual, still carries an overall cultural significance, as an image of progress. The densely written pages of other cultural traditions are laid out differently – as, for example in the Talmud, which has the oldest text, the Mishna, in the centre, the Gemara written around it; and later, medieval commentaries again, around the Gemara, in concentric layers. In such cases, however, every page is still read the same way. In the case of magazine pages and the pages of modern computer screens, each successive page may have a different reading path.

This development beyond the densely printed page began in the late nineteenth-century mass press, in a context in which the ruling class, itself strongly committed to the densely printed page, attempted to maintain its hegemony by taking control of popular culture, commercializing it, and so turning the media *of* the people into the media *for* the people (see Williams 1977: 295). Their own comparable media – 'high' literature and the humanities generally – became even more firmly founded on the single semiotic of writing. Layout was not encouraged here, because it undermined the power of the densely printed page as, literally, the realization of the most literary and literate semiotic mode. The genres of the densely printed page, then, manifest the cultural capital ('high' cultural forms) controlled by the intellectual and artistic wing of the middle class, to use Bourdieu's terms (1986). Yet it is this same social group which has been instrumental in spreading the new visual literacy to those who were not, or not yet, to be initiated into the forms of literacy which constituted its own mark of distinction (the 'masses', or children), and to embrace it, for example in 'high' culture avant-garde manifestations, as an expression of their oppositional role within the middle class as a whole. As so often in the twentieth century, they turned out, in the end, to have been sawing off the branch on which they were sitting. The distinction between 'high' and 'low' forms is now everywhere in crisis, and new ways of maintaining cultural hegemony are required, for instance the development of different and differently valued ways of *talking* about forms which, themselves, are no longer differentiated in the old way (the 'discourses' of different 'audiences'). But the most highly valued ways of talking (and semiotics is one of them) remain themselves bound to methods that cannot adequately describe the new forms. If we are to understand the way in which vital text-producing institutions like the media, education and children's literature make sense of the world and participate in the development of new forms of social stratification, a theory of language is no longer sufficient and must be complemented by theories which can make the principles of the new visual literacy explicit, and describe, for instance, the role of layout in the process of social semiosis that takes place on the pages of the texts produced by these institutions – as we will try to do in this chapter.

GIVEN AND NEW: THE INFORMATION VALUE OF LEFT AND RIGHT

Many of the double-page spreads in the Australian women's magazines we used as one of our data sets when we wrote the first version of this chapter use the layout shown in figure 6.2. Their right pages are dominated by large and salient photographs from which the gaze of one or more women engages the gaze of the viewer (what, in chapter 4, we called 'demand' pictures). These pages show women in specific and sometimes contradictory roles, with which the readers of the magazine are invited to form a positive identification: a mother; a former 'soapie star' turned housewife and happy in that role; working women capable of coping with 'tough', 'masculine' jobs. Their left pages contain mostly verbal text, with graphically salient photographs on the right. The spread shown in figure 6.2 has a

Fig 6.2 Gold-diggers (*Australian Women's Weekly*, November 1987)

photograph on the left also, but this photo is smaller and, in contrast to the photo on the right page, it is a 'fly on the wall' photograph, which does not acknowledge the presence of the photographer, nor therefore that of the viewer. It is what, in chapter 4, we called an 'offer' picture. On such pages there often is a sense of complementarity or continuous movement from left to right, as in figure 6.2, where the photograph on the left is tilted to form a vector that leads the eyes to the photograph on the right, and where the colour gold, with its obvious connections to the theme of the story, is used as another integrating device: it occurs in the photograph as the colour of the helmets and of the liquid being poured, and is used also as the background against which the verbal text is printed.

On such pages the right seems to be the side of the key information, of what the reader must pay particular attention to, of the 'message' – whether it is the invitation to identify with a role model highly valued in the culture of the magazine or something else; for example, an instance of what is to be learned in a textbook. It follows that the left is the side of the 'already given', something the reader is assumed to know already, as part of the culture, or at least as part of the culture of the magazine. In figure 6.2, gold mining is Given, and the fact that women can engage in it, and that you, the reader, should identify with such 'tough' women, is New, the message, the 'issue'.

Looking at what is placed on the left and what is placed on the right in other kinds of visuals has confirmed this generalization: when pictures or layouts make significant use of the horizontal axis, positioning some of their elements left, and other, different ones right of the centre (which does not, of course, happen in every composition), the elements placed on the left are presented as Given, the elements placed on the right as New. For something to be Given means that it is presented as something the viewer already knows, as a familiar and agreed-upon point of departure for the message. For something to be New means that it is presented as something which is not yet known, or perhaps not yet agreed upon by the viewer, hence as something to which the viewer must pay special attention. Broadly speaking, the meaning of the New is therefore 'problematic', 'contestable', 'the information "at issue" ', while the Given is presented as commonsensical, self-evident. This structure is ideological in the sense that it may not correspond to what is the case either for the producer or for the consumer of the image or layout. The important point is that the information is presented as though it had that status or value for the reader, and that readers have to read it within that structure, even if that valuation may then be rejected by a particular reader.

A similar structure exists in spoken English (see Halliday, 1985: 274ff.). As in visual communication, the structure of a 'tone group', an intonational phrase, is not a constituent structure, with strong framing between elements, but a gradual, wave-like movement from left to right (or, rather, from 'before' to 'after', since in language we are dealing with temporally integrated texts), and it is realized by intonation. Intonation creates two peaks of salience within each 'tone group' – one at the beginning of the group, and another, the major one (the 'tonic', in Halliday's terminology), as the culmination of the New, at the end. Just as in figure 6.2 we have one peak of salience on the left, in the bold headline and the red bar which separates it from the article itself, and another on the right, in the photo of the two women, so we would have one peak of salience on the syllable *gold* and another on the syllable *wo* – of *women* in:

GOLD-digging can now be done by women

And just as the image of the two women is the New in figure 6.2, so the word *women* would be the New, the key point of the message, in the clause above. In other words, there is a close similarity between *sequential* information structure in language and *horizontal* structure in visual composition, and this attests to the existence of deeper, more abstract coding orientations which find their expression differently in different semiotic modes. Such coding orientations are culturally specific, certainly where the horizontal dimension is concerned. In cultures which write from right to left, the Given is on the right and the New on the left, as shown in figure 6.3, where the English and the Arabic language versions of Sony's Middle East website are compared.

So far we have taken a composite text as our example, but the Given–New relation applies also within an image. Figure 6.4 shows a fourteenth-century relief depicting the creation of Eve. God is the Given, agreed origin and departure point of all that exists. 'Woman', on the other hand, is New and, in the context of the Genesis story, problematic, the temptress who leads Adam into sin. Michelangelo, on the other hand, in his famous painting *The Creation of Adam* on the ceiling of the Sistine Chapel, placed God on the

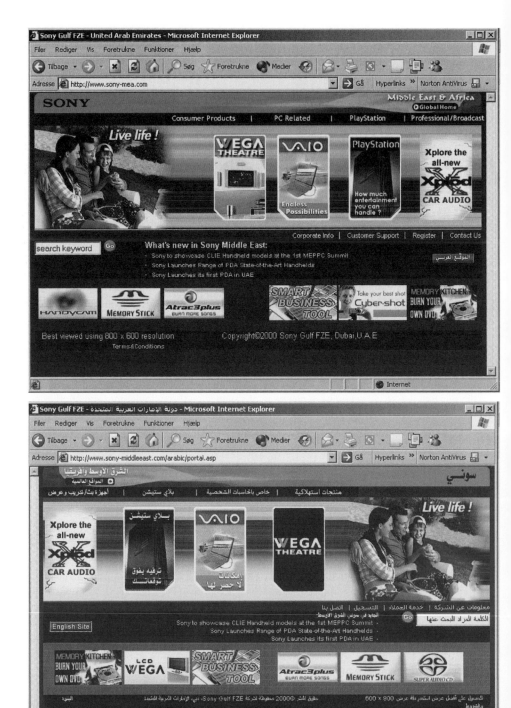

Fig 6.3 English and Arabic language versions of Sony's website (http://www.sony-middleeast.com)

▲ Fig 6.4 *The Creation of Eve* (Lorenzo Maitani, fourteenth century) (from Hughes, 1969)

right, in keeping with the new, humanistic spirit of the Renaissance. In this period God suddenly became New, and problematic. Generations of philosophers were to attempt to redefine Him in ways commensurate with the new science, and to try to prove His existence by the use of logic. In this picture the movement is no longer from God to 'Man', but from 'Man' to God. 'Man' reaches out, aspiring to divine status, and almost achieving it – but not quite.

In magazine layouts such as the one shown in figure 6.2, the space of the Given is filled by verbal text, and the space of the New, or at least a large part of it, by one or more images. But this is not always the case. A double-page advertisement for Mercedes-Benz showed, on the left, a Mercedes photographed objectively (rather than, for example, from the driver's point of view), and with the well-known Mercedes emblem in the centre of the composition. The right page contained only verbal text, with a headline saying, 'Mercedes-Benz agrees with its competitors. You should drive their cars before you drive a Mercedes-Benz.' In other words, the advertisement treated the Mercedes as an already-known, 'Given' symbol of status, and the message that 'you, too, might own a Mercedes' as the New. More generally, if the left contains a picture and the right is verbal text, the picture is presented as Given, as a well-established point of departure for the text, and the text contains the New. If the left page has text and the right page a picture, the text contains the Given, and the picture the New. The example points to the social effects and uses of this structure. What is taken for granted by one social group is not taken for granted by another. We might expect to find, therefore, systematic differences in the dispositions of material in layout across different magazines – for instance, according to their readership.

The concepts of Given and New can be applied also to the design of diagrams. In Shannon and Weaver's (1949) communication model (figure 2.2) it might seem that the horizontal order of the elements is motivated representationally: the process of 'sending information', for instance, must take place before the information can be received. But the left does not always signify 'before', nor does the arrow of time always point to the right. A diagram from a 1990 issue of *Time Magazine* which we were not allowed to reproduce here showed, on the right, a stick figure whose very large head was a pie chart representing the composition of the workforce in the year 2000 (i.e. ten years into the future at the time of publication). Another pie chart, on the left, was superimposed on a massive office building and represented the present composition of the work force. An arrow showed that the stick figure was walking towards the door of the massive office building, i.e. that a change in the composition of the work force was gradually coming closer to the present, but it was *not* moving towards the right, because the current composition of the work force had to be treated as Given and the future additions (more women, minorities and immigrants) as New and problematic. This shows how the Given–New structure can be ideological even in diagrams. If the horizontal order of the communication model were rearranged in a similar way (see figure 6.5), it would no longer depict communication from the point of view of the 'sender', with the 'receiver' as New, and problematic (Will the message 'hit the target'? Will it have the intended effect?). Instead, the reader would become the origin and departure of the communication process, and the 'sender' ('author') problematic, as has indeed happened, for instance, in literary reception theory.

Given–New structures can also be found in film and television. Media interviews, for example, often place the interviewer on the left of the interviewee (from the viewer's point of view). Thus interviewers are presented as people with whose views and assumptions viewers will identify and are already familiar, indeed, as the people who ask questions on behalf of the viewers. The interviewees, on the other hand, present 'New' information – and are situated on the right (see Bell and van Leeuwen, 1994: 160–4). The relation between Given and New may be emphasized by horizontal camera movements ('pans'). In a current affairs item from an ABC *7.30 Report* (March 1987), the children from a Muslim Community School were initially shown as 'ethnic', 'different' from 'us', viewers –

△ Fig 6.5 Reversed communication model

there was much emphasis on their non-Western dress, and there was Arabic music in the background. But it was the point of the programme to establish that they were, despite this, 'just like ordinary Australian children', playful, spontaneous, creative, etc. This was realized, among other things, by various horizontal camera movements: a shot which panned from children in non-Western clothes to the teacher, a young woman in a Western dress, tying a bow in the hair of a little girl; a shot which panned along a classroom wall from an Arabic sign to a picture of a clown, etc. In other words, 'difference', ethnic prejudice, was treated as Given; the fact that at least these children should be accepted as 'like us' was treated as New, and formed the message the programme was trying to get across.

In ongoing texts, each New can, in turn, become Given for the next New. The opening pages of the chapter 'In search of a straw' from the Dutch junior high-school geography textbook *Werk aan de Wereld* (Bols *et al.*, 1986) have, on the far left, a single column of text, occupying about a fifth of the page, which has a 'landscape' format, favouring a horizontally oriented layout. The text contains assertions such as 'Many people in the Third World have nothing' and questions such as 'What prospects do all these people have?' Given is, in the first place, the Third World as a problem. The remainder of the left page has a large colour photo of a man sleeping on the street, covered by a blanket (there is no indication where this photo is taken). This more emotive way of presenting the 'problem' therefore functions as New in relation to the text. The right page features a single photograph, showing a large crowd of people searching a rubbish dump, armed with cane bags and baskets. In relation to this photo, the image of the homeless man (an image now also familiar in Europe) becomes Given, while the photo itself, with its (in Northern Europe) less familiar image of shocking mass poverty, is presented as New. Together with the introductory text, the two images constitute the Given of the chapter as a whole. Thus each new item of information, once received, becomes, in turn, Given for the information which follows, as shown in figure 6.6. This pattern of the New becoming Given is characteristic of language also, both in speech and in writing.

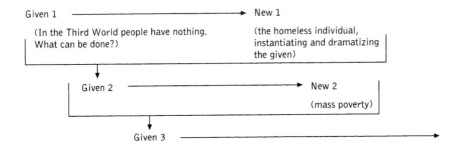

△ **Fig 6.6 Cumulative Given–New structure**

IDEAL AND REAL: THE INFORMATION VALUE OF TOP AND BOTTOM

Like many other magazine advertisements and marketing oriented websites (see Myers, 1994: 139), the Bushells advertisement (plate 2) and the Sony website are structured along the vertical axis. In such texts the upper section visualizes the 'promise of the product', the status of glamour it can bestow on its users, or the sensory fulfilment it can bring. The lower section visualizes the product itself, providing more or less factual information about it, and telling the readers or users where it can be obtained, or how they can request more information about it, or order it. There is usually less connection, less ongoing movement, between the two parts of the composition than in horizontally oriented compositions. Instead, there is a sense of contrast, of opposition between the two. The upper section tends to make some kind of emotive appeal and to show us 'what might be'; the lower section tends to be more informative and practical, showing us 'what is'. A sharp dividing line may separate the two, although, at a less conspicuous level, there may also be connective elements. In plate 2 this is created by the way the jar of coffee forms a bridge between the upper and the lower section of the ad, while in the Sony website it is created by the colour scheme which unites the page as a whole: in both the top and the bottom part of the page the dominant colours are shades of beige, with some blue and blue-grey elements added (the jacket of the girl, the pictures in the bottom part of the page) as well as some red elements (e.g. the girl's lips and the words 'What's new' in the top half, and the headings of the four sections in the bottom half). Overall, however, the opposition between top and bottom is strongly emphasized, with products placed firmly in the realm of the real, as a solid foundation for the edifice of promise, and with the top section as the realm of the consumer's supposed aspirations and desires.

In other contexts, the opposition between top and bottom takes on somewhat different values. In a fairly conservative but (in the early 1990s) still widely used Dutch geography textbook (Dragt *et al.*, 1986), the upper half of the first page of a chapter on, again, 'The Third World', is fully verbal, presenting generalized assertions and definitions such as 'A large part of the world has a low development' and 'These underdeveloped countries we call poor countries or developing countries'. This provides a more neutral and less emotive (but not less ideological) kind of idealization, a representation of the world which is divested of contradictions, exceptions and nuances. The lower half of the page is given over to a map of the world which uses colour-coding to divide the world into regions according to the average income of the inhabitants, thus providing specific and detailed evidence to support the assertions in the top half. Directions for action – for instance, coupons for ordering a product in advertisements, or assignments or questions in textbooks – also tend to be found on the lower half of the page, usually at the bottom right (hence also New).

The information value of top and bottom, then, can perhaps be summarized along the following lines. If, in a visual composition, some of the constituent elements are placed in the upper part, and other different elements in the lower part of the picture space or the page, then what has been placed on the top is presented as the Ideal, and what has been placed at the bottom is put forward as the Real. For something to be ideal means that it is presented as the idealized or generalized essence of the information, hence also as its, ostensibly, most salient part. The Real is then opposed to this in that it presents more specific information (e.g. details), more 'down-to-earth' information (e.g. photographs as documentary evidence, or maps or charts), or more practical information (e.g. practical consequences, directions for action).

As is already evident from the examples given so far, the opposition between Ideal and Real can also structure text–image relations. If the upper part of a page is occupied by the text and the lower part by one or more pictures (or maps or charts or diagrams), the text plays, ideologically, the lead role, and the pictures a subservient role (which, however, is important in its own way, as specification, evidence, practical consequence, and so on). If the roles are reversed, so that one or more pictures occupy the top section, then the Ideal, the ideologically foregrounded part of the message, is communicated visually, and the text serves to elaborate on it.

As with the Given and New, the Ideal–Real structure can be used in the composition both of single images and of composite texts such as layouts. Figure 6.7, reproduced from one of the Dutch geography textbooks we have discussed (Bols *et al.*, 1986), includes a photo which may have been taken in India – its origin is not mentioned, but to the left of the picture, as its Given, we see a map of India. A young mother, carrying a baby, occupies, by herself, the top section of the vertically composed photo, as a 'Third World' Madonna with

⬥ Fig 6.7 Overpopulation (Bols *et al.*, 1986)

child. The bottom section shows a group of women and children, sitting on the ground, tightly packed together. The young mother looks at this group, a worried expression crossing her face. In this way the picture as a whole expresses a contradiction between the deep-rooted Ideal of motherhood and the Real of overpopulation. Immediately below the photo we find a collage of newspaper headlines ('India struggles against overpopulation', 'Unemployment nightmare in India') as Real (the newspaper as source of 'hard facts', of evidence) with respect to the more symbolic, idealized and emotive representation of the problem in the picture.

Ideal and Real can also play a role in diagrams. It is striking, for instance, that diagrams based on a vertical timeline sometimes idealize the present, sometimes the past. The already-mentioned Dutch geography textbook *Werk aan de Wereld* (Bols *et al.*, 1986) features a diagram which represents the decrease of living space per head of the population, by means of a vertical arrangement of what look like chessboards of different sizes. On these 'chessboards' stand cartoon figures. On top we see a gentleman from 1900, complete with top hat, on a large ('6285 m^2') 'chessboard'. At the bottom, on the smallest 'chessboard', we see a 'punk' character from 1980. Here, as in many advertisements, the past, the 'good old days', is presented as Ideal. The other Dutch geography textbook we mentioned (Dragt *et al.*, 1986) features a 'geological calendar' in which the present ('development of vertebrates', complete with a small drawing of a naked woman) becomes the Ideal, the culmination of progress and evolution.

Many visuals combine horizontal and vertical structuring. In figure 6.8 (as in figure 6.4) God is Given, and Adam and Eve are New. But their fall from grace has introduced a (New) opposition, between the Ideal of Paradise, of the Garden of Eden, and the Real of death and decay – and the two are visually separated by the river which surrounds the Garden of Eden.

The communication model in figure 6.9 also combines horizontal and vertical structuring, in an intricate piece of visual thinking about the impossibility of knowing reality 'as it is', objectively. Given is the 'event', as it exists 'out there', separate from our perception of it. New, and therefore problematic, is our perception of the event and, at the lower level, the way we communicate our perceptions through language. Ideal is the 'empirical', the world 'as it is', and our perception of it, unmediated by communication, culture, language (which are positioned in the lower section). Real are our interpretations of these perceptions, as mediated by communication. Clearly, this diagram could have been vertical, or horizontal. But it is not. Communication is positioned *below* the 'event' and its perception. The 'empirical' world and 'pure' observation are Ideal. But this Ideal is also depicted in isolation from our 'statements' about it, and our perceptions of these statements. This is what the lower section of the diagram, the Real, tells us. Perception is secondhand, filtered through culture and language, which, as the double-headed arrows indicate, feed back into our perception of nature, and hence into nature itself. The diagram tells us that reality *does* exist, but that our perception of it can only be 'subjective, selective, variable and unpredictable' (McQuail and Windahl, 1993: 25).

Figure 6.10 is another one of our original examples from late 1980s Australian women's magazines, but it remains a good example of the combination of horizontal

○ Fig 6.8 *God Shows Death to Adam and Eve* (French, fifteenth-century miniature from ms. of *De civitate Dei*) (from Hughes, 1969)

and vertical structuring. Ideal is the moment, one might say, that 'marriage was made in Heaven'. Modality is 'distant', representing the 'not now', the 'out of time'. The bottom section, by contrast, represents the world of 'is', 'now', 'in our time'.

Given is the royal couple, presented as the quintessential couple, the well-established symbol of family values. New are Sydney's Gwen and Ray Kinkade, an instance, an example of these values. Hence what is Given is the pre-eminence (historically, socially, semiotically) of the royal couple as the paradigm example of the married couple. What is New is one instance of the paradigm – where many others of a set of acceptable instances would have served equally well. This distinction is perhaps sharpest in the bottom part. The two pictures in the top part become, at the safe distance of forty years, almost identical, an equation between equal terms.

In one, and a very real sense, the place of the New seems merely perfunctory: it is the place of the replication of the paradigm, of the reproduction of the existing classifications of the culture, the place where the underlying values of the culture are reaffirmed. The New

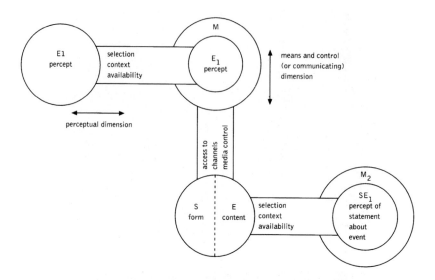

⬥ **Fig 6.9 Gerbner's communication model (Watson and Hill, 1980: 77)**

instantiates and 'naturalizes' these values. But that very fact also makes the position problematic, for it is at the same time the place of the affirmation of what is, the place of the reproduction of social meanings, and the place where the contestation of paradigmatic values can take place, the place therefore of the constant production of social meanings (e.g. of new definitions of 'women's work' in figure 6.2), even when that production seems to be mere reproduction and hence conservative in its effects. Could there, for instance, have been a Vietnamese or Lebanese or Aboriginal couple in this position (in 1987), not to mention a gay couple? This contestation over 'established', 'Given' values may happen in one or two ways: a reader who is not Anglo-Australian will either identify with the syntagm of Anglo-Australianness, 'assimilate', in other words; or will refuse the syntagm as having no relevance or value to him or her. In the latter case there will be pressure on this place in the syntagm, and this in turn will result in pressure on the paradigm as a whole.

There is another aspect to this: while the syntagm declares itself as unquestionably established, its appearance points at the same time to a problem with the paradigm, to the need precisely for a testing and (re)affirmation of its legitimacy. Read from the right to the left, the syntagm declares that it is the willingness of readers to read it as a relation of identity (within a hyponymic structure) which gives legitimacy to the royal couple. Royalty is the established, the Given. What has to be reaffirmed anew is that subjects are still prepared to enter into this paradigmatic relation. A monarchy trying to establish itself, on the other hand, might need to utilize a structure where the power of the people is represented as Given, and the identity of the monarch is to be established – that is, the royal couple would appear on the right.

Fig 6.10 Royal couple (*Australian Women's Weekly*, November 1987)

Thus this syntagm reveals a number of social facts: what is regarded as established and Given; what the cultural classification system is with respect to a certain feature; and whether the system is progressive or reactionary. It is above all a syntagm which does not permit deviance; or, rather, once an item is in the syntagm, it has to be read as being in the paradigm. Where it does permit deviance is on the part of the reader, who can refuse to be part of the community defined by this paradigm.

In the Western visual semiotic, then, the syntagmatic is the realm of the process of semiosis, and the top–bottom structure the result and record of semiosis, the realm of order, the paradigm, the mimetic representation of culture (Hodge and Kress, 1988). To maintain and unsettle top–bottom structures, one has to work on the left–right structures. That this system goes back a long way in Western art can be seen in genres such as fifteenth-century Flemish diptychs, which, for instance, may have the Virgin and the Child as Given, and a donor or Saint as New, as in the diptych by the master of Bruges in the Courtauld Gallery, and polyptychs from the same period, which may parallel a Real (earthly) and Ideal (heavenly) version of the same theme in the lower and upper part of the panels, as in Bosch's *Last Judgement,* where the lower part of one of the left panels shows Adam and Eve being driven from the Garden of Eden and the upper part the expulsion of the Rebel Angels from Heaven.

As we have said in the Introduction, we are largely concerned with the description of the visual semiotic of Western cultures. Cultures which have long-established reading directions of a different kind (right to left, or top to bottom) are likely to attach different values to these positions, as shown in figure 6.3. In other words, reading directions may be the material instantiations of deeply embedded cultural value systems. Directionality as such, however, is a semiotic resource in all cultures. All cultures work with margin and centre, left and right, top and bottom, even if they do not all accord the same meanings and values to these spatial dimensions. And the way they use them in their signifying systems will have relations of homology with other cultural systems, whether religious, philosophical or practical.

We will end this section with one further example of the uses of Given and New, the way in which Rembrandt used Given and New for the expression of affective aspects of meaning, and this especially in relation to the source and direction of light and the effect produced by that. In many, perhaps the majority, of Rembrandt's paintings, whether in landscapes such as *Landscape with a Stone Bridge* or in portraits such as *A Young Woman in Bed* or *Double Portrait of the Mennonite Preacher Cornelius Claesz Anslo and his Wife Aeltje Gerritsdr Schouten* (figure 6.11), the light source is outside the left frame of the picture and illuminates mainly the left part, leaving the right of the painting in greater or lesser darkness. Iconographically speaking the metaphoric range of light is wide – light can signify 'the divine', 'illumination', 'hope', etc. In these paintings light, whatever its meaning, is in the area of the Given, the taken for granted, the now/present. 'Light' is Given, 'darkness' New.

The height of the unseen light source also varies: in *Young Woman* it is on or just below the centre; in *Double Portrait* it comes from a position above the halfway mark, perhaps two-thirds of the way up; and in *Landscape* it comes from somewhere high up, near the top corner and in the near middle distance. That is, light may be in the area of the Real coming from a 'mundane' source or it may be 'divine'. In other paintings the light comes from within the painting; for instance, in *The Holy Family on the Flight to Egypt,* where it forms the (divine) light 'in the world' (there is also a second, faint light coming from outside, in the sky above). In *Belshazzar's Feast,* by a most unusual contrast, the light source (the glowing script announcing the doom of the king) is situated in the top-right quadrant – the space of the New and the 'Ideal'/'divine'. The variation in the source and directionality of light thus has a complex set of meanings. It can contrast the secular/mundane and the

⬤ Fig 6.11 *Double Portrait of the Mennonite Preacher Cornelius Claesz Anslo and his Wife Aeltje Gerritsdr Schouten* (Rembrandt, 1641) (Staatliche Museen, Preussischer Kulturbesitz, Gemäldegalerie, cat. no. 828L)

divine/ideal; light as Given and taken for granted, and light as New and astonishing: and all these in variable combinations. In *Double Portrait*, for example, the light comes from outside the depicted world, is situated in the area of the Given (the area where the scriptures are depicted), and comes from just above the midway point between Ideal and Real, so that it could be interpreted as 'divine', yet close to the Real. One overwhelming effect is the brightness of the area of the Given, and the total darkness of the area of the New (the future?) to which the two figures have, in any case, turned their backs. Are we entitled to read from this autobiographical, affective meanings – perhaps a deep, pervasive pessimism about both the future, the New, and the present, the Real, which then contrasts with a feeling of security about what was, a faith in a divine light from the past certainty, which entails that we must turn our back on the New, on the future? If so, these affective, personal meanings are surely as significant as social and cultural meanings and, of course, related to them.

THE INFORMATION VALUE OF CENTRE AND MARGIN

Visual composition may also be structured along the dimensions of centre and margin. The most typical manifestations of this can be found in children's drawings or, for example, in Byzantine art. As Arnheim (1982: 73) notes,

> In the Byzantine churches the dominant image of the divine ruler holds the centre of the apse. In portrait paintings, a pope or emperor is often presented in central position. More generally, when the portrait of a man shows him in the middle of a framed area, we see him detached from the vicissitudes of his life's history, alone with his own being and his own thoughts. A sense of permanence goes with the central position.

Figure 6.12 is an example – a Buddhist painting in which the central figure is surrounded by a circle of subordinates. Arnheim in fact makes the centre the crucial element of his theory of composition, conceiving of the visual objects in a composition as 'so many cosmic bodies attracting and repelling one another in space' (1982: 207).

In contemporary Western visualization central composition is relatively uncommon, though here too there may be changes in train. Most compositions polarize elements as

⬤ Fig 6.12 Buddhist painting (Arnheim, 1982)

Given and New and/or Ideal and Real. But when one of us was teaching on a media design course in Singapore, he found that central composition played an important role in the imagination of young Asian designers. Perhaps it is the greater emphasis on hierarchy, harmony and continuity in Confucian thinking that makes centring a fundamental organizational principle in the visual semiotic of their culture. Much of the work produced by these students had strong dominant centres, surrounded or flanked by relatively unpolarized marginal elements.

While many Anglo-Western tabloid newspapers tend to adhere to a basic left–right structure in the layout of their front pages, others place the main stories and photographs in the top section. The front pages of the business sections of the *Sydney Morning Herald*, however, for a time invariably used central composition, featuring a large photo (or, frequently, drawing) in the centre of the page: for instance, Asian students entering the neo-Gothic Quadrangle of the University of Sydney when the page featured articles on education as a money earner for the country's economy; a cartoon-like drawing of two men playing Monopoly (based on Van Doesburg's *Card-players* – see figure 5.6), when corporate takeovers dominated the news; and so on. Such pictures provided a symbolic kernel for the issues of the day, and a centre for the elements arranged around them – news stories at the top and to the left, as, still, the Ideal and the Given of the newspaper, even if now somewhat marginalized; advertisements as the Real; and a column of expert commentary as New, hence as the element to which readers should pay particular attention. Figure 6.13

Fig 6.13 Going on holiday (from Prosser, 2000: 117)

shows a diagram from a tourism studies textbook in which 'going on holiday' is the core issue, and in which a range of reasons for going on holiday is arranged around this Centre, without any sense of polarization.

To generalize, then, if a visual composition makes significant use of the Centre, placing one element in the middle and the other elements around it, we will refer to the central element as Centre and to the elements around it as Margins. For something to be presented as Centre means that it is presented as the nucleus of the information to which all the other elements are in some sense subservient. The Margins are these ancillary, dependent elements. In many cases the Margins are identical or at least very similar to each other, so that there is no sense of a division between Given and New and/or Ideal and Real elements among them. In other cases – for instance, the newspaper pages we discussed above – Centre and Margin combine with Given and New and/or Ideal and Real.

Not all Margins are equally marginal. Circular structures can create a gradual and graded distinction between Centre and Margin, as for instance in the communication model by Andersch *et al.* in figure 6.14, where the process of 'structuring' is more marginal than the process of 'evaluating'. In this model, nature (the 'environment') is Centre, origin and prime mover of communication. Compared to the dominant position of nature, communication is a marginal phenomenon, just as, in the medieval maps of cities we discussed in chapter 3, the cities themselves were placed in the centre and depicted with topographical

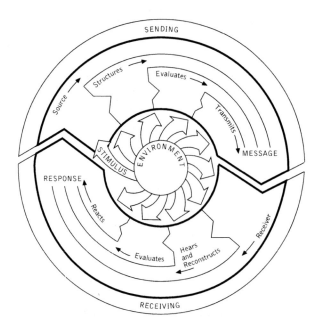

△ Fig 6.14 Andersch *et al.*'s communication model (from Watson and Hill, 1980: 14)

accuracy, while the surrounding countryside was represented on a smaller scale, and with less accuracy. Verbal commentaries do not necessarily try to 'translate' such meanings. Watson and Hill (1980: 76), for example, say that in this model the 'message' is 'interacting with factors in the environment'. Yet, the model itself represents the relation between communication and the 'environment', not as interaction, but as a one-way process, a 'non-transactive reaction', according to our terminology in chapter 2 (there is an arrow only from the 'environment' to the communicative processes that surround it). And 'interacting' suggests greater equality between the 'message' and the 'factors in the environment' than does the centred composition of the model.

As we have seen, Given–New and Ideal–Real can combine with Centre and Margin. Dividing visual space according to these dimensions results in the figure of the Cross, a fundamental spatial symbol in Western culture (see figure 6.15). Just how marginal the margins are will depend on the size and, more generally, on the salience of the Centre. But even when the Centre is empty, it continues to exist *in absentia*, as the invisible (denied) pivot around which everything else turns, the place of the 'divine ruler'. The relative infrequency of centred compositions in contemporary Western representation perhaps signifies that, in the words of the poet, 'the centre does not hold' any longer in many sectors of contemporary society.

One common mode of combining Given and New with Centre and Margin is the triptych. In many medieval triptychs there is no sense of Given and New. The Centre shows a key religious theme, such as the Crucifixion or the Virgin and Child, and the side panels show Saints or donors, kneeling down in admiration. The composition is symmetrical rather than polarized, although the left was regarded as a slightly less honorific position. In the sixteenth century altarpieces become more narrative, showing, for instance, the birth of Christ or the road to Golgotha in the left panel, the Crucifixion on the centre panel, and the Resurrection on the right panel. This could involve some polarization, albeit subordinated to the temporal order, with the left as the 'bad side' (e.g. the transgression of Adam), the

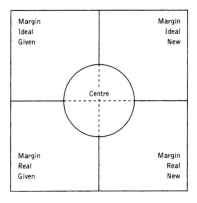

△ Fig 6.15 The dimensions of visual space

right as the 'good side' (e.g. the Resurrection) and the middle panel representing Christ's role as Mediator and Saviour (e.g. the Crucifixion). Bosch's *Last Judgement* (and also his *Earthly Delights*) inverts this, showing on the left the Garden of Eden and on the right a cataclysmic vision of Hell in which there is no place for the 'ascent of the blessed'.

The triptychs in modern magazines and newspaper layouts are generally polarized, with a 'Given' left, a 'New' right, and a centre which bridges the two and acts as 'Mediator'. In August 2004, the top banner of Nokia's website showed on the left an image of a fashionable woman and on the right a Nokia imaging phone. The text in the Centre connected the two. In fact it consisted of two alternating texts. First we read 'Inspiringly. Welcome to London Fashion Week', then this first text made way for 'Inspiringly different. The new official imaging phone of London Fashion Week'. The concept of fashion is Given, and the Nokia imaging phone as a fashion accessory New.

Triptychs can also be used to structure diagrams. Iedema *et al.* (1994: 217) shows how the left column of the organizational chart of a local council lists that council's 'Corporate Services', so making the 'administrative and financial backbone of the organization' Given, while the council's 'Development and Environmental Services', the department which 'connects all other departments', is described in the central column, as the Mediator. In a lecture on social cognition attended by the authors, the lecturer used the blackboard (conventional blackboards also have a triptych structure!) to list, on the left panel, a number of key issues in linguistics (this was Given because most of those present were linguists and students of applied linguistics), on the right panel a number of issues in sociology (this was New, as the linguists were meeting to discuss the social relevance of discourse analysis), and on the central 'panel' an outline of his own theory of social cognition, which he presented as the necessary link between the two fields, and as an issue that should be the central concern of those present at the meeting.

Vertical triptychs are also common in websites. The triptych from the University of Oxford website (figure 6.16) can be interpreted as a simple Margin–Centre–Margin structure, though there is some polarization in that the top image is a 'long shot' and the bottom image a close up. Overall, however, the student is Centre here, while images of history and tradition surround and support her. The triptych in figure 6.17 comes from a German junior high-school politics textbook (Nitzschke, 1990). As the Ideal, we see (in colour) immigrants (*Ausländer*, 'foreigners') in high-status professions. As the Real, we see 'foreigners' in low-status professions. This Real is divided into a Given and a New, with a colour photo as Given and a black-and-white photo as New, as though, in the 1990s, the low status of immigrants should be looked at in a more sober light, and no longer as 'Given' as it once was. In the Centre we see, again in black and white, a single immigrant worker cleaning a train. The accompanying text encourages students to explore what would happen if 'one day all foreign workers had to leave'. What, it asks, would be the consequences for the building industry, the children of the workers, the owners of hostels, the workers themselves, the managers of hospitals and cleaning firms? In other words, this triptych (itself the New on the double page in which it appears) tells us that foreign workers should, perhaps, ideally be able to move into high-status positions, but in reality are needed to do 'our' menial jobs. The central image is an attempt to overcome, or at least mitigate, this

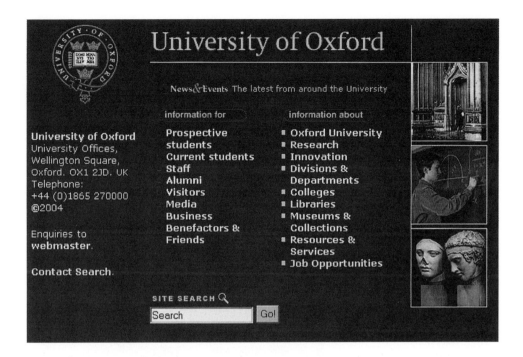

⬤ Fig 6.16 Vertical triptych from the University of Oxford website (www.oxford.ac.uk)

contradiction. It shows a worker who, like the high-status immigrants in the Ideal, is depicted as an individual, and as involved in 'clean' work, but who, also like the workers shown in the Real, has a low-status job – and is shown in the sober, documentary modality of black-and-white realism.

The structure of the triptych, then, can be either a simple and symmetrical Margin–Centre–Margin structure or a polarized structure in which the Centre acts as a Mediator between Given and New or between Ideal and Real (see figure 6.18).

In this and the preceding section of this chapter, we have not drawn any parallels with language. Though spoken English has its own Given–New structure, this is not the case with the Ideal–Real and the Centre–Margin structures. This is not to say that the meanings these structures express cannot, in some form, be expressed in language, but rather that they are more readily and frequently expressed visually, and that language, unlike visual communication, has not developed 'grammatical' forms to express them. As we have emphasized throughout this book, sometimes language and visual communication express the same kind of semantic relations, albeit in very different ways, but there are also many types of semantic relation which are more often and more easily expressed visually, just as there are others which are more often and more easily expressed linguistically, with epistemological consequences of the kind we discussed in the Introduction and chapter 1.

A Wieviele Kinder ausländischer Eltern sind in eurer Schule?
Fragt sie, seit wann ihre Eltern in Deutschland sind, was sie arbeiten, warum sie hierher kamen, ob sie bleiben wollen und warum.

Stellt im Atlas fest, woher ausländische Arbeiter kommen, woher Flüchtlinge. Laßt euch erzählen, wie es dort aussieht. Lest in Erdkundebüchern oder Reiseführern nach. Achtet dabei besonders auf die Arbeits- und Lebenssituation.

H Im Sekretariat eurer Schule gibt es Zahlen über ausländische Schüler.

Vorschläge zum Gespräch:
○ Gibt es Probleme mit ausländischen Schülerinnen und Schülern?
○ Welche Lösungsmöglichkeiten seht ihr?
○ Was denken ausländische Schüler über die Bundesrepublik?
○ Was denken deutsche Schüler über Ausländer?

A Stellt euch vor, daß an einem Tage alle ausländischen Arbeiter die Bundesrepublik verlassen müßten. Bildet Gruppen und überlegt, was z.B.
○ Bauunternehmer,
○ Kinder der Arbeiter,
○ Gaststättenbesitzer,
○ die Arbeiter selbst,
○ Leiter von Krankenhäusern,
○ Leiter von Reinigungsfirmen für Probleme hätten, tun müßten ...
Tragt die Ergebnisse zusammen und besprecht sie.

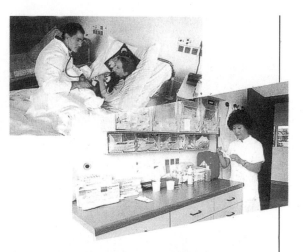

⬆ Fig 6.17 Vertical triptych from a German school textbook (Nitzschke, 1990)

Fig 6.18 Horizontal and vertical triptychs

SALIENCE

The fundamental function of integration codes such as composition is textual. Integration codes serve to produce text, to place the meaningful elements into the whole, and to provide coherence and ordering among them. So far we have discussed how composition determines 'where things can go' and how the positioning of the elements in a composition endows these elements with different information values in relation to other elements. But the composition of a picture or a page also involves different degrees of salience to its elements. Regardless of where they are placed, salience can create a hierarchy of importance among the elements, selecting some as more important, more worthy of attention than others. The Given may be more salient than the New, for instance, or the New more salient than the Given, or both may be equally salient. And the same applies to Ideal and Real and to Centre and Margin.

The same phenomenon occurs in temporally integrated texts. Rhythm always involves cycles which consist of an alternation between successive sensations of salience (stressed syllables, accented notes, etc.) and non-salience (unstressed syllables, unaccented notes) and these cycles repeat themselves with the time intervals that are perceived as equal even when, measured objectively, they are not. The perception of salience, in speech as in music, results from a complex interplay between a number of auditory factors: the duration of the strong and weak elements of the cycle ('long'–'short'), the pitch of the strong and the weak elements ('high'–'low') their loudness ('loud'–'soft'), and in speech also the vowel colour (vowels may be fully pronounced, for instance the first 'e' in *element,* or pronounced as a 'schwa', like the second 'e' in *element,* or the second 'a' in *alabaster*). Indeed anything that can create an auditory contrast between successive sounds can serve to realize salience. And even when objective clues for salience are absent, the first element of each cycle can be perceived as 'stronger': perception imposes rhythm, waves of salience and non-salience on sound (and on movement) even when, strictly speaking, there is none.

When composition is the integration mode, salience is judged on the basis of visual clues. The viewers of spatial compositions are intuitively able to judge the 'weight' of the various elements of a composition, and the greater the weight of an element, the greater its salience. This salience, again, is not objectively measurable, but results from complex interaction, a complex trading-off relationship between a number of factors: size, sharpness of focus, tonal contrast (areas of high tonal contrast – for instance, borders between black and white – have high salience), colour contrasts (for instance, the contrast between strongly saturated and 'soft' colours, or the contrast between red and blue), placement in the visual field (elements not only become 'heavier' as they are moved towards the top, but also appear 'heavier' the further they are moved towards the left, due to an asymmetry in the visual field), perspective (foreground objects are more salient than background objects, and elements that overlap other elements are more salient than the elements they overlap), and also quite specific cultural factors, such as the appearance of a human figure or a potent cultural symbol. And, just as rhythm creates a hierarchy of importance among the elements of temporally integrated texts, so visual weight creates a hierarchy of importance among the elements of spatially integrated texts, causing some to draw more attention to themselves than others.

Being able to judge the visual weight of the elements of a composition is being able to judge how they 'balance'. The weight they put into the scales derives from one or more of the factors just mentioned. Taken together, the elements create a balancing centre, the point, one might say, from which, if one conceived of the elements as part of a mobile, this mobile would have to be suspended. Regardless of whether this point is in the actual centre of the composition or off-centre, it often becomes the space of the central message, and this attests to the 'power of the centre' (Arnheim, 1982) to which we have alluded already, a power which exerts itself even if the Centre is an empty space around which the text is organized – cf. Barthes' remarks about the 'empty heart of Tokyo' (1970: 44).

Perspective produces centres of its own, and by doing so contributes to the hierarchization of the elements in compositions. As a result viewers may relate to compositions in two ways: perspectively, in which case the composition is ostensibly based on the viewer's perspective/position; or non-perspectively, in which case the composition is not based on the viewer's position/perspective. In the former case the viewers, face-to-face with the infinite recess of perspective, become themselves the centre of the composition, thus taking the place of, for example, the deities in Byzantine or Buddhist paintings. In the latter case the representation is coded from an internal point of view, as is borne out by the fact that what is left and what is right is judged from the point of view of the represented participants rather than from the point of view of the viewer. Uspensky (1975: 33–9) has documented this with respect to icon-painting. He cites traditional guides for icon-painters which state, for instance, 'On the right, or good side, is Mount Sinai, on the left, or bad side, Mount Lebanon', and then shows how, from the viewer's point of view, Mount Sinai is on the right and Mount Lebanon on the left. He adds that this is a general feature of pre-Renaissance art, and also of primitive cartographic drawing.

In the theory of art, composition is often talked about in aesthetic and formal terms ('balance', 'harmony', etc.). In the practice of newspaper and magazine layout it is more often discussed in pragmatic terms (does it 'grab the readers' attention'?). In our view these two aspects are inextricably intertwined with the semiotic function of composition. As we have seen, in many magazine advertisements (e.g. plate 2) the top section, the 'promise of the product', is the most salient element due to its size. This suggests, not just that such advertisements attempt to make readers notice the attractive picture first, so as to 'hook' them, but also that Ideal and Real are ranked in importance and opposed to each other in this way. Composition is not just a matter of formal aesthetics and of feeling, or of pulling the readers (although it is that as well); it also marshals meaningful elements into coherent texts and it does this in ways which themselves follow the requirements of mode-specific structures and themselves produce meaning.

Rhythm and balance also form the most bodily aspects of texts, the interface between our physical and semiotic selves. Without rhythm and balance, physical coordination in time and space is impossible. They form an indispensable matrix for the production and reception of messages and are vital in human interaction. Moreover, it is to quite some degree from the sense of rhythm and the sense of compositional balance that our aesthetic pleasure in texts and our affective relations to texts are derived.

FRAMING

The third key element in composition is framing. In temporally integrated texts framing is, again, brought about by rhythm. From time to time the ongoing equal-timed cycles of rhythm are momentarily interrupted by a pause, a *rallentando*, a change of gait, and these junctures mark off distinct units, disconnect stretches of speech or music or movement from each other to a greater or lesser degree. Where such junctures are absent, the elements are connected in a continuous flow. In spatially integrated compositions it is no different. The elements or groups of elements are either disconnected, marked off from each other, or connected, joined together. And visual framing, too, is a matter of degree: elements of the composition may be strongly or weakly framed.

The stronger the framing of an element, the more it is presented as a separate unit of information. Context then colours in the more precise nature of this 'separation'. The members of a group, for instance, may be shown in a group portrait (as in group photos of school classes or employees of a company) or in a collage of individual photos, marked off by frame lines and/or empty space between them (as with photos of the managers of a company in a company brochure). The absence of framing stresses group identity, its presence signifies individuality and differentiation. In figure 6.1, framing acquires *dramatic* significance. The left post of the door and the dividing line between the light and dark boards on the roof create a frame line which, literally and figuratively, separates Minus from his sister, expressing the communicative gap between them. In film and video a similar effect can be created by the choice between showing two or more actors together in one shot, or editing between individual shots of the actors in which each is isolated from the others by frame lines.

The more the elements of the spatial composition are connected, the more they are presented as belonging together, as a single unit of information. In the Nokia triptych referred to above, for instance, there are no frame lines to demarcate the elements of the triptych strongly from each other. There is a sense of continuous flow from left to right. But in figure 6.16 the 'panels' of the triptych are separate units – there is a sharp demarcation here between past and present. The same applies to figure 6.17, where the empty space between the top and the central 'panel' and the colour contrast (the top panel is in colour, the middle panel in black and white) create a strong division between the Ideal and the reality of immigration. The example also illustrates the many ways in which framing can be achieved – by actual frame lines, by white space between elements, by discontinuities of colour, and so on.

Connectedness, too, can be realized in many ways. It can be emphasized by vectors, by depicted elements (structural elements of buildings, perspectively drawn roads leading the eye to elements in the background, etc.) or by abstract graphic elements, leading the eye from one element to another, beginning with the most salient element, the element that first draws the viewer's attention. In figure 6.2 the tilting of the left-hand photo forms a vector leading the eye from left to right, and the repetition of the colour gold in all the elements of the two pages provides a strong sense of unity and cohesion – visual 'rhymes' of this kind, repetition of colours and shapes in different elements of the composition, form another key connection device, often used in advertisements to stress the connection between the 'promise of the product' and the product itself (cf. also the colour-coordination in the Sony homepage).

It should finally be noted that, at a deeper level, there is also an element of framing in styles of drawing and painting. In line drawings, for instance, the outlines of objects strictly demarcate them from their environment, whereas in certain styles of painting (e.g. Impressionism) they are set apart from their environment only by subtle transitions of colour.

LINEAR AND NON-LINEAR COMPOSITIONS

In densely printed pages of text, reading is linear and strictly coded. Such texts must be read the way they are designed to be read – from left to right and from top to bottom, line by line. Any other form of reading (skipping, looking at the last page to see how the plot will be resolved or what the conclusion will be) is a form of cheating and produces a slight sense of guilt in the reader. Other kinds of pages (e.g. traditional comic strips) and images (e.g. timeline diagrams) are also designed to be read in this linear way.

The pages we have described in this chapter are read differently – and can be read in more than one way. Their reading path is less strictly coded. Readers of magazines, for instance, may flick though the magazine, stopping every now and again to look at a picture or read a headline, and perhaps later returning to some of the articles which drew their attention, and websites are specifically designed to allow multiple reading paths. Yet in many pages composition does set up particular hierarchies of the movement of the hypothetical reader within and across their different elements. Such reading paths begin with the most salient element, and from there move to the next most salient element, and so on. Their trajectories are not necessarily similar to that of the densely printed page, left–right and top–bottom, but may move in a circle, as in figure 6.2, where the gold being poured is the most salient element, because of its extreme brightness (somewhat reduced in reproduction), the photo of the two gold-diggers the next most salient, the headline the third most salient, and the text the next most salient – but it may also be that the vector formed by the tilting of the left photograph leads the eye back to the larger photo, and so on, in circular fashion. Whether the reader only 'reads' the photos and the headline, or also part or all of the verbal text, a complementarity, a to and fro between text and image, is guaranteed. For any one reader the photograph or the headline may form the starting point of the reading. Our assumption is that the most plausible reading path is the one in which readers begin by glancing at the photos, and then make a new start from left to right, from headline to photo, after which, optionally, they move to the body of the verbal text. Such pages can be 'scanned' or read, just as pictures can be taken in at a glance or scrutinized for their every detail. We deliberately make a modest claim here and speak of the 'most plausible' reading path, for this type of reading path is not strictly coded, not as mandatory, as that of the densely printed page or the conventional comic strip. Different readers may follow different paths. Given that what is made salient is culturally determined, members of different cultural groupings are likely to have different hierarchies of salience, and perhaps texts of this kind are the way they are precisely to allow for the possibility of more than one reading path, and hence for the heterogeneity and diversity of their large readership.

As non-linear texts become more common, even densely printed pages of text begin to be read differently. The scientist, reading a journal of organic chemistry, will glance at the diagrammatic representations of organic compounds before deciding whether or not to read the paper or, when reading that only one rat has been used in the experiment, skip to find out first why this was done (Gledhill, 1994). Students preparing for their exams will use the index of the textbook to find out and highlight the passages they need, rather than read the textbook from cover to cover. The more a text makes use of subheadings, emphatic devices (italics, bold type, underlining), numbered lines of typical elements or characteristics of some phenomenon, tables, diagrams and so on, the more likely it is to be scanned, skip-read, 'used' rather than read: linear reading is gradually losing ground.

We noted that reading paths may be circular, diagonal, spiralling, and so on. As soon as this possibility is opened up, as soon as there is a choice between differently shaped reading paths, these shapes can themselves become sources of meaning. If the reading path is circular, one reads outwards, in concentric circles, from a central message which forms the heart, so to speak, of the cultural universe. If the reading path is linear and horizontal, it constitutes a progression, moving inexorably forwards towards the future (or backwards, towards the 'origin' of all things). If it is vertical, a sense of hierarchy is signified, a movement from the general to the specific, from the 'headline' to the 'footnote'. The shape of the reading path itself conveys a significant cultural message.

Sixteenth-century books of emblems explicitly described the meanings of different kinds of reading path. The reading path of figure 6.19, an illustration from a Flemish book of emblems, is a spiral, which was an emblem for the inexorable progress of time. It is also a serpent, so that the reading proceeds from the tail, a low, base element, to the head, a

Fig 6.19 A page from Alciato's *Book of Emblems* (from Bassy, 1975)

superior element. Alain-Marie Bassy (1975: 303–5) explains the sequence of the emblem-atically expressed meanings one encounters as one follows the spiral from the centre outwards: the hand ('work'), the head ('intelligence'), the tail of the serpent (a 'base' element), the hand which holds down and imposes its will on the tail. Joining these mean-ings together results in the visual proposition also expressed in the title of the picture: 'Ex literatum studiis inmortalitem acquiri' ('Through intellectual endeavours I gained immor-tality'). Today, the study of the meaning of new kinds of reading paths has barely begun.

Analysing reading paths with students, we found that some are easy to agree on, others harder, again others impossible. This was not, we think, because of a lack of analytical ability on our part or on the part of our students, but because of the structure of the texts themselves. Texts encode reading paths to different degrees. Some, though no longer densely printed pages, still take the readers by the hand, guiding them firmly through the text. Others (we might call them 'semi-linear' texts) at best provide readers with a few hints and suggestions, and for the rest leave the readers to their own devices. In again others we can, with the best will in the world, not detect any reading path that is more plausible than any number of others. In figure 6.20, a comic strip from the magazine *Cracked*, the headline stands out and this, together with the strong vector formed by the waterslide

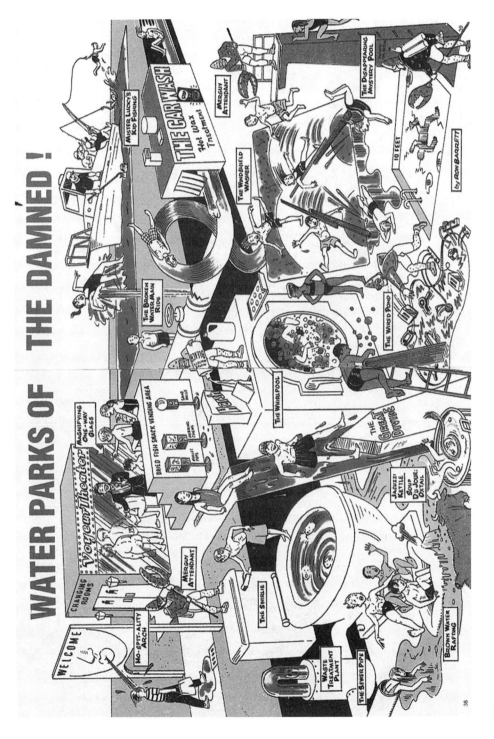

● Fig 6.20 Water parks of the damned (*Cracked*, October 1994)

on the left page, predisposes us to start our reading top left. But where the eye will move from here is difficult to predict. There is neither chronology (despite the resemblance to a flowchart) nor a clear hierarchy of salience.

Increasingly many texts (newspapers, billboards, comic strips, advertisements, websites) are of this kind. They offer the reader a choice of reading path and, even more so than in the case of texts where a plausible reading *can* be discerned, leave it up to the reader how to traverse the textual space. They are 'interactive' – and it is perhaps no accident that they have their clearest antecedent in the genre of the 'activities' books which offer children a choice of puzzles, riddles, colouring-in pictures, etc. for a rainy day during the holidays. This is not to say that the order of the elements on such pages is random. The comic strip, for instance, still has its 'welcome' sign at top left, and its most gruesome images in the Real, a division between depictions of holiday fun and of sadistic torture that recalls the division between the Garden of Eden and Death in figure 6.8.

Linear texts, then, are like movies, where the viewers have no choice but to see the images in an order that has been decided for them, or like an exhibition in which the paintings are hung in long corridors through which the visitors must move, following signs perhaps, to eventually end up at the exit. In non-linear texts viewers can select their own images and view them in an order of their own choosing. They are like an exhibition in a large room which visitors can traverse in any way they like. But, again, the way these exhibits are arranged will not be random. It will not be random that a particular major sculpture is placed in the centre of the room, or that a particular major painting has been hung on the wall opposite the entrance, to be noticed first by all visitors entering the room.

Linear texts thus impose a syntagmatics on the reader, describe the sequence of, and the connection between, the elements. As a result the meanings of individual elements can be less strictly coded, as for instance in documentary films, where the meaning of the individual shots can be largely determined by the editing, rather than by the intrinsic meanings of the shots. Non-linear texts impose a paradigmatics. They select the elements that can be viewed and present them according to a certain paradigmatic logic – the logic of Centre and Margin or of Given and New, for instance – but leave it to the reader to sequence and connect them. In the design of such texts there will be pressure to put more of the meaning in the individual elements of the composition, to use more highly coded images – symbolic and conceptual images, tightly written, self-contained items of information, stereotyped characters, drawings or highly structured images rather than realistic photographs, and so on. Linear and non-linear texts thus constitute two modes of reading and two regimes of control over meaning, exactly in the same way as we discussed in chapter 1, in connection with *Baby's First Book* (figure 1.1) and the page from Dick Bruna's *On My Walk* (figure 1.2).

A SUMMARY

Figure 6.21 provides a summary of the distinctions we have introduced in this chapter. The double-headed arrows (↕) stand for graded contrasts ('more or less', rather than 'either–or'). The superscript 'I' means 'if' and the superscript 'T' means 'then'. In other words, 'if there is no horizontal polarization, then there must be vertical polarization' – the opposite follows from this. In the next section we will discuss a number of examples in greater detail.

REALIZATIONS

Centred	An element (the Centre) is placed in the centre of the composition.
Polarized	There is no element in the centre of the composition.
Triptych	The non-central elements in a centred composition are placed either on the right and left or above and below the Centre.
Circular	The non-central elements in a centred composition are placed both above and below and to the sides of the Centre, and further elements may be placed in between these polarized positions.
Margin	The non-central elements in a centred composition are identical or near-identical, so creating symmetry in the composition.
Mediator	The Centre of a polarized centred composition forms a bridge between Given and New and/or Ideal and Real, so reconciling polarized elements to each other in some way.
Given	The left element in a polarized composition or the left polarized element in a centred composition. This element is not identical or near-identical to the corresponding right element.
New	The right element in a polarized composition or the right polarized element in a centred composition. This element is not identical or near-identical to the corresponding left element.
Ideal	The top element in a polarized composition or the top polarized element in a centred composition. This element is not identical or near-identical to the corresponding bottom element.
Real	The bottom element in a polarized composition or the bottom polarized element

	in a centred composition. This element is not identical or near-identical to the corresponding top element.
Salience	The degree to which an element draws attention to itself, due to its size, its place in the foreground or its overlapping of other elements, its colour, its tonal values, its sharpness or definition, and other features.
Disconnection	The degree to which an element is visually separated from other elements through frame lines, pictorial framing devices, empty space between elements, discontinuities of colour and shape, and other features.
Connection	The degree to which an element is visually joined to another element, through the absence of framing devices, through vectors and through continuities or similarities of colour, visual shape, etc.

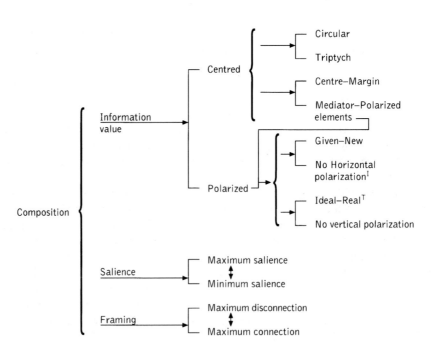

● **Fig 6.21 The meaning of composition**

GIVEN AND NEW IN CHILDREN'S DRAWINGS AND CD-ROMs

In any sequential structure, that which is about to be said or shown is by definition always New, not yet known. By contrast, what has (just) been seen, heard, discovered is, by comparison, now known, Given. In visual media, sequence can of course be represented in a number of dimensions, right to left, bottom to top, in a spiral from outside, etc. (and in medieval painting perspective can indicate sequence, with the foreground as the present and the background as the future). Such dimensions have been used throughout history, and are still used by different cultures, as primary visual sequencing orientations. The medium of the book, bringing the possibility of turning the page, adds a further means of reprinting sequence visually, the left page/right page structure and the possibility of the two-page structures (right page and following left page).

Figure 6.22 shows a double page from a book produced by a six-year-old boy while staying in Paris for half a year with his parents. It records events and experiences he was involved in, and sights and objects he encountered during his stay in Paris. Clearly, in this situation everything was New for the child, literally. He was faced with the question of how to represent new information, new ideas, new objects, without the possibility of relating them to already-established, known domains.

The book opens with the name and address of the author, on the first lefthand page. This is the Given for the book as a whole, an element of security and familiarity in the new environment. On the first righthand page that new environment is represented visually: a picture of the Eiffel Tower. It is only when this page is turned that the picture is named, commuted into language. Once named, the Eiffel Tower becomes Given, and on the adjoining righthand page the child faces the next aspect of his new environment. Thus the book continues: the new picture, too, is only identified on the next lefthand page – the Arc de Triomphe. The child obviously realized that this structure could be misunderstood, and used left-facing arrows to refer the reader to the picture on the previous page. But his impulse was to first visually represent Paris as the New, and then to master it, make it known and Given by means of language, by means of naming it. His attitude was empirical and he used language as an 'anchorage' in his effort to come to terms with his new experiences.

We will end with an example that brings all the elements of this chapter together. Figure 6.23 shows the first screen of an 'edutainment' CD-ROM for children, titled '3D Body Adventure'. The top of the screen shows a range of media on a desktop. A slide is projected on a screen. A video monitor shows an animated sequence. Half-hidden behind the monitor, a loudspeaker plays soft music. In other words, the Ideal here is what we might call 'information media', media to read, look at and listen to. The Real, on the other hand, presents things the user can *do*. It offers games to play, media to interactively engage with. 'Emergency', for instance, is a game which mixes laser surgery and the shooting gallery – the player zaps brain cells in a race against time ('Hurry doctor, save the patient'). And in 'Body Recall' body parts must be matched with their names. Thus the composition of the screen uses the vertical dimension to separate information-as-knowledge from information-as-action, or information-as-knowledge from information-as-entertainment.

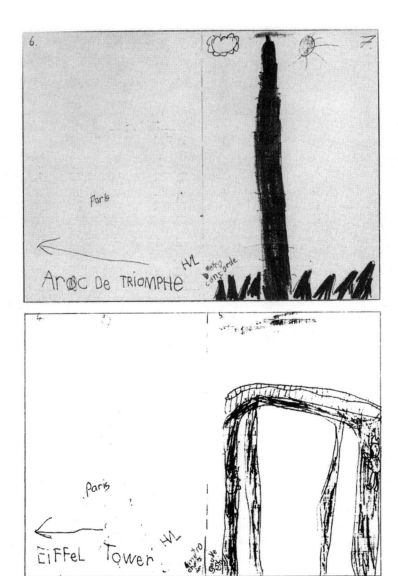

⬛ Fig 6.22 Paris diary of a six-year-old boy

And, while it continues to put the former, literally and figuratively, on a pedestal, it places real learning squarely in the zone of interactive activities. We might say that 'entertaining activities' are here represented as 'consolidating' (giving a firm 'footing' or 'grounding' to) authoritatively presented, 'high' knowledge. Reversing the two – putting the games on top

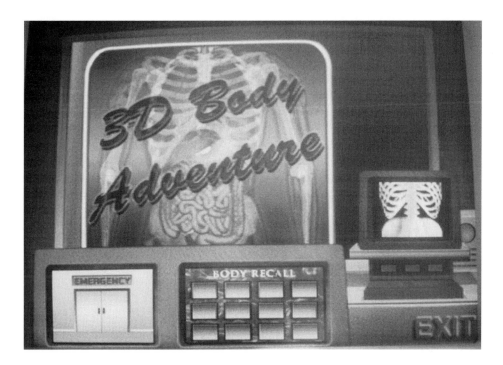

Fig 6.23 Page from 3D Body Adventure (Knowledge Adventures, 1993)

and the information media at the bottom – would create a very different meaning, perhaps something like 'knowledge provides a "foundation" for ("highly" regarded) active experiences'.

The screen also uses the horizontal dimension, and this in two ways. First, the left is the domain of the still image, and the right the domain of the animated '3D' images, of the move from two-dimensional representation to 'virtual reality'. Second, the left is the domain of what has already been formulated for the users, while the right is the domain of what users can do themselves: they can rotate the skeleton with their mouse so as to view the image from whichever angle they choose, and they can exit the screen at will. Note that the monitor straddles the boundary between Ideal and Real: like interactive games, user-activated 3D viewing has (still) some entertainment value, because of its novelty; but, like information media, it also has instruction value – the animated skeleton can serve as a stand-in for a real or reproduction skeleton and make a good learning aid for students. In other words, as we move from left to right, we move from the traditional 2D diagram to the new animated 3D diagram or drawing, and from the traditional 'passive learner' to the new 'interactive' mode of learning.

Another dimension used here is that of foreground and background. The loudspeaker is placed behind the monitor, which is congruent with the role played by sound and image in this CD-ROM: all information is provided visually, and the soundtrack only offers soft background music.

Most salient on the screen is the monitor image of the moving skeleton, and this for two reasons: it moves, and it displays the greatest tonal contrast. Next most salient are perhaps the names of the games. Although they do not occupy much space, their colours – bright red and yellow – contrast strongly with the cool whites, blues and greys that dominate the rest of the screen. And the images (the doors of the Emergency Ward and the 'Body Recall' keyboard) are both sharper and more saturated in colour than the rest of the screen. Relative size can also establish salience, and as a result the 'slide' with the X-Ray picture of the body and the title of the CD-ROM is perhaps the next most salient element. Which leaves the loudspeaker and the 'exit' sign.

From the point of view of framing, finally, the most significant 'disconnection' is that between the space of the interactive games and the rest of the screen. The games, against a brighter, more garish blue than can be found elsewhere on the screen, insert themselves into the more traditional, naturalistic continuity (and natural palette) of the desktop. They could have been placed on the desktop. But they are not. They are represented as a quite separate, 'alien' element, disrupting the natural perspectival homogeneity of the semiotic space. Within the picture of the desktop on the other hand, there is a sense of continuity, both because of the harmony of the muted colours, and because of the way the elements form part of a continuous, homogeneous, non-fragmented space. Thus the traditional media are represented as naturalistic and complementary to each other, but also as radically different from the new 'interactive' media.

The example shows that the composition of this screen positions the component modes of the multimodal text in relation to each other, making some play a foreground role, some a background role, presenting some as complementary to each other, others as each other's opposites, and so on. It *visually* realizes a discourse of 'edutainment', and *visually* defines its characteristic relations and values, and the part played in it by different semiotic modes.

7 Materiality and meaning

MATERIAL PRODUCTION AS A SEMIOTIC RESOURCE

The semiotic resources we have discussed in this book abstract away from the materiality of the signifier. They can be applied, we have claimed (and tried to demonstrate through our examples) to the production and understanding of visuals which, materially, are quite different from each other: photographs, movies, websites, drawings, paintings, and so on. One of the major features – explicitly and implicitly – of the development of our ideas since we wrote the first edition of this book has been to pay more attention to the semiotic role of the material production of the sign. In music, the performance of a composition contributes a great deal to its meaning, and in many cases it is difficult, if not impossible, to separate composition and performance. In visual communication, similarly, the material production of a design is not just the execution of something already complete, but a vital part of meaning-making. Here we will focus on that aspect of semiosis in some more detail by looking at the materials used in what, in the first edition of this book, we called 'inscription', and have since come to call 'production' (Kress and van Leeuwen, 2001).

When, some time in 1988, we first presented our initial ideas on the visual to the Sydney Semiotics Salon, one of our friends said, 'But what about brushstrokes? How can you describe brushstrokes as semiotic units?' Our fumbled response was to say, 'You have to start somewhere. We'll get to brushstrokes later, when we are further on with our work.' But the question stayed with us, and regularly kept coming up in our discussions. It was a question that responded to our view – then an odd one – that in a message all aspects matter and mean, and at the same time showed a profound scepticism about that assumption. However, it is and remains an important question. Nearly twenty years later, our answer would in principle be the same, though maybe a little less fumbled and somewhat more thought through. In our 'grammar' of visual design, we wanted to move away from a totalizing view of semiotic resources, a view in which semiotic resources are homogeneous systems in which there may be differences in the 'size' of units, but in which all the units are of the same kind, all 'belong' to 'the same system', so that all texts are, in the end, built up from a single kind of 'minimal unit', be it the brushstroke, the 'iconic figure' (Eco, 1976a), the 'coloureme' (Saint-Martin, 1987), or the phoneme and morpheme – in their respective 'tactic' arrangements. By contrast, we wanted to maintain that a given form of semiosis – for instance, 'painting' – involves a *range* of signifying resources. Some of these are like the signifying systems we have discussed in this book, resources which can be used, not just in painting, but also in photography, or in drawing, to mention just some examples. Any given type of production medium can, at least in principle, realize most of the choices from the ideational, interpersonal and textual networks we have presented in this book, though there are, in practice, historically and culturally specific restrictions on the combination of choices from these signifying systems; for example, restrictions on what can be painted and how. But other semiotic resources are more specifically tied to specific forms of material production and can be realized, for instance, only in the medium of paint or only in the medium of the photograph.

In the realm of art this is a relatively uncontentious point of view. Materiality matters: oil- and water-based paints offer different affordances, and hence different potentials for making meaning. The manner of production also matters, as we discussed with the examples of Robert Ryman in chapter 5. In the realm of linguistics it has been less obvious. If we ask the seemingly simple question 'What is a text?' or 'Is a written text the same object or a different one when it is written with a pencil or with pen and ink or is word-processed?', the answer of most *linguists* would be, 'No question. It is the same text.' The material, graphic expression of the text would not be seen as a relevant issue. If we asked a non-linguist the same question, the answer might be different – the teacher who responds negatively to an essay presented on scrappy bits of paper, badly handwritten (perhaps badly spelled), but responds favourably to a 'well-presented', typed version of the same text, uses a quite different criterion. So does the marketing executive when presenting a proposal to a client. Their notion of what a text is differs from that of the linguist. Like us, they would see 'presentation' as a significant part of the making of the text, increasingly often equal to, or even more important than, other aspects. For them, as for the painter or the viewer of a painting, the medium of inscription changes the text.

It is our impression that this aspect of text is rapidly gaining in importance, perhaps aided by new technologies of writing. The boundaries between the criteria prevailing in 'art' and those prevailing in everyday writing are no longer as sharply drawn as they once were. We do not want to engage in an argument with linguistics here, and the linguistic theory from which we draw much inspiration is in any case semiotically oriented. But we do want to say that the linguistic notion of text is an artefact of linguistic theory; as, indeed, is our notion of text – whether written and linguistic or painted and visual, or both. The question about the significance of brushstrokes comes, we think, out of a view in which everything representational is seen as belonging to the same unified, homogeneous representational system (language, or painting). The boundaries around what is 'in' and what is 'out' used to be strictly patrolled: in the linguistic training of one of the authors, phonetics was not part of linguistics, and everyone knew what was extra-, para- or simply non-linguistic. The material aspects of handwriting and typography were not even touched upon.

In our approach the material expression of signs, and therefore of the text, is always significant; it is what constitutes 'signifier material' at one level, and it is therefore a crucial semiotic feature. So is the process of sign- (and therefore text-) production. Texts are material objects which result from a variety of representational and production practices that make use of a variety of signifier resources organized as signifying systems (we have called these 'modes'), *and* a variety of 'media', of 'signifier materials' – the surfaces of production (paper, rock, plastic, textile, wood, etc.), the substances of produc-tion (ink, gold, paint, light, etc.) and the tools of production (chisel, pen, brush, pencils, stylus, etc.).

Every culture has systems of meanings coded in these materials and means of production. Here, as in all areas of semiosis, signs in their materiality are fully motivated, though as always the motivations are those of a particular culture in a particular period, and those of the maker of the sign; they are not global, nor are they a-historical. Precious metals are precious because of their scarcity, and perhaps because of their malleability. But scarcity is not a globally uniform characteristic, and the preciousness of one metal need not be equally marked in another culture. It was one of the particular calamities of the cultures of Central and South America that they had attached different semiotic values to the material signifier *gold* from those of the invading Spaniards.

We regard material production as particularly significant because often it is in its processes that unsemioticized materiality is drawn into semiosis. At times production is therefore somewhat less subject to the various forms of semiotic policing than are other regions of the semiotic landscape, and thus leaves more room for individual possibilities of expression than those regions which have better-known cultural histories, are more foregrounded and have better-understood conventions. To explore material production is therefore also to explore the boundaries between the semiotic and the non-semiotic, and between individual expression and social semiosis.

PRODUCTION SYSTEMS AND TECHNOLOGY

Like all cultural technologies, forms of production are entirely related to the overall state of a society's technologies. Indeed, dependence on technology may be one of the strongest features of graphically realized semiotics; it distinguishes them from semiotic modes in which signs are articulated by the body without any technological aids (as, for instance, in speech, singing, 'non-verbal communication', dance). Modes like music straddle the two categories; yet the boundaries between them are in any case always fuzzy: one can draw or write with one's finger in sand, using only the body and a natural surface. But generally the surfaces, substances and tools of the visual semiotic are made available by technologies, as much in the case of pencil and paper as in the case of the modern word processor. Technology enters fundamentally into the semiotic process: through the kinds of means which it facilitates or favours, and through the differential access to the means of production and reception which it provides.

We distinguish three major classes of production technologies: (1) production in the narrower sense – that is, technologies of the hand, technologies in which representations are, in all their aspects, articulated by the human hand, aided by hand-held tools such as chisels, brushes, pencils, etc.; (2) recording technologies – that is, technologies of the eye (and ear), technologies which allow more or less automated analogical representation of what they represent, for instance, audiotape, photography and film; and (3) synthesizing technologies which allow the production of digitally synthesized representations. While remaining tied to the eye (and ear), these reintroduce the human hand via a technological 'interface', at present still in the shape of a tool (keyboard, mouse), though in future perhaps increasingly through direct articulation by the body (e.g. through issuing spoken commands to the computer, or through other gestures).

The boundaries between these categories are not clear-cut; and are always subject to further transformative semiotic work. A photograph can be hand-coloured once it has been printed, for instance, or digitally altered, and many artists experiment with precisely these mixed production systems. It should also be noted that the possibility of 'mechanical reproduction', to use Benjamin's term, is not uniquely tied to any of the three categories. Printing can be done from a hand-carved master, photographically, or with a modern laser printer. But we think the categories are useful, particularly as they can be tied to major periods in the history of production and to the epistemologies that went with them.

While production technologies – technologies of the hand – have continued to play a role, the development of recording technologies has dominated the visual semiotic from the moment Renaissance artists began to use the camera obscura as an aid in painting, and particularly during the last two centuries or so, when a variety of recording technologies were developed, beginning with photography. They, in their turn, are now beginning to be superseded by synthesizing technologies. Quite different ontological orientations go with these different technologies. Walter Benjamin (1973) commented on the transition between manual production and recording, stressing reproduceability rather than the modes of representation themselves, and linking it to the dissolution of traditional forms of social organization in 'mass society' and to the disappearance of the 'aura' of the work of art.

Today the transition from recording to synthesizing technologies is the more pressing issue. The 'crisis of representation' which has characterized theoretical debate over the last two decades or so may be an indication of this. 'Recording' leads, we believe, to ontologies of referentiality, a view of representation being founded on direct, referential relations between the representations and the world. In an earlier publication we developed this idea in more detail (van Leeuwen and Kress, 1992). Synthesizing technologies undermine or even abolish such notions of referentiality, whereas as recently as in the 1970s, 'Electronic News Gathering' was ubiquitous enough to have developed an acronym, 'ENG', a deceptively naive metaphor reminiscent of other unproblematic gatherings – wild mushrooms, apples, the children. That metaphor is now entirely untenable; not only because news never was simply 'out there' to be gathered, but even more so because the technology now exists literally to *produce* it – a development anticipated by the critical media theory of the 1970s. 'Reference' has given way to 'signification', the production, out of existing semiotic resources, of new semiotic means, new signs, new texts, new images, new visions, new worlds. This does not mean that representation has ceased. Rather, the formerly naturalized relation, the identity of representation and reference, has broken down, irreparably for the time being. A new relation is becoming established instead, between representation and signification. If present social and technological developments continue, this relation will, in its turn, first become naturalized and dominant, and then come into crisis. In the year that we revised this book for its second edition, the 'production' of photographs of abuses of prisoners by British troops in Iraq was one (notorious) case in point. (Leaving the crucial matter of veracity aside, it is interesting to note that the much earlier 'production' of the same 'news event' by means of writing produced no outcry of any kind.)

These technological and semiotic developments perhaps help us understand contemporary theoretical developments. With 'recording' goes an older semiotics of 'representation' and of naturalistic modality, which itself gave rise to particular ontologies of truth, of fact (hence the interminable debates of prior decades around 'bias'). To deconstruct representation as recording, representations ('texts') themselves had to be 'deconstructed', which was done by emphasizing 'production' and therefore displaying the 'constructedness' of representations, in texts, images, etc. This can be seen as the period of 'critique' – with the adjective 'critical' used as a descriptor of many practices. Inherent in this there was already a theorizing of one new stage of semiotic practice, namely synthesis, through new practices of construction and production – making new representations out of (constructed) representations – in the visual arts maybe some of the practices of 'Brit Art' or of the American artist Jeff Koons, and in music the currently ubiquitous practices of scratching, mixing.

From such a history and perspective, which both heralds and legitimizes the present stage of synthesis, we could project a further development, which will be to deconstruct current practices of production by showing that 'underneath' production there is an already-existing, already-produced 'programme', a system which defines the limits of production. This system, of course, is still a system of representation, a representation of the social/cultural system. We could also point to the present tendencies in semiotic theories (in cultural studies, in education, in literacy theory) to collapse reading into writing, or vice versa. The dissolution of that distinction ('reading is writing') was initiated in theory in the 1960s by Roland Barthes, though it is now enacted in electronic technologies which combine the acts of reading and (re)writing someone else's text, whether in changes to an attachment to the email or, differently, in playing computer games. In other words, when the analogically based mode of 'recording' was dominant, the tendency of critical theory was to deconstruct representation-as-reference, and to emphasize the 'constructedness' of the sign, or the text.

As the synthetically based mode of production is becoming the dominant technology, critical theory will have to turn to deconstructing representation-as-programme, representation-as-design; that is, deconstructing the combinatorial possibilities and laying bare their cultural/social sources. It is for this reason that we concentrate on representational *resources* in this book, rather than (only) on texts. However, given the deconstruction of formerly stable frames – whether semiotic or social, cultural and economic – for the time being there exists newly the need for conceiving of social semiotic practice in terms of rhetoric and 'design', where the term 'rhetoric' focuses on the social relations which obtain in the process of communication, and the term 'design' focuses on the arrangement of the available semiotic resources in the making of the representation as a message.

Before we leave this subject, we should note two other aspects of the relation between production and technology. Our classification of production media was based on the way representations are produced, whether by hand, by more or less automated recording or by electronic synthesis. But production media also favour *modes of reception,* and here the surface plays a particularly important role. Some surfaces (walls, cinema screens) favour public reception, for instance, and others (pages, and paper generally, the computer screen) favour individual reception. Also – and more difficult to describe – there is the effect of the physicality, the tangibility of the surface, the difference between the forms carved in the hard rock and the fleeting flickers of light on the glass screen (we return to this in the next section). What matters is the site as much as the kind of surface on which the text is received. Now, unlike in previous periods, the surface of reception is no longer necessarily at all the same as the one on which the text was/is produced. Transcodings/transpositions of a wide variety may take place. An image may be produced in one medium – as a painting, say – and be received in a different medium – as a photograph, for instance. Or it may be produced in a recording medium, as a photograph, for instance, and received in a synthesis medium, retrieved from the image bank of a computer.

Finally, technology has also developed different *distribution media*, and it is here that the issue of (mass) reproduceability belongs, together with that of communication at (long) distance. The latter, although of crucial social importance, bears less directly on our subject. Whether images are distributed via electrical wires, optical fibres or the airwaves is irrelevant, semiotically, at the level of representation – though not at the level of dissemination. The fact that the internet is crammed full with images is in large part a matter of available technology; and it has profound semiotic consequences. At another level what matters most is the production medium in which images are produced, and the distribution medium in which they are received, if the latter is different from the former, be it because of transcoding (e.g. the photographic reproduction of paintings) or because of recoding at the other end of the telecommunication channel. Or, to be more precise, we would say that the mode of transmission is relevant only in relation to the potentials which it offers for reception as (re-)production.

BRUSHSTROKES

If one looks at Rothko's *Seagram Murals* from a distance of 4–5m, the boundaries between the large blocks of colour seem sharp and clear-cut. The closer one moves to the paintings, however, the more uncertain and fuzzy the boundaries become, the more they overlap and run into each other. Yet a postcard of one of the paintings, taken from much more than 5m distance, shows nothing of this. An aspect of meaning is lost, because of the distance from which the photograph was taken, and because of the transcoding, from painting to photograph, from one production medium into another. This brings us back to the starting point of this chapter, to the argument about brushstrokes and about the status of 'text'.

Painting allows the viewer a choice between different ways of relating to the text, even though this choice may be restricted in practice, as when a line on the floor in front of a painting prohibits the gallery visitor from coming too close to the painting. I may wish to view the painting as 'a representation', concentrating on what the painting 'is about', or view it in terms of its various techniques ('the effective use of colour'), or effects ('depression'). In each case I will stand at the requisite distance. I may wish to engage with its materiality and with the way in which the hand of the artist 'inscribed' the canvas – the matter of the application of the paint; the brushstrokes – and in that case I would need to move very close up. Photography allows me choice of distance of viewing, but without any of these effects in meaning. This 'recording' medium is representational and can only be representational. It abstracts away from the imprint of the hand that made it, even when it reproduces art.

Certain discourses about art put much emphasis on material production, particularly in relation to a handful of great painters: the fine brushstrokes of Rembrandt, the violent brushstrokes of Van Gogh, the treatment of volume by the Pointillists. This encourages a focus on the 'graphology' of the painting as a symptom, a trace of the individual temperament of the artist. That is, it takes a semiotic approach to the matter of brushstrokes. Most of the descriptions of paintings in art galleries and in catalogues, however, focus on representation rather than on inscription. The preference of art historians for black-andwhite reproductions or even for drawings of paintings also points to an overriding concern with representation.

The question of transcoding is closely related to this. What does it signify when I purchase a print of Monet's *Poppies* to hang on my living-room wall? That I want to show my appreciation and admiration of Monet? That I have been to a gallery where the painting was exhibited? That I like the theme of the painting? That I am familiar with the intellectual histories of which Impressionism is a part? The print will allow me to signify all of these, but it will not allow me to signify my interest in the material production of the work, simply because it does not enable me to focus on that; it does not even make it available as a question.

To take another example, in an original painting by Mondrian the lines are, in close-up, not straight, but overpainted and the colour of the various rectangles is modulated rather than plain and flat. Postcards and other reproductions of the same painting make the lines appear straight, remove the overpainting and present flat, unmodulated colour. It is these reproductions which produce the Mondrian of innumerable high-school art lessons, and so reinforce and reproduce a particular (incorrect) version of Mondrian and a particular (ideological) version of abstract painting. It is through these ideologized readings that such paintings have their effect on, and in, other practices.

As a final example, consider Kandinsky's *Cossacks* (plate 5). Representation is strongly reduced in this painting: one can 'see' Cossacks on horseback and drawn and flashing sabres, but figuration is not foregrounded; or, we might say that what is represented ideationally is 'violent action'. Colour differentiation, on the other hand, is amplified. And colour is used, not in a representational/referential function (shades of white to represent the 'real' shades of the white of uniforms, for instance), but to allow the substance of the production medium and the traces of the act of production themselves to signify. Colour is, in this painting, the key semiotic resource: jagged blocks of white, flashes of red, curves of yellow and blue. Action, energy, movement and violence are represented through the way the production medium has been handled. And this takes us back to the issue of individuality with which we ended the first section of this chapter, and perhaps also to the distinction between 'art' and 'design'. The handling of paint is close to the individuality of handwriting, and it was precisely this mark of individuality which came to be lauded as the distinguishing characteristic of art and as its mark of difference from 'recording'. On the other hand, this celebration of individuality was also somewhat of a last- ditch stand for art, in its losing battle with photography, and the very same art which came to stand for individual expression had its principal social effects in the form of photographic reproductions – that is, without the marks of individuality – while the originals became the priceless relics of a past ethos. In most other domains such marks of individuality became proscribed. Handwriting, for instance, has now become unacceptable in all but the most private forms of writing, despite the increased emphasis on 'presentation' which we noted earlier: this new valuation of 'presentation' is in no way a return to the kind of individual expressiveness that hovers on the border between the individual and the social, the ostensibly unsemioticized and the semioticized; it is thoroughly semiotic and social.

The individuality of the brushstroke not only became a symbol of individual expression, of 'the essence of things seen through an individual temperament', but it also came to be drawn into the domain of the semiotic, the domain of culture. It 'made school'. It was reproduced, faked, developed, imitated, and so entered into the world of semiosis as a transformative element, in a process which then transformed the brushstroke itself, as witnessed by Roy Lichtenstein's pop art parody (figure 7.1). Thus the brushstroke becomes a paradigm case of how inscription (the 'how' of painting) is allowed to play a key role in

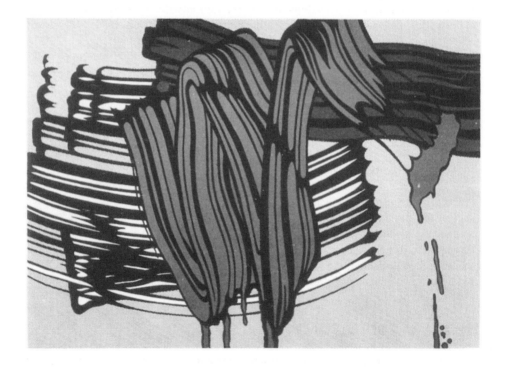

▲ Fig 7.1 *Big Painting, 1965* (Roy Lichtenstein)

some domains – for instance, the domain of the great Modernist art of the immediate past – but required to play a humbler role in others, where representation (the 'what' of painting) dominates, and where product matters more than process and practice. The division exists within painting also. A painter such as Robert Ryman, whose work we discussed in chapter 5, focuses on the 'how', on the inscriptional practices of painting, whereas a painter such as Gainsborough focused on the 'what', on the analysis of social arrangements, the recording of social states of affairs; in short, on the referential. (Though maybe the better way of describing it would be to say that for Ryman the 'how' has become the 'what'. In that view the question that painters ask is, 'What is painting for?' and that question has different answers in different periods and in different cultures.)

Such shifts of emphasis are themselves 'signs'. Interest in the materiality of representation and representational practices reflects wider social and cultural concerns with questions of substance and materiality in a world in which the concrete becomes abstract, the material immaterial, the substantial insubstantial and reality 'virtual'. Today we have, side by side, a hankering for the individual, the subjective, the affective, the non-semiotic and non-social 'punctum' of the photograph or the 'grain' of the voice (Barthes, 1977, 1984), and at the same time (and in large part as a result) the increasing semioticization of all these phenomena and more. As we have noted already, it is as representations rather than as material productions that modern art has informed and shaped practices in other domains, that paintings such as those of Mondrian came to be transformed into blueprints for designed objects, buildings, cities, and that paintings such as those of Kandinsky had their effect on the layout of European newspapers such as the *Bildzeitung* and *The Sun*, which are further translations/reductions of other translations/reductions, but no less potent for that.

Any systematizing semiotics of materiality (of the brushstroke, or of handwriting) would follow the trend of semioticizing the not yet semioticized. Reluctance to do so would follow the opposing trend set by Barthes to 'protect' the non-semiotic, to protect the 'unspoilt nature' after which the tourist hankers. In this chapter, we (like him) are also at least a little reluctant to follow the path of relentlessly making everything semiotically accounted. In reality, we think that the choice is not one between turning the unsemiotic into the semiotic – if I as an interpreter take meaning from some phenomenon, then it is semiotic by virtue of that action. The choice rather is one between assisting in laying bare, in making overtly visible meanings which are as yet not visible and made systematic; and being clear about the consequences of that process. Nevertheless, as material production is semioticized, it becomes more important to be able to talk about it. Simply asserting the value of the non-semiotic at the very moment when everywhere around us it is being semioticized, marginalized or repressed seems at least equally problematic.

THE MEANING OF MATERIALITY

From the 1920s onwards, there has been a 'functionalist' current in Modernism, a trend to 'let materials speak for themselves', which is only now beginning to change. This had various roots, but it culminated in now happily clichéd styles of 'plainness': whether of steel or timber furniture, or of 'brutalist' architecture, with its love of unadorned concrete. Behind this trend were notions of 'authenticity', themselves explicit or implicit critiques of the 'distortions' of representation, the 'falsities' introduced by 'decorative' art and its ideologies. This trend had its origins in art, where it could even become the subject matter of artworks, as in Ryman's paintings. In some periods or genres of art, artists have no choice of materials: all paintings are painted on cave walls with ochres, or on canvas with oil paints, all photographs are printed on paper. In other periods or genres, the material becomes a fully exploitable and exploited resource. Modern sculpture is perhaps the best example. The smoothly turned wood of Brancusi's *Head* (1919–23) or the veined redness of the alabaster of Epstein's *Jacob and the Angel* (1940) (see figure 8.1) become part of the meaning.

In some cases it is precisely the opposition between the materiality of the material and the mimetic quality of the product which becomes the issue. In Rodin's *The Kiss* (1880), the figures are perfectly worked when seen from the front. The material resistances of marble have been entirely and successfully overcome. The material has become 'invisible', just as the materiality of the canvas is invisible in most paintings. If we change our viewing position by walking around the sculpture, however, we are permitted to see that this first impression is 'produced', and therefore ideological. The contrast poses the question of the sculptor's work, his semiotic action. It forces us to reflect on the borderlines between the seemingly unsemioticized materiality of the representation and the semioticized, fully cultural work of the sculptor, and on the dialectic between the expression of individuality and the social semiotic framework in which it takes place. The two are connected: the 'handwriting' effect, so clearly visible in the less 'polished' parts of Rodin's sculpture, becomes increasingly possible as we move from the highly policed, the highly conventionalized, the fully semiotic, towards the less semioticized, therefore less policed and less conventionalized. The uncertain lines of a Mondrian painting signal individuality, affect and art as clearly as the certain lines of a blueprint signal conventionality, reference and design. A painting by Ben Nicholson (1945) makes the same point in a different way. It consists, quite simply, of two circles: a perfect, compass-aided circle on the left, as the Given; and a hand-drawn circle on the right, as the New. Drawing by hand, with all its subtle marks of individuality, may once have been unproblematic, as there was no other way of drawing, but has now become problematic, an issue for concern.

Architects who develop blueprints for buildings also work with 'unsemioticized' materials. Their intentions are usually less semiotic or, to put it another way, it is harder for them to put the semiotic in the foreground. Other considerations may weigh more heavily: functional considerations (the fact that they are designing an office building, for instance), financial considerations, the wishes of a client. Art, on the other hand, has, since the 1960s, attempted critiques of mass society and in particular of mass production methods, which led it towards the very practices it sought to critique. When the American artist Jeff Koons commissions sculptures from factories, from artisans or from other artists, and then signs them with his name, he works with attenuated, abstract 'surfaces': the whole global domain of cultural production becomes the material of the work. Choice serves as the production tool, and industrialized cultural production as the material surface. Our focus on physical materiality should therefore be taken as a metaphor. In the highly semioticized world we live in, Jeff Koons' work may be both more relevant and more usual than that of Giacometti or Moore, of Rothko or Ryman. The notion of artists producing objects 'with their own hands' dates back to the pre-industrial period, and had already come into crisis in the period of industrialization. It may be that in the post-industrial world it has lost much of its relevance.

The relative freedom of the artist, perhaps greater in the visual than in the verbal, remains, for the time being, in force, albeit on the margins. It lies in the possibility of *foregrounding* – either of the materiality of the means of production or of the object produced, or of the semioticization of this material in (referential or significatory) acts of representation. Wallpaper draws attention away from the materiality of a wall. A room without a hint of decoration on concrete or pine walls draws attention away from the facts of the wall itself and on to the materiality of the material.

What, then, is the meaning of material? Our assumption remains that signs are motivated. It is no accident that the statues erected to commemorate heroic figures are made of durable materials, or that tombstones are still carved: the durability of the materials makes them usable signifiers for the meanings of permanent feelings we intend to produce. Nor is it an accident that certain flowers or stones become signifiers for love: their rarity may make them precious, or else their colour, shape or perfume may make them suitable signifiers. Bone-china teacups do not produce the same meanings as tin mugs. Australian money is printed on plastic, a shock still to the returning expatriate, as if it is too boldly a signifier of what should not be signified.

To summarize, material production comprises the interrelated semiotic resources of surface, substance and tools of production. Each has its own semiotic effects, and in their interaction they produce complex effects of meaning. Production exists on many planes; that is, there are serial relations between surfaces. As with Barthes' notion of the sign, signs at one level become available as signifiers at a higher level. And there are serial relations of translation *between* production media also, as in the case of the relation between paintings and their photographic reproductions.

COLOUR AS A SEMIOTIC MODE

Our focus so far has been on materiality of the sign – on surfaces, substances and tools. We now want to turn to the question of materiality as a means for representation more centrally. Of course we have touched on this many times, indirectly or more directly, but our question now is, 'How does materiality actually enter into and shape the resources for representation, the modes?' We referred to this when we pointed out that our 'grammar' of the visual could not be, simply, a transposition of the terms of a grammar of the linguistic mode, because it had to pay due attention to the material differences of the resource for representation – not the material of sound as in speech, but the material of graphic stuff as in images, not the ordering logic of *time* as in speech, but that of the *space* of surfaces of images.

One theoretical issue to be 'got out of the way', so to speak, is that of 'abstraction'. If transpositions of linguistic terminology to other modes have been quite commonplace in the past, it has been because 'grammars' of language paid attention to an abstract entity, 'language', and did not see it or its elements in terms of their materiality. That is one reason why phonetics (as a discipline) had been excluded from linguistics (as a discipline). It had been too much concerned with the physicality of its domain. It is also one reason why for much of the twentieth century much of mainstream linguistics was concerned with 'language' as such, as an abstraction, rather than with the distinctiveness of the grammatical organization of speech and writing. At that level of abstraction it seemed possible to move from one medium to another: materiality was not seen, and hence did not figure and did not need to be accounted for.

In our approach the twin factors of materiality and of culture (always set in the social organizations in which cultures exist) are *the* means to an explanation of the resources for representation. Materiality enters into semiosis through tangible physical facts: speech happens as sound, and sound happens in temporal sequence. However, what culture does with these 'facts of nature' is then another matter. In any temporal sequence, something is first and therefore something else is second and something else last; cultures cannot get around that fact. But what meanings may be attached to that ordering is quite another matter, a matter for makers of signs in their cultures. 'Being first' may have any number of meanings: 'that which is most important to me the speaker', or 'that which is my starting point, from where I can proceed', or 'the entity which is responsible for the action which is represented', and so on. Using 'speech sounds' means using the possibilities of changes in pressure in the air, as well as the potential of changes in the frequency of vibration of the vocal cords and changes in the volume and frequency of oscillation of a column of air in the 'vocal tract' to fashion a semiotic resource – speech sounds and intonation. Again, the same considerations apply: some cultures use the potentials of pitch for syntactic/semantic means, to make questions; others use it to produce differences in lexis – in the so-called tone languages, such as Cantonese, Mandarin, Igbo, etc. difference in pitch produces difference in lexis.

What material a culture chooses to fashion into a resource for making representations, into a *mode*, is a matter of the contingencies of that culture and of its history; though it is also a matter – a fundamental point neglected in traditional linguistics – of the bodilyness of humans as makers and as receivers/remakers of signs. A mode is a means for making representations, through elements (sounds, syllables, morphemes, words, clauses) and the possibilities of their arrangement as texts/messages. Colour is such a material, and here we will explore the question of colour as mode in social semiotic terms, letting colour stand in for all other instances of the relations of material, culture and mode as semiotic resource.

We begin with a bit of history, to demonstrate the point we made above. In the Middle Ages, pigments had value in themselves. Ultramarine, as the name indicates, had to be imported from across the sea and was expensive, not only for this reason, but also because it was made from lapis lazuli. Hence it was used for high-value motifs, such as the mantle of the Virgin Mary. Such pigments were not mixed, but used in unmixed form, or at most only mixed with white. The material identities of specific pigments had to remain visible, and it was these material qualities which motivated their use, their meaning. As a result 'colour' was a collection of distinct material substances, rather than a 'system' – 'lexis' rather than 'grammar'.

Around 1600, in Dutch painting, the technology changed. New techniques allowed each particle to be coated in a film of oil, which insulated it against chemical reaction with other pigments and made more extensive mixing possible. As a result the status and price of specific paints went down and colour became to some extent disengaged from its materiality. Colour was no longer used and thought of as a *collection*, an extensive catalogue of distinctly different individual pigments, each with their own affordances, and hence semiotic potentialities, but as a *system* with five elementary colours (black, white, yellow, red and blue) from which all other colours could be mixed. But this system was not a semiotic system. It was a (practical) physics of colour, just as phonetics is a physics of speech. Nevertheless it involved considerable abstraction, and this made it possible to apply the system to different media, just as the system of language is applied to the medium of speech as well as to the medium of writing. Newton drew a comparison between the elements (tones) and rules of combination (harmony) of music and the elements (colours) and rules of combination ('colour harmony') of colour. Colours would be 'consonant' or 'dissonant' on the basis of the same intervals between seven ordered 'elements' (green, blue, indigo, violet, red, orange and yellow) as music (the seven different tones in the octave). In his time it inspired Castel to built an 'ocular harpsichord', a type of experiment which has cropped up again and again since – for instance, in the interest in synaesthesia and *audition colorée* of early twentieth-century psychologists and, more recently, in the work of abstract film and computer animation artists. The point is, 'colour' was no longer a collection of material substances, pigments; it became 'colour'. As Kandinsky would later say, 'Colour is only loosely attached to objects. . . . It has a grammar of its own, akin to the grammar of music.'

What, then, of meaning? Of course, colour has always been used as a semiotic resource. In the Middle Ages there were many theoretical and practical debates about colour symbolism. Should monks wear black (penitence, humility) or white (glory, joy)? But there was no unified system. Green could mean 'justice' as well as 'hope', red 'charity' as well as 'life' and so on. Learned tomes such as F.P. Morato's *On the Meaning of Colours* (1528) argued with and against each other about the symbolic meanings of colour, and in their arguments the meanings of colour were always motivated. Green could be the colour of unity, for instance, because it was used as a background in representations of the Trinity. Red could mean 'life' because it is the colour of blood. Some modern artists have tried to revive this kind of symbolism. For Malevich black denoted a worldly view of economy; red, the revolution; and white, action. With these elements, he thought, more complex ideas could be constructed. But as in the Middle Ages, contemporary 'colour codes' have limited domains of application, and specific colours can have very different meanings in different contexts. The work of Malevich, Mondrian, Kandinsky and others was an attempt to explore the possibility of a broader, more widely applicable 'language of colour'. But they did not manage to bring such a language into being. As Gage has said, their experiments 'offered the prospect of universality, [but became] thoroughly hermetic' (1999: 248).

So colour has, on the one hand, developed into a 'mode', a systematically organized resource. But on the other hand, this system is a physical, rather than a semiotic system, a kind of 'phonetics', although the basic elements of the system, the 'primary' and 'secondary' colours, have played a key role in visual semiotic practices and in accounts of the meaning of colour. *Semiotically*, a single 'system' has not developed. 'What people do' with colour varies enormously, and social groups which share common purposes around uses of colour are often relatively small and specialized – they do not constitute a large group, as is the case with speech, or with the systems of visual communication we have discussed in this book. But if we stay with the notion that 'what people do' shapes the tools, and bear in mind that very different things are done by different groups, we might be able to make some sense of how colour becomes a usable resource for making meaning. If we relate the meanings of colour both to their materiality *and* to what people do with that, we might be able to ask the crucial questions: Is colour a mode of representation in its own right? Does it offer the full affordances of mode?

So the task is to discover the regularities of the resource of colour as they exist for specific groups; to understand them well enough to be able to describe what the principles for the use of the resource in signs are (that is, to understand how a specific group's interest in colour shapes their signs of colour). From that we might begin to understand general principles of the semiosis of colour and of semiosis generally, and these in turn might provide a principled understanding of all uses of colour in all sociocultural domains.

THE COMMUNICATIVE FUNCTIONS OF COLOUR

In Halliday's metafunctional semiotic theory, a communicational system simultaneously fulfils three functions: the *ideational function*, the function of constructing representations of the world; the *interpersonal function*, the function of enacting (or helping to enact) interactions characterized by specific social purposes and specific social relations; and the *textual function*, the function of marshalling communicative acts into larger wholes, into the communicative events or texts that realize specific social practices. We can ask the questions that we have asked of images generally of colour specifically. Can it create specific relations between 'participants'; that is, between represented people, places, things and ideas? Can it represent social relations and help enact social interaction? And can it realize textual meanings – for instance, in a system of reference or in creating cohesion in an text?

In the preceding chapters we have, we hope reasonably plausibly, applied this model to a number of resources of visual communication (composition, gaze, angle and size of frame, and so on), thereby (re)constituting these resources as part of the 'grammatical system' of images, in Halliday's terms. We did not, however, in the first version of this book, deal with colour in this way, because we found it difficult to assign colour plausibly to just one – and only one – of Halliday's three metafunctions. It is true that there is a dominant discourse of colour in which colour is primarily related to affect, and Halliday and others (e.g. Poynton, 1985; Martin, 1992) see affect as an aspect of the interpersonal metafunction. But the communicative function of colour is not restricted to affect alone. We think that colour is used metafunctionally, and that it is therefore a mode in its own right.

Starting with the ideational function, colour clearly can be used to denote people, places and things as well as classes of people, places and things, and more general ideas. The colours of flags, for instance, denote states, and corporations increasingly use specific colours or colour schemes to denote their unique identities. Car manufacturers, for instance, ensure that the dark blue of a BMW is quite distinct from the dark blue of a VW or a Ford, and they legally protect 'their' colours, so that others will not be able to use them. Even universities use colour to signal their identities. The Open University, for example, stipulates:

> Two colours . . . for formal applications such as high-quality stationery and degree certificates – blue (reference PMS 300) for the shield and lettering, and yellow (PMS 123) for the circular inset. Single colour stationery should be in blue (PMS 300) if possible.
>
> (quoted in Goodman and Graddol, 1996: 119)

On maps, colours can serve to identify water, arable land, deserts, mountains, and so on. In uniforms, colour can signal rank. In the safety code designed by US colour consultant Faber Birren (Lacy, 1996: 75), 'green' identifies first-aid equipment, while 'red' identifies hoses and valves (which play a role, of course, in fire protection). On the London Underground, 'green' identifies the District Line and 'red' the Central Line, and on both Underground maps and in Underground stations many people look for those colours first, and speak of the 'green line' and the 'red line'.

Colour is also used to convey 'interpersonal' meaning: it allows us to realize 'colour acts' (as language permits 'speech acts'). It can be and is used to *do* things to or for each other: to impress or intimidate through 'power-dressing', to warn against obstructions and other hazards by painting them orange, or to subdue people – apparently the Naval Correctional Centre in Seattle found that 'pink, properly applied, relaxes hostile and aggressive individuals within 15 minutes' (Lacy, 1996: 89). According to the *Guardian*'s 'Office Hours' supplement (3 September 2001: 5):

> 'Colours are very powerful and can reduce or raise stress levels,' believes Lilian Verner-Bonds, author of *Colour Healing*. Bright reds are energising and are good for offices in the banking or entertainment fields. Green is useful if there's discord or disharmony as it is soothing. Blue is rated as the best colour for promoting calm and pastel orange is good for gently encouraging activity.

Elsewhere in the same article we learn that adding colour to documents can increase the reader's attention span by more than eighty per cent and that 'an invoice that has the amount of money in colour is thirty per cent more likely to be paid on time than a monocolour one'. In all these cases colour represents, projects, enables or constructs social relations – it is interpersonal. It is not just the case that colour 'expresses' or 'means' things such as 'calm' or 'energy'; rather, people actually use colour to try to energize or calm down other people. Putting it more generally, colour is used to act on others, to send managerial messages to workers, or parental messages to children, as we have shown in an analysis of a child's room (Kress and van Leeuwen, 2001). It is used by people to present themselves and the values they stand for, to say in the context of specific social situations, 'I am calm' or 'I am energetic', and to project 'calm' or 'energy' as positive values. We will address this in more detail below, when we analyse the use of colour in home decoration.

Colour also functions, maybe even most obviously, at the textual level. In many buildings, the differing colours of doors and other features – the colour schemes of floors – distinguish different departments from each other on the one hand, while creating unity and coherence within these departments on the other. Colour can be used to create coherence in texts. Textbooks make wide use of this, whether in 'reading schemes' or in mathematics texts to indicate 'levels' of difficulty, or in science textbooks to provide topical unity. In *Pasos*, a Spanish language textbook (Martín and Ellis, 2001), the chapter headings and page numbers of each chapter have a distinct colour, all section headings (*'Vocabulario en casa'*, *'Gramática'*, etc.) are red throughout the book, and all 'activities' (e.g. 'Make phrases with *es* or *está'*) have a purple heading and number. In an issue of the German edition of *Cosmopolitan* (November 2001), film reviews have orange headlines and other uses of orange in the typography, as the background of textboxes, etc. The art reviews use green in a similar way, book reviews use red, and so on. In some cases this is cued by a salient colour in the key illustration of the first page of the relevant review section; for instance, Cate Blanchett's orange hair in a still from the film *Bandits* in the film review section.

'Colour-coordination', rather than the repetition of a single colour, can be used to promote textual cohesion. In this case the various colours of a page, or a larger section of a text (or of an outfit, or a room), may have roughly the same degree of brightness and/or saturation. In computer software such as PowerPoint, this feature is already built in, a kind of analogue of the spell-checker, showing just the development in the direction of a broader use of grammar. Choosing the initial background automatically selects a range of colours as a colour scheme. For instance, if the initial colour is a pastel, then the other colours will also be pastels. It is possible to override this by selecting another colour from a Munsell atlas type display, but this takes more effort and skill.

There are two points to make. First, colour fulfils the three metafunctions simultaneously. The colours on a map retain their ideational and their interpersonal value, their appealing brightness, or stuffy dullness; on maps colours are coordinated to enhance textual cohesion. And contemporary scientific visualizations are thought of as primarily ideational: veins and arteries will be represented using different colours to indicate the amount of oxygen – or the level of its depletion. Second, we are not arguing that colour always has and always will fulfil all three of these functions equally. Colour does what people do with it, in making a sign and in remaking the sign in its reception. We are not 'discovering' universal and suprahistorical facts about colour here. We are trying to document what kind of communicative work colour is made to do in today's increasingly global semiotic practices, and how. The examples provide an indication that some of these uses of colour have fairly specific, limited domains, where they clearly relate to the specific interests of sign-makers (e.g. map-making, subduing prisoners) while others may have wider distribution (e.g. the use of colour-coding in magazines as a means of cohesion).

Finally, the central question: If we are right, if colour fulfils all three metafunctions, is it a semiotic mode in its own right, along with speech, image, writing, music? Maybe. But is there not also a difference? Language, image and music have been conceived of (and have in various 'purist' practices often operated) as relatively independent semiotic modes. Although a novel is a material object, and a page a visual artefact, its communicative work is done primarily through writing. In an art gallery images usually come with no words – the small descriptive sign on the wall nearby is not a part of the image but a part of the environment of display in the gallery or museum. In the concert hall everything is concentrated on the music, while expression through semiotic modes such as dress, bodily performance, etc., is held back, certainly by comparison to contemporary popular music shows. There is a choice for the audience to focus on the music 'as such' or on the whole as 'performance', the 'concert'.

Is this the case with colour? Painters have tried to make paintings that use only colour and nothing else ('field painting', Rothko, etc.), but this does not appear to have led to a whole new artform. Then again, maybe colour is a characteristic mode for the age of multimodality. It can combine freely with many other modes, with architecture, typography, product design, document design.

Let us step back for a moment. As one of us writes this – it is a day in mid-August, just before lunchtime – I am sitting looking out through the open French windows, on a tranquil French countryside. I see low hills, trees, forest in the background, some Charolais cattle in the pasture beyond the fence. There are a very few fluffy clouds, though above and beyond the forested hill there is a denser bank of cloud, just appearing, making me think of a late afternoon thunderstorm. I am describing this scene by selecting out specific elements, naming them, putting them here on the screen of my laptop as words in a particular order. I have avoided using any colour words.

Now let me try this again. I am looking out through the open French windows at a world of colour. Overwhelmingly, greens of the most varied hues dominate, though there are greys of various kinds and browns, dark purples, blues, off-white. Everything that I see I see as colour. And if I represent it here on my screen again as words, it is because I have *translated* the world *as I see it* into the mode that my culture has made most readily available to me. Usually I don't even regard that action as translation, but as representation: that is how my culture has taught me to understand it. The elements of this translation code have to be inscribed – first on to this screen in ways I do not understand, later on to a printed page – though until about eight years ago or so I would have transcribed them on to the paper-page directly, using a pen.

I might, however, have learned (or might still learn) to paint. I would be able to represent this scene – it would of course not be a recording (even a photograph would not be that) – in a mode which is closer to the manner of my perception. Colour would be represented by colour, whereas at the moment colour is represented by words (in syntactic order). The colours would of course be organized, as blocks, splashes, lines, dots: the greys and browns would appear as thinner, differently vertical elements – as the trunks of the trees I see, or as the flecks of grey in the bank of cloud, the greens of various hues and brightness as leaves and blades of grass, and the purples as the dots of various sizes of plums and ripening elderberries. Colour would appear entirely by itself – on an inscriptional surface, of course, no less, but also (are we right in saying?) no more so than the words I used above need the inscriptional surface of page or, if spoken, the inscriptional surface of air and, if heard, the receptor organs of the ear.

In my banal account of this framed segment of the landscape I used words as my descriptional resource, having become so used to it that it also served as my means of analysis of the countryside. The mode gave me the terms with which to analyse that which I saw, and it gave me the means for its description. The mode of colour – if we see it as a mode – would give me different terms (not of course as here in my transcription as words), if I were able to *paint* what I see having mixed my own colours on my palette, using now a quite different set of analytical and descriptive 'terms'.

None of this is new; and the Impressionists were just one 'school' of painters who worked with ideas such as these, even if more subtly thought and expressed, and focused on the materiality of *light* rather than of colour. However, what would be new for us now is to see colour for what it is and what it does. Does colour here exist on its own? Well, yes, of course – at least as much as do words spoken or written. Once posed and seen in this context the answer becomes somewhat oddly self-evident. Can colour be or become a mode only in a multimodal environment? Well, yes, in the same way – no more no less, even if differently – as every other mode. And the experiments of Mondrian, of Rothko or Nicholson, as of others, would now be seen not so much as experiments in turning colour into mode, but as experiments in abstracting away from the (attempted) realisms of blocks (as tree trunks), slashes (as blades of grass), lines (as edges of all kinds) and dots (berries or plums), turning realism of the ideational kind into its abstraction.

A DISTINCTIVE FEATURE APPROACH TO THE SEMIOTICS OF COLOUR

In Kress and van Leeuwen (2001), we argued that signifiers – and colours are signifiers, not signs – carry a set of affordances from which sign-makers and interpreters select according to their communicative needs and interests in a given context. In some cases their choice will be highly regulated by explicit or implicit rules, or by the authority of experts and role models. In other cases – for instance, in the production and interpretation of art – it will be relatively free. In our brief analysis of the use of colour in home decoration below, we show how in most situations these two poles, constraint and creativity, are both in evidence and mixed in complex ways.

Like Kandinsky, we distinguish two types of affordance in colour, two sources for making meaning with colour. First there is association, or provenance – the question of 'where the colour comes from', 'where we have seen it before'. The associations taken up in many of the communicative uses of colour, such as in advertising or the entertainment media, will usually be with substances, objects, etc. that carry significant symbolic value in the given sociocultural context. While the affordances of a colour may be wide in theory, in practice they are not when the context of production and interpretation is taken into account, as we will try to do in the analysis below.

The second type of affordance is that of the 'distinctive features' of colour. Here we want to show some aspects of the affordances of the materiality of colour, and hence make a connection, not with the 'grammar', but with phonetics and phonology. In Jakobson and Halle's distinctive feature phonology (1956), the features named real material phenomena – such as the point of articulation of a consonant, or the aperture of the mouth in the making of a vowel – and in description they were deployed as operating in opposition. So one consonant could be distinguished from another by an opposition, such as /+voiced/ as against /–voiced/, an opposition which would distinguish /b/ from /p/, or /d/ from /t/, in English. We focus less on opposition than on the quality, the characteristics of the features, and talk about values on a range of scales, such as the scale that runs from light to dark, the scale that runs from saturated to desaturated, and so on. Unlike Jakobson and Halle, we see these features not just as serving to distinguish different sounds or colours from each other, but above all as meaning potentials; that is, as their potential to become signifiers. Any specific instance of colour can be defined as a combination of specific values on each of these scales – and hence also as a complex and composite meaning potential, as we will try to show below.

Value

The scale of value is the grey scale, the scale from maximally light (white) to maximally dark (black). In the lives of all human beings light and dark are fundamental experiences, and there is no culture which has not built an edifice of symbolic meanings and value systems upon this fundamental experience – even though different cultures may have done so in different ways. Painters who emphasize value – for instance, Rembrandt – are often able to exploit this meaning potential in complex and profound ways.

Saturation

This is the scale from the most intensely saturated or 'pure' manifestations of a colour to its softest, most 'pale' or 'pastel', or dull and dark manifestations, and, ultimately, to complete desaturation, to black and white. Its key affordance lies in its ability to express emotive 'temperatures', kinds of affect. It is the scale that runs from maximum intensity of feeling to maximally subdued, maximally toned-down, indeed neutralized feeling. In context this allows many different more precise and strongly value-laden meanings. High saturation may be positive, exuberant, adventurous, but also vulgar or garish. Low saturation may be subtle and tender, but also cold and repressed, or brooding and moody.

Purity

This is the scale that runs from maximum 'purity' to maximum 'hybridity', and it has been at the heart of colour theory as it developed over the last few centuries. Many different systems of primary and mixed colours have been proposed – some physical, some psychological and some a mixture of both – and this search for primaries or basics has not resulted in a generally accepted system, but 'has proved to be remarkably inconsequential and . . . freighted with the heavy burden of ideology' (Gage, 1999: 107). Some writers have seen the issue as closely related to the question of colour names. Colours with commonly used single names, such as brown and green, would be considered pure. The names of other colours, like cyan, are mainly used by specialists, and non-specialists would refer to them by means of a composite name, for instance, blue-green. Such colours would then be perceived as mixed.

Terms like 'purity' and 'hybridity' already suggest something of the meaning potential of this aspect of colour. The 'pure' bright reds, blues and yellows of the 'Mondrian' colour scheme have become key signifiers of the ideologies of modernity, while a colour scheme of pale, anaemic cyans and mauves has become a key signifier of the ideologies of post-modernism, in which the idea of hybridity is positively valued. This is by no means the only way in which the affordances of this scale have been taken up, but it is a culturally salient one, and hence one which is currently quite widely understood.

Modulation

This is the scale that runs from fully modulated colour (for example, from a blue that is richly textured with different tints and shades, as in paintings by Cézanne) to flat colour, (as in comic strips, or paintings by Matisse). It was already recognized as a feature of colour in Goethe's *Farbenlehre (Theory of Colour)* (1970 [1810]). The affordances of modulation are various and, again, strongly value-laden. Flat colour may be perceived as simple and bold in a positive sense, or as overly basic and simplified. Modulated colour, similarly, may be perceived as subtle and doing justice to the rich texture of real colour, or as overly fussy and detailed. And, as we have discussed in chapter 5, modulation is also closely related to the issue of modality. Flat colour is generic colour, it expresses colour as an essential quality of things ('grass is green'), while modulated colour is specific colour ('the colour of grass depends on the time of day and the weather'), it attempts to show the colour of people, places and things as it is actually seen, under specific lighting conditions. Hence the truth of flat colour is an abstract truth, and the truth of modulated colour a naturalistic, perceptual truth.

Differentiation

Differentiation is the scale that runs from monochrome to the use of a maximally varied palette, and its very diversity or exuberance is one of its key semiotic affordances, as is the restraint involved in its opposite, lack of differentiation. In our analysis of an article from a home decoration magazine below, a couple 'uses nearly the whole spectrum in their house' and comment that 'it's great that there are so many bright shades in the house. It's a shame people aren't more adventurous. It's when you start being timid that things go wrong' (*House Beautiful*, September 1998: 21). So here high differentiation means 'adventurousness' and low differentiation 'timidity', but it is clear that in another context restraint might have a more positive value.

Hue

This is the scale from blue to red. In a distinctive feature theory of colour it becomes only one of the factors constituting the complex and composite meanings of colour, and maybe not even the most important one. Nevertheless, although 'the' meaning of red-in-general, of the abstract signifier 'red', cannot be established, the red end of the scale remains associated with warmth, energy, salience, foregrounding, and the blue end with cold, calm, distance, backgrounding. The cold–warm continuum has many correspondences and uses. Itten (1970) lists transparent/opaque, sedative/stimulant, rare/dense, airy/earthy, far/near, light/heavy and wet/dry. In an actual red, meanwhile, its warmth combines with other features. An actual red may, for instance, be very warm, medium dark, highly saturated, pure and modulated, and its affordances for sign-makers and sign interpreters flow from all these factors. In the next section we will see how such sets of affordances are actually taken up in a specific context, and what context-specific interests and values are at work in this process.

HOME DECORATION: COLOUR, CHARACTER AND FASHION

What colours are used in home decoration and why? The answer depends on the socio-cultural context. There have been many different traditions, including, for instance, regional differences, such as the bright blues and greens of the doors and windows of farmhouses in Staphorst, a village in the Netherlands where traditional dress is still worn. But today a new approach has developed, in which the expertise of the colour consultant plays a key role. According to Lacy (1996: 29), the entrance hall of a home signals the identity of its owner or owners:

> A yellow entrance hall usually indicates a person who has ideas and a wide field of interests. A home belonging to an academic would probably contain a distinctive shade of yellow as this colour is associated with the intellect, ideas and a searching mind. . . . A green entrance hall – say, a warm apple green – indicates a home in which children, family and pets are held in high importance. . . . A blue entrance hall indicates a place in which people have strong opinions – there could be a tendency to appear aloof as they can be absorbed too much in their own world.

In expert discourse of this kind the colours of a home above all express *character*, express the identity, the personal characteristics, and the values and interests of the home owner or owners, while the colours of workplaces (and prisons, schools, etc.) are more often discussed in terms of their *effects* on workers (prisoners, students, etc).

Most people will encounter this discourse in magazines and television makeover programmes where it is mediated by journalists, although the expertise of colour consultants and interior decorators is often explicitly drawn on. In magazines aiming at different sectors of the market, different types of home owners or celebrities may be introduced (for instance, the owner of a London art gallery versus an actor in a popular soap opera). Compare the following two quotes:

> Her latest habitat (she moves as regularly and happily as a nomad) is surprisingly spare and elegant, as you might expect from someone with a sense of the aesthetic in her genes. After all, Jane's great aunt was Nancy Lancaster, of Colefax and Fowler fame, while her brother, Henry Wyndham, is chairman of Sotheby's.
>
> (*Ideal Home and Lifestyle*, September 1998: 60)

> Guessing what Hamish and Vanessa Dows do for a living isn't too difficult – a pair of feet on the house numberplate is a dead giveaway for a couple who are both chiropodists, but it's also an indication of the fun they've had decorating their home.
>
> (*House Beautiful*, September 1998: 20)

In such articles colour choice is presented as an original and unique expression of the character and values of the home owners – as fully personal, rather than mediated by social codes. The two fun-loving chiropodists above, for instance,

> use nearly the whole spectrum in their house, from mustard yellow and leaf green in the sitting room, to brick red and blue in the dining room. Their bedroom is a soft buttery yellow combined with orange, there's lemon and lime in the breakfast room and cornflower and Wedgwood blues on the stairs. 'It's great that there are so many bright shades in the house', says Hamish. 'It's a shame people aren't more adventurous. It's when you start being timid that things go wrong.'
>
> (*House Beautiful*, September 1998: 21)

This shows the reader how colour semiosis works, but at the same time avoids the suggestion that such models can be slavishly followed, and suggests that colour semiosis should naturally flow from people's unique character and values. It is here that the affordances of colour are taken up. High colour differentiation and high saturation become signifiers of 'adventurousness', with differentiation standing for the absence of monotony and routine, and saturation for an intensity of feeling, for 'living to the full' and not being 'timid'.

A look at the actual colours in the illustrations of the article (e.g. plate 6) shows that the distinctive features are selectively used in the discourse. There are, on those bright walls, painted gold leaves and sunflowers which, Hamish and Vanessa say, 'give such a lovely Victorian feel'. Indeed, the photos show a very cluttered interior, with many retro objects, including fringed lampshades and statuettes of servile black servants. But, even without the quote and without these objects, the provenance of the leaves and sunflowers would be clear. While the colours may be highly saturated, they are also relatively dark and relatively impure, certainly by reference to Modernist bright and light interiors (and Mondrian-type pure colours), and *this* aspect of the colours, their provenance as 'historic' colours, is not explicitly discussed in the article.

Such 'historic' colours were very much in fashion in the 1990s: 'The specialist paint firm Farrow & Ball whose colours were used to recreate eighteenth- and nineteenth-century England in television adaptations of *Pride and Prejudice* and *Middlemarch*, reports that its sales have consistently risen by 40% each year over the past ten years' (*Guardian* Weekend Magazine, 19 January 2002: 67). It may be that Hamish and Vanessa's interior is not just an original expression of their character, but also follows fashion, and also takes its cues from the media. It may be that Hamish and Vanessa not only use the affordances of the distinctive features of colour to express their unique interests and values, but also base their choice of colour on 'provenance', and thereby also express the values of the place and the time where these colours come from. It may be that Hamish and Vanessa, through the way they decorate their home, symbolically identify with the values of that era, and with the nostalgia for a 'lost' Englishness which had been so salient throughout the 1990s. In this article, this is expressed in a covert way in which colour plays an absolutely crucial role. It may be that what seems so uniquely their own is socially constructed in and through the media, in discourses realized through colour.

COLOUR SCHEMES

In this last section we will discuss one final example in order to focus briefly on the question of the colour scheme. The example is a pamphlet produced to describe and explain the corporate identity change of a major publishing house in the UK (plate 7).

A number of modes are involved – colour, typeface, icons of several kinds. The pamphlet briefly describes the function of each. In the case of colour, a caption states that 'The colour palette provides a harmonious selection of 16 colours, all carefully chosen to complement the corporate colour Palgrave silver, and they should be used wherever possible.' So the deliberateness and intent is clear. Rather than the traditional layout of the colour chart, here the corporate colour is central, to indicate its status and role, and the subsidiary colours cluster around it in a regular display. This clustering is organized – in part – on the principle of gradations in hue, though given the colours chosen this cannot be achieved entirely in the manner of the traditional chart; there are gaps. Coherence has been deliberately aimed for: all the hues have to be able to collocate with the corporate colour, in its support. There is, consequently, already a strong sense of structure – both in the explicit hierarchy of colours and in the delimiting of the range of permissible 'units'. But one colour changes the overall effect of the scheme, the bright-yellow top left. Its introduction in effect makes all the colours in its palette different in their meaning-potentials. It puts this colour palette into the domain of the sharp, the bright, the upbeat – in the words of the pamphlet, 'active pursuit of ideas', 'rapid change', 'a world of challenges to be met', 'a new company and a global force in publishing', etc.

Today, colours increasingly are colours in a 'colour scheme', colours in systems of colour which can be defined on the basis of specific uses of the distinctive features we have discussed. We have come across several such schemes already: the 'historic' colour scheme, based on differentiation, relatively high saturation and dark value; the modernist 'Mondrian' colour scheme, based on purity and high saturation; the postmodern colour scheme, based on hybridity and pastel values. All these colour schemes have distinct historical placements. But they live on beyond their historical period as recognized semiotic resources which can continue to be used and combined (for instance, the bright-yellow accent in the overall postmodern scheme of Palgrave) to realize distinctly different ideological positions.

8 The third dimension

THE THIRD DIMENSION: FROM 'READER' TO 'USER'

So far we have restricted ourselves to still rather than moving images, and to two-dimensional forms of visual communication rather than three-dimensional ones such as sculpture, product design, architecture or stage set design. In this chapter we will explore to which degree the descriptive framework we have developed in this book can be applied also to the three-dimensional visual and the moving image. Our three-dimensional examples will mainly be drawn from the fields of sculpture and children's toys. Toys are of particular interest as they occupy a space somewhere in between sculptures, which are primarily symbolic objects, objects for contemplation and veneration, and 'designed objects', which are primarily objects for use, even though they may also convey symbolic messages. In addition we will consider everyday objects such as cups and motor cars, and architecture. The chapter is intended as a first exploration. We are not able, within the space of this book, to present a systematic account of all aspects of three-dimensional visual communication, as this would require too many additional concepts (some of these are discussed in van Leeuwen, 2003). Instead, we will concentrate on the concepts we have described in the preceding chapters, to show what role they play in three-dimensional visual communication. In this way we will at least be able to indicate in which ways three-dimensional visual communication is similar to and different from two-dimensional communication, and to outline the theoretical issues which follow from this.

Starting with the issue of visual representation, we found that the key categories we introduced in chapters 2 and 3 can be applied also to three-dimensional visuals, and do indeed seem sufficient to describe a wide range of such objects. Many sculptures, for example, have what we called in chapter 2 a 'narrative' structure. Take Epstein's *Jacob and the Angel* (1940), shown in figure 8.1: the arms of Jacob and the Angel form powerful vectors, relating the two participants in a complex and interesting way. The Angel's action is transactional. It has a Goal, as he holds Jacob in a firm grip. But Jacob's action, though foregrounded, is non-transactional – his arm hangs limply, and he does not hold or grab anything.

Kenneth Armitage's *People in the Wind* (1952), shown in figure 8.2, also has strong vectors, formed by the way the figures are bent forwards as they struggle against the wind. But here (as in sculptures of discus throwers, ballerinas and other active subjects) the action is 'non-transactional'. The vectors do not point at or lead to another participant, a Goal. The figures, it seems, 'strain forwards', but they do not 'strain towards something'.

'Reactions' are also common, although in sculpture the eyes do not usually form as strong a focus of attraction as they do in two-dimensional images, because they lack the strong tonal contrast between the whites of the eyes and the pupils, which, in pictures as in nature, makes eyes so salient. It is as if the added naturalism of the third dimension must

● Fig 8.1 *Jacob and the Angel* (Jacob Epstein, 1940) (Granada Television Ltd)

be counteracted by greater abstraction in other means of expression, such as colour, to prevent sculpture from crossing the line between art and the uncannily real make-believe of the waxworks show (or of certain contemporary forms of art). Nevertheless, in a sculpture like Rodin's *The Kiss* (1880), the man and the woman not only hold each other with their arms, they hold each other with their gaze as well, in a 'transactional reaction', and it is not difficult to find examples of 'non-transactional reactions' also. Jacob (figure 8.1) looks up, in a non-transactional reaction, while the Angel looks at Jacob, in a transactional reaction. Again, the Angel acts on Jacob, but Jacob does not act on the Angel. Arnheim's description of Michelangelo's Moses provides another example. 'The deflection of the lawgiver's head and the fierce concentration of his glance introduce an oblique vector that moves outwards like the beam of a lighthouse. But no goal object is included' (Arnheim, 1982: 46).

Even the design of objects and buildings can be vectorial and hence 'narrative', as shown in figure 8.3. The vector formed by the tailfins of 1950s cars, for instance, repre-sented (in an abstract way) the idea of dynamic motion, as if it was not enough that cars are in fact dynamic moving objects, regardless of whether they have tailfins or not. The fact that cars do not have tailfins now points to the ideological dimension of sculptural representation: the meanings represented were those of the 'jet age'. But here an important

🔺 Fig 8.2 *People in the Wind* (Kenneth Armitage, 1952) (Tate Gallery)

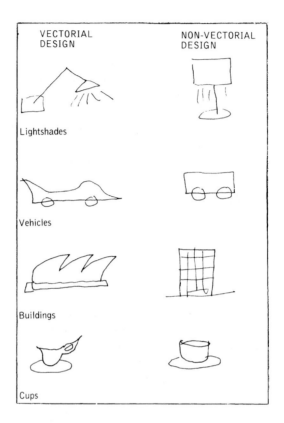

VECTORIAL DESIGN	NON-VECTORIAL DESIGN
Lightshades	
Vehicles	
Buildings	
Cups	

⬥ **Fig 8.3 Vectorial and non-vectorial lightshades, cups, cars and buildings**

complication occurs. In the case of objects, the ideational relations we have discussed in chapters 2 and 3 can be realized in two ways: they can be realized by the designer, as forms to be 'read' by a viewer, as when a cup has a 'dynamic', vectorial handle (and also, of course, in the case of the pictorial or decorative designs printed or painted on, or moulded or carved in, the cup); or they can be realized by the user of the object, as when the cup is held or drunk from, in a 'transactional action' with its user – the vectorial handle is then a 'non-transactional action' from the point of view of the design of the cup, and a potential for transactional action, a means, from the point of view of its use.

Reactions can even occur in objects. The toy telephone shown in figure 8.4 not only includes the dog's tongue, as an oblique vector signifying a non-transactional speaking; it also has eyes. The inclusion of eyes is in fact quite common in toys for young children, particularly in toys with the themes of time (clocks), communication (toy telephones) and transport (toy locomotives and cars), as if to encourage the child to form an emotive, personalized bond with these three key technologies as early as possible.

⚫ **Fig 8.4 Toy telephone**

In contrast to two-dimensional visuals, sculptures rarely include a Setting. Their setting is the environment in which they are displayed, a gallery, a niche in a church, or a public square. It is not a *represented* Setting. Of course, sculptures *can* include a Setting, as in the works of Edward Kienholz and George Segal, for instance, or Asian sculpture gardens, such as the Tiger Balm Gardens in Singapore. But in contemporary Western sculpture the inclusion of a Setting is relatively rare. Decontextualization, it seems, has to counteract the added naturalism of the third dimension. Sculptures do, however, often have another participant, the pedestal on which they stand. Such pedestals can be (mere) framing devices, creating a degree of separation between the sculpture and its environment, and so enhancing its status as a representation, an object for contemplation, set apart from its environment. But they can also and at the same time form part of the representation, as in Canova's *Paolina Borghese* (1805), which has Paolina resting on a couch which forms also a sarcophagus-like support for her reclining body. The absence of such framing can have a strong effect, as in the lifesize bronze of a middle-aged, corpulent man in a raincoat and hat placed as if mingling with the shoppers in the middle of the footpath of a busy shopping street in Amsterdam.

Turning now to 'conceptual' rather than 'narrative' structures of representation, these, too, can be found in sculpture. Miró's *Woman* (1970), reproduced in figure 8.5, is what, in chapter 3, we called an 'analytical' representation. The sculpture does not just play with the forms of found objects, making eyes of the headlights and a mouth of the windscreen of a car; it is also an 'analysis' of 'Woman'. 'Woman', in all its generality, is the 'Carrier', and the parts, the 'Possessive Attributes', are, in Miró's conception: a head which is also the empty shell of a car; an upper body which is also a tray on which two aggressively pointed breasts are presented to the viewer; and a lower body which is a barrel-shaped container with a vagina-like slit and two handles to hold her by. When we visited an

○ Fig 8.5 *Woman* (Joan Miró, 1970) (Parellada, Barcelona)

exhibition of Miró's sculptures we noted that the misogynistic quality of Miró's 'analysis' was not lost on the viewers. There was a guest book in which the visitors of the gallery could write down their impressions. Many had used the opportunity to draw a quick caricature of a Miró woman with a contemptuous comment such as 'woman????' These readings contrasted sharply with the artspeak in the catalogue, which described the formal qualities of the sculptures only, and did not dwell on Miró's way of representing the female gender.

Giacometti's *Hour of the Traces* (1930), shown in figure 8.6, is an analysis of the genderless human being, of the human condition in general. The parts: a kind of antenna, with an abstract eye, forms an active sensory tentacle and protrudes from the sculpture at an angle, constituting an oblique vector; a rigid rusty frame, the body; and, within the

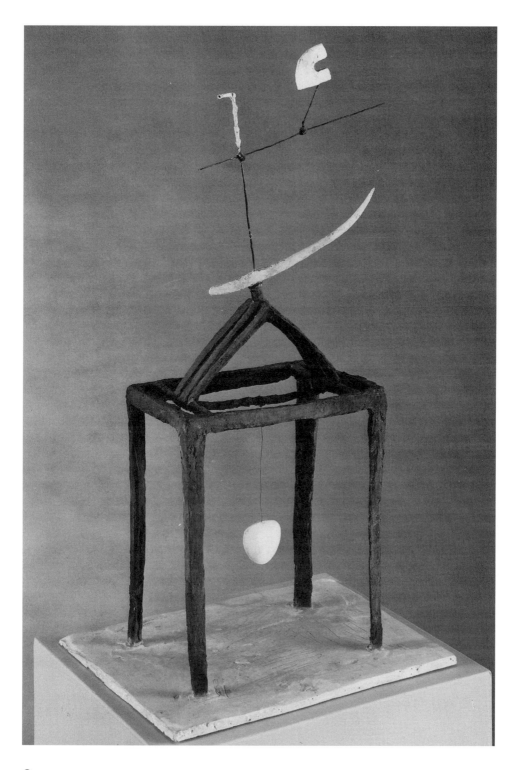

△ Fig 8.6 *Hour of the Traces* (Alberto Giacometti, 1930) (Tate Gallery)

open frame, a plaster heart, suspended on a thin string, and moving slightly to and fro. Thus two actions are embedded in the analysis, both non-transactional: the action of the sensory apparatus, and the movement of the heart – the human being as a skeletal frame that is alive and surveys its environment.

We might add that analytical sculpture is used not only in art but also in science – for instance, to show the construction of a molecule; or as a teaching aid, for instance in anatomy, in which case the parts can often be detached from the whole. The kinetic design of sculptures and other objects, the way they can move or be made to move, taken apart and put back together again, and so on, is a subject to which we cannot do justice in this chapter, as it would again demand the introduction of a new set of concepts (but see van Leeuwen and Caldas-Coulthard, 2004).

The third dimension creates an additional option in representation, a relation between the representational structure and the position of the viewer. Seen from the side Epstein's *Jacob and the Angel* (figure 8.1) has a narrative structure ('transactional action'). It is in the first place about what Jacob and the Angel *do*. But if we look at the Angel from behind (figure 8.7), we are faced with an 'analysis' of the Angel, and a very striking one: the three

⬤ Fig 8.7 *Jacob and the Angel* from behind (Jacob Epstein, 1940) (Granada Television Ltd)

principal 'Possessive Attributes' Epstein emphasizes are the Angel's long hair, his wings – and his balls.

Not all sculptures use this possibility. One can imagine a continuum running from reliefs, which perhaps differ from two-dimensional images only in terms of modality, to fully 'multifaceted' sculptures such as *Jacob and the Angel*. In between there are sculptures which, though free-standing, are clearly not designed to be seen from behind and leave the back 'unworked', perhaps because they were meant to be placed against a wall or in a niche. And even when a sculpture is a fully multifaceted representation, like *Jacob and the Angel*, its placement in a particular environment can block access to alternative viewing positions, and hence to alternative readings. This may be because the work is placed with its back against the wall, or because a barrier prevents the viewer from access to other than more or less frontal viewing positions. But it may also be done in subtler ways. When we first analysed *Jacob and the Angel*, it was placed in the centre of the octagonal entrance hall of the Tate Gallery, in such a way that the viewer first saw it from the side, with the Angel on the left. In other words, its position favoured the narrative reading, the drama of the sculpture, rather than Epstein's striking 'analysis' of the Angel. But the viewer did have access to the other sides, as the sculpture was placed in the centre of the hall.

Playmobil figures such as those shown in figure 8.8 are also analytical structures. They show the significant attributes, the significant characteristics, of (for example) an 'ethnic family'. The family has five members – a father, a mother and three children. Each member of the family has black hair and dark skin. Note the difference from the neutrally labelled 'family set': the composition of the family is the same, and all the members of the family have pink skin, but they differ in the colour of their hair and therefore have individual characteristics as well as social characteristics, whereas (lesson number one) the members of the 'ethnic family' are 'others' who 'all look the same'. The children of the two families are dressed identically, but the parents are not. Lesson number two: second-generation immigrants are already 'more like us'. The Playmobil company brochure says that these

⬥ Fig 8.8 Playmobil 'family set' and 'ethnic family'

toys 'form an aid to the training of your minds' and will 'acquaint children with what they will meet in the big real world' – but not in an entirely neutral fashion. As we have said in chapter 3, any analytical structure is only one of the many ways in which a given 'Carrier' can be analysed.

We have to remember, of course, that Playmobil figures enter into representation in two ways, like our earlier example of cups with vectorial handles (figure 8.4). On the one hand, they are like sculptures, pre-designed representations, to be 'read' by the child; on the other hand, they have movable limbs and detachable parts and they can hold objects in their hands. Children can therefore use them to create a variety of representational structures, narrative 'scenes', and they can even subvert the pre-designed representations, for instance by giving an 'ethnic' child red hair. They can also create their own classificatory or analytical arrangements, for instance by making a display of different kinds of Playmobil children on their toy shelf or by creating a new analysis of the 'family', with only a mother, perhaps, or with five children of different 'ethnic' origins (the arrangement of *Our Society and Others*, figure 3.29, could be reconstructed with Playmobil figures!). In the same way a cup can be used, not only in the 'transactions' of holding or drinking, but also: to create an analytical structure, as when the cup is arranged on a sideboard together with the other parts of the set to which it belongs, or on the kitchen shelf, to become a 'Possessive Attribute' of the 'Carrier' 'dishes'; or to create a classificational structure, as when a number of different cups are arranged symmetrically in a shop window or in a design exhibition.

The *Vitrinen* (display cases) of the German avant-garde artist Joseph Beuys are an intriguing example of the classificational sculpture. They are the kind of sculpture which is usually referred to as an 'installation' – glass display cases containing a variety of objects, some of them altered by Beuys. *Vitrine 2* (1960–70), for instance, contains a film can (itself containing a film which features a performance by Beuys), a pair of boxing gloves, a sausage, a cassette player (with a tape of music performed by Beuys), a Beethoven score with a small blackboard eraser on it, two wineglasses (one coated with a white substance, the other looking as though something has been burnt in it), and a zinc box. Clearly a work like this raises the question of what these objects have in common (what their 'superordinate' is, in our terms), and this is exactly the question Beuys' interpreters have asked. According to Theewen (1993: 139), *Verwandschaft* ('relatedness') is the key to understanding Beuys' *Vitrinen*: 'By bringing related objects together an association between them is created', and in the case of the *Vitrine* we have just described this association is that all the objects 'have played a role in performances of Beuys, and [that they] all contain something' (1993: 29).

The third kind of conceptual structure discussed in chapter 3 was the symbolic relation. We saw how in pictures an overall colour – a blue haze, or a golden glow – could realize what we called a 'suggestive symbolic' process, endowing the depicted scene with an overall significance, 'saying', as it were, 'this scene is cold and desolate' (in the case of the blue haze) or 'these objects are very valuable' (in the case of the golden glow). Colour can play this role also in the case of three-dimensional objects – think of the colours of cars, for instance, the difference between a black, a bright-red and a white Mercedes, say.

But in addition to colour there are other factors, such as the material from which an object is made, the way the surface of a sculpture or other object is 'worked', or the overall shape of the objects, in so far as these are not determined by considerations of naturalistic representation, or by the functions served by an object. Giacometti's *Man Pointing* (1947) is much less 'analytical' than the sculptures we have so far discussed. It places no emphasis on the distinctness of the parts of the human body. Even the facial features are hardly stated – small indentations to indicate a mouth and eyes. The sculpture does of course have a clear vector, as the man is making an expansive oratorical gesture. The most striking characteristic of this sculpture, however, is its rough, black, craggy surface. It is difficult to put into words exactly what is suggested by this surface, but whatever transcoding we attempt it will have to express somehow that this figure is 'weather-beaten', affected by exposure to – but here we can fill in a number of things – the elements suffering, ageing and so on. The sculpture is abstract enough to allow all these readings and more.

The same applies, again, to other kinds of three-dimensional objects. Cups can be smooth, made of delicate china, suggesting, perhaps, an overall quality of elegance and refinement; or they can be sturdy and solid and made of brick-red terracotta, suggesting, perhaps, an overall quality of down-to-earth simplicity. Cars can be elongated and streamlined, suggesting power and speed, or, as in the case of the currently fashionable 'retro' look, rounded and egglike, suggesting a safe cocoon, a kind of womb.

The second kind of symbolic relation we discussed was the 'symbolic attributive' process, where one represented participant has no other function than to endow another with symbolic significance. This occurs, for instance, in some of Miró's sculptures, where birds and eggs attribute symbolic qualities to the figures depicted (usually 'women'). But it occurs also in toys for young children, where telephones can have wheels (an early lesson about the concept of communication as 'transport of information' and 'bridging the distance' rather than 'sharing of information'), and 'interactive learning centres' for children aged 2½ to 5 ('6 built-in functions which teach the alphabet, numbers, shapes, colours, sound effects and nursery rhymes', and all this for £29.50) have a steering wheel and dashboard, as a symbol of the power and control afforded by knowledge. Or in adult toys: emblems and other decorations on cars, for instance. Or in architecture, where sculptures and murals can become symbolic attributes for buildings.

On the whole, then, we feel that the account of visual representation we have presented in chapters 2 and 3 can be applied to three-dimensional visual communication. Yet there are some significant differences. First, three-dimensional objects can be placed on a continuum which runs from objects that allow only one reading (by offering the reader only one aspect, usually the front) to objects which allow more than one reading, depending on the position of the viewer relative to the object.

Second, three-dimensional objects can be placed on a continuum which runs from objects which have been designed only to be looked at, only to be 'read', to objects which enter into representational relations in three ways: (1) the relations encoded in the design of the object itself, to be 'read' only by the viewer; (2) *interactive* relations between the object and its *user* (e.g. holding the cup, or drinking from it); and (3) *conceptual* relations created by the user (e.g. creating a classificational syntagm with a number of different cups).

Third, even when an object does have a potential for multifaceted representation and/or for being 'used' as well as 'read', external conditions can inhibit this potential, block the viewer's access to alternative reading positions, or to interactive engagement with the representational potential of the object.

INTERACTIVE VIEWING

We will now turn to the interactive relations we discussed in chapter 4, trying to explore, again, how applicable they are to three-dimensional visual communication. In that chapter we distinguished between 'demand' pictures from which represented participants address the viewer directly with their gaze and 'want something from the viewer', and 'offer' pictures which position the viewer as an observer only, and offer the represented participants as 'information' to be taken in by the viewer.

Clearly, this distinction can be applied also to sculpture – but, again, with a difference. Henry Moore's *Recumbent Figure* (1938), shown in figure 8.9, addresses the viewer

Fig 8.9 *Recumbent Figure* (Henry Moore, 1938) (Tate Gallery)

powerfully. Although the eyes are little more than indentations in the surface of the stone, the whole attitude of the figure suggests a concentrated look. But, as viewers, we can take up a position from which that look *will* directly address us (as did the photographer, in the case of figure 8.9), so that the picture forms a 'demand'; or a position from which the figure looks past us, at something else, or at nothing in particular, in any case, at something not included in our view, and in that case the look will become a 'non-transactional reaction'. In the two-dimensional medium we cannot, as viewers, decide whether or not we will allow ourselves to be directly addressed by a represented participant; the decision has been made for us. In the three-dimensional medium we can – that is, if the placement of the sculpture allows us to do so. In the Tate Gallery, Moore's sculpture could have been placed in such a way that the figure's gaze would fix the viewer immediately upon entering the room. But this was not done when we viewed the sculpture there, and as a result the figure became just one of a number of Moore's works, presented as part of a classificational syntagm, and favouring the 'offer' rather than the 'demand'.

The same would be true of the toy telephone (figure 8.4). The gaze of this telephone can only become a 'demand' by virtue of an active decision on the part of its user. Some toys, of course, lend themselves more to this than others. Playmobil characters have small black dots for eyes. They are biased more towards the 'offer for information' than towards the interactive 'demand'. And the eyes of many 'boys' ' dolls (Batmen, Crash-dummies, Megazords, etc.) are often obscured by helmets, masks or dark glasses. The eyes of 'girls' ' dolls (and of many cuddly animal toys), on the other hand, tend to be large and highly detailed. While boys are steered towards a more manipulative relation to their dolls, for girls the look, the interactive dimension, is made to matter more. And the same is true for very young children: even their bedclothes, pillowcases, cups, plates may have eyes, and are thus personalized, animated, capable of entering into a 'direct address' relation with the child. As with many other things, some of this may well live on, unconsciously, in the adult relation with objects.

The same reasoning can be applied to the other interactive dimensions we discussed in chapter 4. In principle the viewer can decide whether to see the object from close up or from a distance, frontally (hence with 'involvement') or from an oblique angle (hence with 'detachment'); from above (hence from a position of power over the object) or from below (hence from a position in which the object has power over the viewer). We say 'in principle', because here, too, the viewer's choice may be restricted by external factors, by barriers that prevent viewers from coming up close or seeing the object from a different angle. And large objects can make the high-angle viewpoint and the close distance impossible. What towers over us has, by design, power over us, and is, by design, socially distant: the vertical dimension is the dimension of power and reverential distance, the dimension of 'highly placed' people, places and things. In this connection it is also significant that sculptures, as works of 'high' art, cannot usually be approached from the most intimate distance, the distance that makes touching possible: as soon as the gallery visitor comes too close, a guard will become alert.

When sculptures are taken out of their original context and moved into another, their interactive meanings may change significantly. They may be, literally, taken down from the pedestal – in a church perhaps – where they were to be looked at from below, with reverence, to be moved into a gallery, where they are positioned at a level of equality, and viewed from a more 'familiar' distance: Michelangelo's *David*, removed to the rotunda of a museum, no longer calls to the citizens of Florence and is unaware of their calling on him, and now 'can be explored by the viewer, but makes no advances to him' (Arnheim, 1982: 50; also Hodge and Kress, 1988: 201–3).

MODALITY IN THREE DIMENSIONS

In chapter 5 we described visual modality as resulting from the degree to which certain means of pictorial expression (colour, representational detail, depth, tonal shades, etc.) are used. Each of these dimensions can be seen as a scale, running from the absence of any rendition of detail to maximal representation of detail, or from the absence of any rendition of depth to maximally deep perspective. And on each of these scales there is a point that represents the way the given pictorial dimension is used in what could be called standard naturalism. To the degree that the use of a dimension is reduced, it becomes, at least in one respect, more abstract, 'less than real'. To the degree that it is amplified, it becomes 'more than real', and we associated this with a 'sensory coding orientation', an emphasis on sensory pleasure (or displeasure, as in the case of 'more than real' horror images), and an attempt to come as close as possible to a representation that involves all the senses.

Some of these play much the same role in three-dimensional visuals. Clearly, sculptures and toys can represent what they represent in naturalistic detail or more abstractly. And when the shape of everyday design objects no longer betrays their function, when, for instance, refrigerators, washing machines and kitchen storage cabinets all become sleek featureless white boxes, there is also a strong sense of abstraction. The same can be argued for buildings. Also, like pictures, three-dimensional representations can include several levels of modality. The heads of Henry Moore's *King and Queen* (1952–3), for instance, shown in figure 8.10, are abstract symbols, while their hands are rendered in naturalistic detail. This expresses the contradictory nature of the powerful. Their minds may have lost touch with the detail of everyday concrete reality, but look at their hands – they are after all still human, and their work, their doing, is still the work of humans. Machin and Suleiman (2004) have pointed out that in American computer war games the weaponry is represented in realistic detail, while the settings have lower modality, forming a generic desert that could be anywhere. This foregrounds American technological supremacy and backgrounds the specifics of specific conflicts. In a Lebanese computer war game produced by Hezbollah, the landscape is reconstructed from photographs of the sites of actual conflicts and represented in more detail. Here the specifics of historical and geographical accuracy matter.

The representation of detail in toys is particularly interesting. Barthes' still highly readable essay about the semantics of toys (1973: 53ff.) is now perhaps overtaken by semiotic events. He describes French toys as highly detailed, highly naturalistic miniature

Fig 8.10 *King and Queen* (Henry Moore, 1952–3) (Tate Gallery)

versions of adult objects – and notes how unsatisfactory they are, therefore, both from the point of view of pleasure, of the sensory dimension, and from the point of view of their interactive potential, as objects to play with: 'the child can only identify himself as owner, as user, never as creator; he does not invent the world, he uses it: there are, prepared for him, action without adventure, without wonder, without joy' (1973: 54). Toys of this kind can be seen in museums such as London's Museum of Childhood. One's first impression on seeing Victorian toys is that children are addressed as miniature adults, their subjectivity 'scaled down', but not 'reduced', from that of the adult world. This is represented through a large number of semiotic modes: the materials (glass, clothes of various kinds, metals, etc. – all of them rarely, if at all, used in contemporary toys) as much as the miniature naturalism of the represented objects. Today's toys vary in their detail. Toys for young children are abstract. Shapes and textures are brought down to their essentials. Locomotives have featureless wheels, one featureless chimney, two yellow circles for windows. They are, from the point of view of detail of representation, like the simplest line drawings. As the child gets older, detail increases. The wheels of the locomotives get spokes and driveshafts. The texture of the machine's body acquires detail. Headlights with miniature Fresnel lenses are added. But on the whole the contemporary toy remains simple, essentialized, as for instance (again) in the popular Playmobil figures, where the eyes are two dots, the mouth a curved line, the hair an almost featureless helmet, with a few indentations suggesting texture and the length signifying gender. Girls' dolls, on the other hand (and other girls' toys: realistic washing machines, 'beauty shops', vacuum cleaners, dolls' cots), imitate the adult world, or at least that of the glamour girl, the housewife and the mother, much more so than boys' toys, which depict a make-believe world of science-fiction vehicles and weapons, or a world of dinosaurs and other monsters. The latter are often 'more than real', with highly textured, glistening scales, irregular teeth, and menacing eyes, set behind wrinkled lids. They are designed to create the kind of sensory, visceral reaction also sought, for instance, in horror films. Cuddly animal toys also tend to be 'more than real', with exaggeratedly soft furs and large moist eyes, this time to enhance the sensory pleasures of holding and touching. Researching this chapter, we spent many hours in toy shops as well as in toy museums, and could not help being struck by the contrast between the 'bourgeois' naturalistic toys Barthes described and today's make believe world of brightly coloured plastic and creatures and objects from fantasy stories.

The role of colour in the modality of three-dimensional visual representation also resembles that of the two-dimensional visuals. Some of Miró's sculptures of 'women', for instance, are painted in bright, primary colours – yellow, blue and red. As a result they are schematic and analytical from the point of view of representational detail, a simplified, abstract view of 'woman', but 'more than real', 'sensory' from the point of view of colour. Miró's women are not just machine-like assemblages of parts, they are also pleasurably colourful ('woman' as a machine for pleasure). Many toys, especially toys for young children, have exactly the same kind of modality configuration: abstract and schematized, 'conceptual', from the point of view of colour; 'un-naturalistic' primary colours, colours for the sake of pleasure rather than naturalistic representation. This 'sensory' aspect is then further enhanced by the way these toys appeal to all the senses, and include touch and sound, as stressed in this description of the 'Chicco animal train': 'a locomotive featuring eight different animal sounds and four different train sounds. Sounds are activated by pressing appropriately shaped buttons.' Again, for older children colour can become more naturalistic, as in Thomas the Tank Engine, which replaces bright reds, yellows, blues and greens with more mute steel blue, grey and black, and just a touch of red. And, while the colour in all these examples is unmodulated, the colour of girls' dolls becomes more varied, with blushes on the cheeks, shadows under the eyes, a shine on the lips. And the same applies to the slimy greens and greys and pinks on dinosaurs and monsters.

The materials used in three-dimensional representation, similarly, can be motivated naturalistically, as when toy cars are made of metal, or cuddly animals of soft, furry materials (though, on the other hand, even toy pigs can be furry!). But they can also be 'less than real', abstracting from the variety and specificity of the range of materials available, as in the case of plastic. To quote Barthes again,

> Many toys are now moulded from complicated mixtures; the plastic material of which they are made has an appearance at once gross and hygienic, it destroys all the pleasure, the sweetness, the humanity of touch. . . . Henceforth, toys are chemical in substance and colour; their very material introduces one to coenaesthetics of use, not pleasure.
>
> (1973: 55)

Again, materials can have 'more than real' modality, when their choice is motivated not by an attempt to make the object look like what it represents, but by an attempt to create pleasure or displeasure. And this can apply also to everyday objects, and to buildings, if we replace naturalism by an attempt to reveal the material from which the object is actually made and divergence from naturalism by attempts to conceal these in one direction (say, plain sheets of a synthetic material over bricks) or another (say, timber cladding over bricks or concrete).

In other respects, however, three-dimensional modality differs from two-dimensional modality. There is no need to *represent* depth: the object already has depth, by virtue of its three-dimensionality. And there is no need to *represent* the play of light and shade: it already occurs, naturally. It is to compensate for these intrinsic naturalistic qualities that most Western sculpture (1) is decontextualized, lacking a Setting; (2) refrains from using colour as a means of representation, except in the sense of overall, symbolic colour; and (3) increasingly tends towards highly reduced forms of representation. In this way 'high art', which seeks to go beyond the mere replication of reality by representing an ideal of beauty or an abstract truth, distinguishes itself from everyday sculpture – from the dummies in shop windows, from girls' dolls, from miniature dinosaurs, and so on. These need not themselves be naturalistic in every dimension in any case, and may use reduced naturalism either for didactic purposes, as in toys for young children, or to create class distinctions in taste, as with the more stylized dummies in expensive shops.

COMPOSITION IN THREE DIMENSIONS

Many sculptures and other three-dimensional objects do not clearly polarize between left and right, top and bottom, centre and margin, but when they do, the values of Given and New, Ideal and Real and Centre and Margin apply, we think, in the same way as they do in two-dimensional visual communication. Yet the third dimension does introduce additional factors.

In figure 8.1 we saw Epstein's *Jacob and the Angel* as it would have been seen by visitors entering the Tate Millbank Gallery when the work was positioned in the centre of the gallery's octagonal entrance hall. Like God in figures 6.5 and 6.9, the Angel against whose force Jacob is so helpless is Given, and Jacob's helplessness is New, the focus of the drama. But moving to the other side, the viewer can reverse this, and make Jacob Given and the Angel New, provided access to the other side is not blocked. The same is true for other multifaceted sculptures with two or more 'polarized' participants, such as Rodin's *The Kiss*, where, depending on your point of view, either the man can be Given and the woman New, or the woman Given and the man New. This is why photographs cannot do justice to multifaceted sculptures – a photo can always give only one angle, and hence one reading. The same is not true, however, for Ideal and Real and Centre and Margin. These relations cannot be inverted by changing the angle from which the work is viewed. In other words, the horizontal dimension allows interactivity; the vertical dimension and centrality do not.

Ideal and Real and Centre and Margin are often the most significant compositional dimensions in three-dimensional visual composition. Architecture provides perhaps the clearest example. Left and right are not usually polarized. Horizontally there is symmetry, but vertically there is not. The vertical dimension is used to polarize, to produce difference, with the Ideal, the element(s) that give(s) the building its more general and 'ideal' significance on top – the tower, for instance, with its significant emblems, the cross, or the clock, the gable stone on Amsterdam canal houses, the frieze high up on the Greek temple. Below, on the other hand, is the space of the Real – the forecourts where we meet, the doors through which we enter. More generally, the façade of a building, its vertical dimension, is the building we 'read'; the horizontal dimension, the floor plan, is the building we 'use':

> the compositional spectacle in the upright dimension is essentially visual. It restricts the user to observation from a distance. . . . In the horizontal plane, the corresponding dynamics involves the user directly and is therefore largely social. The level plan is the arena of human action.
>
> (Arnheim, 1982: 213)

Figure 8.11, shows an example of centrality in an architectural façade: the canopy with the Madonna, in the centre of the façade of the Church of Santa Maria della Spina in Pisa.

Multifaceted objects add further dimensions to three-dimensional composition, and allow (at least in principle) front and back, and the left and right side (and, in the case of open structures, an interior centre and the exterior) to be used for the production of difference. Of the latter we have already seen an example in figure 8.6 – the plaster heart in

● Fig 8.11 Church of Santa Maria della Spina (Arnheim, 1982)

the centre of the rigid frame of Giacometti's *Hour of the Traces*. But not all multifaceted objects use these dimensions. As in nature, where trees or mountains do not have a front or back (other than one which stems from our positions towards them, e.g. which side of the mountain we live on), objects can be the same, and have the same meaning, whichever side we view them from. Sculptures of the 'Three Graces', for instance, are usually composed in the round, offering essentially the same view from whichever side one approaches them. And the same pattern can be observed in some children's toys, for instance a kind of ball with symmetrically distributed pictures illustrating nursery rhymes (although 'the one that ends up on top determines which song is heard'). Or you find it in buildings, such as the Queen Victoria Building in Sydney, which, in its latest reincarnation as a shopping centre, has, on every side, a central entrance and shop windows; or perfectly round buildings such as the Temple of Vesta in Rome, or the Pantheon. In other cases, however, front and back especially differ in meaning. It is tempting here to take the human body as a metaphor, with the front as the public side, the side where we articulate how we want to be read, and the back as the non-social side, the private side which is not meant to be viewed and often has no meaning except perhaps for those with whom we are most intimate. This is why, paradoxically, it can also be the most revealing, as in the case of Epstein's Angel (figure 8.7). This idea is worked out in more detail in van Leeuwen (2003).

In chapter 3 we argued that the structures of diagrams (the top–down path of the taxonomy, the left–right path of the flowchart, the digital network) are modelled on forms of social organization. Perhaps it can be argued along the same lines that composition, both two- and three-dimensional, is ultimately modelled either on the 'non-social' round-ness of the natural forms such as trees and mountains, or on the polarized human body, with the head as the Ideal, the feet as the Real, the heart as the Centre, movement and action as the more interactive and dynamic horizontal dimension, and the front and the back as, respectively, the social and public and the non-social and private side. As Lakoff and Johnson said,

> Spatial orientations arise from the fact that we have bodies of the sort we have and that they function as they do in our physical environment. Orientational metaphors have a basis in our physical *and* cultural experience. Though the polar opposites, up–down, in–out, etc., are physical in nature, the orientational metaphors based on them can vary from culture to culture.
>
> (1980: 14, our italics)

THE MOVING IMAGE

The representational, interactive and compositional patterns we have discussed in this book also apply to the moving image, as shown by a number of our examples in this book. Yet the addition of movement does of course lead to differences, and it is these differences we will discuss in the final section of this chapter.

Starting with the narrative processes we discussed in chapter 2, here the principal difference is that the role of the vector is taken over by movement. Instead of, for instance, a vector formed by an outstretched arm, as in figure 2.15, the process will be realized by the action of raising the arm and pointing the hand. Usually these actions are figurative, recognizable as driving, walking, jumping, pointing and so on. But they may also be abstract – as, for instance, in Walt Disney's animation film *Fantasia* (1941) – or in technical films, where arrows may be animated, unfolding in front of our eyes.

But there is a complication. In moving images the relation between Actors and Goals may be represented in a single shot, showing both Actor and Goal; or in two subsequent shots, the first showing the Actor, the second the Goal (or vice versa), as demonstrated in figure 8.12. In both cases we see a soldier (Actor) and civilians (Goal). But in the one case they are spatially connected, shown together in the same shot; in the other they are *disconnected*, shown in separate shots. As every film and television director knows, the two shots in such a disconnected syntagm (usually referred to as a pair of 'reverse angle shots') have to be 'matched' carefully, to restore the connection. They have to be taken from the same side of the imaginary line running between the participants and from approximately the same horizontal angle, to make it appear that the participants are facing each other and looking at each other. The tonality of the two shots has to match as well, for instance by ensuring that they are shot under the same lighting conditions, and through colour grading, removing any discrepancies between the colour rendition of the shots.

Should we see such a 'disconnected' narrative process as one unit of meaning or two? Is it the equivalent of a sentence like 'The soldier shoots the villagers', or of a formulation that expresses the soldier's agency less directly – for instance, 'The soldier fires. The villagers are shot'? But such an attempt at translating moving images into words cannot fully capture the difference. Filmic 'disconnection' has no parallel in language. It does have semiotic potential, however. It can, for instance, show people as 'isolated' individuals, even while they are interacting with others, and it can radically disconnect Actors from the Goals of their actions, and from the effect of their actions on these Goals, just as happens, for instance, in long-distance telephone calls or the firing of long-range missiles.

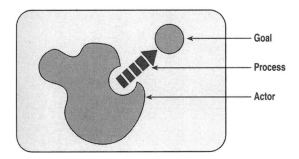

⬘ **Fig 8.12 Connected and disconnected narrative process (Goodman and Graddol, 1996)**

The disconnection between Actors and Goals is an aspect of 'film language' that only developed twenty-five years or so after the invention of the medium, and it has been the subject of much discussion in film theory, not least because it allows 'faking'. No history of the medium omits the experiments of 'Constructivist' film-makers in the Soviet Union of the early 1920s. In one of these experiments, film maker Lev Kuleshov cut together shots of two actors meeting and greeting each other. Each actor was filmed separately, in a different location. They had therefore never actually played out the scene together. Once the two shots were spliced together, however, the two appeared to meet in one and the same place, an effect which Kuleshov called 'creative geography'. In 1930s *Tarzan* films, encounters with wild animals were often faked in this way, by intercutting stock shots of wild animals with shots of actors acting out the appropriate reactions and actions in a studio set. The famous French film critic André Bazin (1967), on the other hand, favoured the 'connected' method. To see a real event happening in real time was for him the quintessential film experience and the quintessential power of the medium. He praised

Actor

Cut to

Goal

⬣ Fig 8.12—Continued

the seal hunt in the documentary *Nanook of the North* (1921), a scene taken as one long, unedited shot of a seal being harpooned through a hole in the ice.

In contrast to the still image, the moving image can realize events that have neither an Actor nor a Goal. Shots of shimmering light on softly rippling water create a sense of pure process, pure movement, in which it is hardly possible to disentangle process and participants, and in which participants, if they can be discerned at all, are 'caught up' in the process in a way that is neither 'active' nor 'passive'. The still image equivalent of such a shot would be a kind of abstract pattern, lacking the dynamic sense of 'action' or 'event'.

The choice between 'connection' and 'disconnection' also exists in the case of reactions. Films can show Reacters and Phenomena either in one and the same shot, or in two subsequent shots. This pattern, known as 'the point-of-view shot', ties together three shots, with the Reacter reappearing in the third shot, so that the Phenomenon is wedged in between two shots of the Reacter. Here too the shots have to carefully 'matched'. If, for instance, the Reacter looks down, the Phenomenon has to be shot from above, and if the Reacter looks at a moving Phenomenon, the angle of his or her head and the direction of his or her gaze should have changed in the third shot, to match the distance travelled by the Phenomenon during the second shot. Disconnected reactions have a particularly strong 'subjective', 'first-person' feel, as the viewer is looking at the Phenomenon 'through the eyes of the Reacter'. A variant shows the Reacter and the Phenomenon in the same image, 'over the shoulder' of the Reacter, hence also from the Reacter's point of view. But here we do not look at the Phenomenon 'through the Reacter's eyes', and the effect is less emotionally involving, as we see the Reacter from behind and therefore do not see his or her reactions to the Phenomenon. It is the angle used in contemporary computer war games, to make players identify with the 'special-ops' soldier characters they play (figure 8.13).

Finally, while still images have developed dialogue balloons to realize verbal processes, in moving images dialogue is not represented visually, through writing, but directly, through speech. The synchronization between the speech and the Speaker's lip movements replaces the vector that connects Speaker and Speech. Without such synchronization, moving images cannot signify that the speech we hear is actually spoken by the Speaker we see. Once the link between the Speaker and the dialogue has been established, the dialogue may become 'off screen', continuing, for instance, while viewers watch the reaction of a listener.

Turning now to the interactive dimension, in chapter 4 we have already seen how camera positions can create symbolic relations between viewers and what is depicted in an image. Moving images are no different in this respect, with one proviso: in moving images the relationship becomes *dynamic*. It can change in front of our eyes. The camera can zoom in to a closer shot, or zoom out to a wider shot; it can crane up to a high angle or crane down to a low angle; and so on. And even when the camera is not moving, the participants themselves can move, walk away from or towards the camera, or walk up or down a flight of stairs with the camera tilting up or down to follow them, thus changing the angle from which viewers see the participants. In other words, the moving image can represent social relations as dynamic, flexible and changeable. Distance and angle can be *dynamicized*, and this in two ways: *subject-initiated*, with the represented participants initiating the change, or *camera-initiated*, with the image-maker initiating the change (the contrast of course

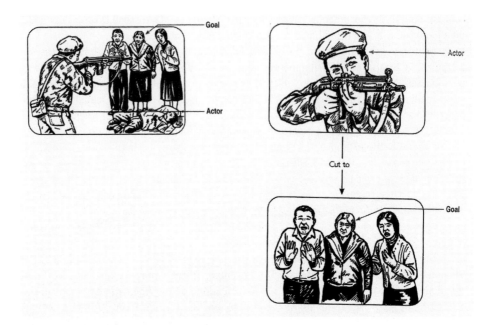

◭ Fig 8.13 'Overshoulder' shot in a computer war game

also applies to synthetic images where a camera is not involved). In the first case, the visual text takes a 'neutral' stance, a stance of 'recording' what is taking place (even though the events may of course be staged). In the second case, the image-maker more overtly positions viewers towards what is being represented.

In most films distance and angle change constantly. In other words, what in the case of still images has never moved in the mainstream, cubism, the use of multiple perspectives, has become so commonplace in movies that it is now hardly noticed. The only difference is that films show the different perspectives one after the other, rather than at the same time. Figure 8.14 shows how such changes of distance and angle can be used to signify both the relations between 'characters', between the people we see on the screen, and the ongoing, constantly shifting relations between these characters and the viewers. It is the opening scene from Howard Hawks' *The Big Sleep* (1947). 'Private Eye' Marlowe (Humphrey Bogart) has been called to the house of General Sternwood (Charles Waldron) to help him deal with a case of blackmail involving his youngest daughter, Carmen (Martha Vickers). As Marlowe waits in the hall to be shown in by the butler, Carmen provocatively confronts him. The interview with Sternwood then follows.

In news and current affairs television, distance and angle create a symbolic relation between the people on the screen and the viewer. Anchorpersons are shown frontally, from slightly below eye level, and in a wider shot than most other participants in the programme. This enhances their authority. They are literally 'higher up' than the viewers and shown

Fig 8.14 **Dynamic interpersonal relations in the opening scene of** *The Big Sleep* (Hawks, 1947)

from a respectful distance – initial shots may even show them from a very long distance, sitting behind large, gleaming desks at the far side of an empty, palatial hall.

The distinction between 'offer' and 'demand' (see chapter 4) also applies to moving images, and it too can be dynamicized: represented participants can turn towards the camera and look at the lens (and hence at the viewer), or can avert their gaze. But the camera cannot initiate this; it must be initiated by the participant, whether on their own initiative or as a result of following instructions from a director.

'Offers' are still the rule in naturalistic drama, in the theatre as much as in film and television. Bertolt Brecht famously sought to reintroduce the 'demand' stance in the theatre, especially by means of interpolated songs, and film-makers like Jean-Luc Godard have followed him in this. In these contexts 'demands' were thought to create an 'alienation effect', to break with conventions meant to naturalize the fictional world of stage and screen, and so to make the audiences more aware that they were watching a fiction and invite them to reflect on its content. In many other contexts – for example, television news – the 'demand' is the accepted convention, although not everyone is given the right to address the viewer directly. Anchorpersons and on-camera reporters may look at the camera, but interviewees may not; in chat shows hosts may look at the camera, but guests may not, and so on. In other words, the 'demand' is a privilege which media professionals have reserved for themselves.

The concept of modality (see chapter 5) is also fully applicable to moving images, but a further factor, movement, needs to be added to the list of means of expression that can cue modality. Like visual detail, background, depth, light and shade, colour, etc., movement can be represented with different degrees of realism or abstraction and hence play a role in modality judgements. Representations of walking, for instance, can range from simple animations in which stick figures raise and lower their legs without any articulation of the joints or any movement of the rest of the body, to highly detailed animations showing the rippling of every muscle involved.

Most films invite us to use the naturalistic criterion, although this is perhaps changing as the use of synthetic images and animation increases. In many animated cartoons, the background has higher (naturalistic) modality than the foreground, a reversal of what normally happens in 'live action' films. There is, of course, a technical reason for this. Backgrounds do not have to be animated and can therefore be painted in detail without breaking the budget. Again, in computer games different characters and actions may be animated more or less intricately. In a Delta Force game one of us played, the movement of enemies falling down as they were killed was decidedly unconvincing and unnatural. Again, there may be pragmatic reasons. Detailed animation costs time and money, and may slow down the action. But that does not negate the semiotic effect of reducing the naturalistic impact of killing.

Finally, the elements of composition discussed in chapter 6 (information value, salience and framing) apply to the composition of the shots in a film or television programme just as much as they apply to still images and other visual compositions, with, again, the proviso that the moving image can make composition dynamic. Something that starts out as Given can move into the New position in front of our eyes. Something that has low salience can become highly salient in the middle of a shot – for instance, by moving or being moved into the light, or by a change of focus of the camera. In chapter 6 we showed how, in figure 6.1, the left edge of the door of the shed frames the two characters in the shot, causing them to inhabit different spaces and so emphasizing the lack of communication between them. But in a moving image characters can move into each other's space and undo the framing between them. And all of these ways of dynamicizing composition can be subject-initiated or camera-initiated.

This brief discussion does not exhaust the 'language of film and television'. It has concentrated on the *spatial* patterns of individual shots and on two specific time-ordered patterns, the 'reverse angle' and 'point of view'. But film is also, and perhaps above all, a temporal mode, structured by intricate semantic and rhythmic patterns of editing (see van Leeuwen, 2004, for a social semiotic approach), and it is also characteristically multimodal, involving not just the visual, but also speech, sound and music. These aspects of the medium fall outside the scope of this book. But we do hope we have shown that the ideas presented in this book can usefully be applied to the spatial aspects of moving images or, more precisely, since movement is a temporal phenomenon, to an area where the spatial and the temporal interact and overlap.

9 Colourful thoughts (a postscript)

We have, in this book, attempted to present a 'grammar of visual design', to make explicit how the available resources of visual grammar form a potential for the representation and communication of meaning through spatial configurations of visual elements. We have travelled a certain distance along the road, but we realize that this work has only just begun. We find ourselves thinking about the limitations of what we have done and the amount of work and the kind of work that remains. Social semiotics is an attempt to describe and understand how people produce and communicate meaning in specific social settings, be they settings such as the family or settings in which sign-making is well institutionalized and hemmed in by habits, conventions and rules. But sign-making in society is so varied an activity that any attempt to capture it in a general theory must look crude by comparison with the richness of the actual semiotic world. In any case the theory which we use tells us that the actions of those who make signs in the environments of their cultural and social worlds is constantly changing the resources which they use, as well as their potentials; and in the increasingly diverse and dynamic world in which we are, this makes the relation of even a general theory to the specific instance tentative. Both the theory and the 'grammar' are always hypothetical and provisional.

We have become increasingly aware of this and have tried to write our grammar not as one which describes fixed 'rules' and a stable 'system', nor as one which seeks to capture the detail of everything people can and do do in visual communication, but as a flexible set of resources that people use in ever new and ever different acts of visual sign-making. We have included as many examples as we have, not in order to achieve comprehensiveness of coverage, but rather to illustrate and demonstrate the semiotic principles which underlie and shape human social semiosis, and thereby to try and show the flexibility of these resources in relation to the representational and communicational needs that humans have in their social lives. But even given this qualification, we feel we have only made a beginning. We wish, for instance, that we could have more fully documented and interpreted the social history of scientific-technical image-making, or the question of modality configurations in different schools of modern art, to mention just some of the questions on which we have touched all too lightly. And, although by now quite a few descriptions exist of how images work in distinct cultures, this is a field of such vast importance in a culturally – as well as economically – globalizing world that we see an absolute imperative for work in that area. As just one practical instance, in any one of the hugely culturally diverse classrooms in cities such as London or Sydney or Johannesburg, children still encounter a curriculum realized in the visual semiotic of the dominant culture and yet are likely to 'read' – and therefore 'misread' – that realization in terms of their 'home culture'.

In beginning to explore the 'third dimension', we saw a whole new field of problems and questions opening up, one which no doubt will itself open up further questions when we begin to delve into it more deeply. Nor have we, in this book, said enough about the impact of the digital media on modes and processes of representation and communication. (We have made comments on this elsewhere; see Kress and van Leeuwen 2001; Kress 2003.)

However, it was our aim to provide at least initially a broad overview, to map one large region of the semiotic landscape, and this we feel we have done, with all the faults that will inevitably cling to such a broad enterprise. We are very much sensitive to the fact that at the very moment when there is a theoretical move in the social sciences towards widening, in often quite radical ways, the framings around the domain to be studied, and hence to expand the scope of the theoretical framework used – we seem, in this book, to have moved in an opposite direction, focusing narrowly on one mode. However, we do see our attempts here actually as an essential part of that broadening – away from the intensity of focus on speech and writing alone, to a reframing of the domain of public forms of representation and communication. That will, we hope, have many advantages: first (and foremost) to show how human (social) semiosis actually works, in whatever sites, of school or work or leisure; and secondly to show the connections which have often been obscured by more limited and highly specialized approaches, whether in art-historical studies or in attempts to study the most banal of everyday events. These are connections such as that between the history of art (and visual communication generally) and the theory of language, in which the social and historical dimensions have, too often, been absent; or the connection between the 'micro' and 'macro' accounts of the social world which characterize different schools of sociology; or the connections between the study of the world in 'practices' and the study of that 'same' world in its representations. For us, the child's relatively 'free' act of sign-making, which for its understanding requires very specific, 'biographical' con-textualizations, is of as much interest as is representation within highly institutionalized genres in which sign-makers must follow well-established rules and conventions, and which, for their understanding, require broader social and historical contextualizations.

To emphasize, once more, the nature of the 'grammar of visual design' as a resource for making and communicating meaning through the convergence of many different signifying systems, we will discuss one final example. This example will also help reiterate another point. In writing such a book as this, one sometimes feels that one is applying a cold, clinical approach to semiotic practices which are, in reality, always coloured by affective factors. How to write about affect? How to steer a path between the mere assertion, or celebration, of the role of affect, which will leave no room for analysis and interpretation, and the cold dissection which threatens to destroy its object as one is writing about it? We have, from time to time, reminded the reader of the omnipresence of affect which we asserted in the Introduction: for instance, in chapter 4, where we discussed the relations between the image and the viewer, relations which are always affective relations, relations of identification or its opposite; in chapter 5, where we discussed the affective quality of 'more than real' values of modality markers; in chapter 6, where we discussed 'balance' as an interface between the biological and the semiotic; and in our discussion of 'handwriting' in chapter 7. Yet we feel that affect has perhaps been too thin a thread in the tapestry. The production and communication of meaning cannot be other than always affective and constitutive of subjectivities, in the domains we tend to regard as self-expressive (e.g. children's drawing and art) as much as in the domains we see as objectivating and impersonal (e.g. scientific and technical drawings). Even the maximally abstract modality of diagrams is an affective choice, by the very fact that it attempts to negate affect. The productive subject is as central here as anywhere else. In much contemporary theory, the old body–mind dichotomy again manifests itself in the strict boundaries drawn between rational and cognitive approaches and more affective approaches, be they grounded in the discourses that eulogize the 'pleasure of the text', in psychoanalytical discourses, or otherwise. We have tried to avoid this. We feel strongly that the cognitive and the affective are not antithetical but inevitably always co-present. This is one reason why we have given such a central place to children's representation: here affect has not yet been covered over by a society's ideological demands for 'rationality' or 'objectivity'.

Our final example will therefore be another example of children's visual sign-making, and its title, *Colourful Thoughts*, indicates that the child who made it sought to fuse the cognitive ('thoughts') and the affective ('colourful'). It is a painting, on plywood, measuring 120 by 90 centimetres; and was made by a ten-year-old girl (plate 8). The mother of the girl who made this painting is a professional artist and, in the size of the work, the medium and the way she has signed the painting, the girl has, perhaps, imitated her mother. But the work itself very much represents her own style of visual thinking. It was painted as a present for her father (separated from her mother), an academic whose study, the girl felt, was too bare and functional, and lacked not only sufficient pictures on the wall, but also – and above all – *colour*.

Looking at the painting from the point of view of ideational meaning, we note first of all that there are no vectors between the main participants, the shapes in the foreground. It is a conceptual picture. Like many of the conceptual pictures discussed in chapter 3, it lacks a concrete setting, shows the participants front-on and at eye level, includes a linguistic element in the picture space and uses abstract representation. The participants are distributed across the picture space in a symmetrical way, and this suggests that the relation between them is classificational. The symmetry is in fact quite striking and the objects are delicately balanced: even though, by itself, the yellow shape top left is heavier than the yellow shape middle right, the balance is restored by the higher position of the small blue 'thought balloon' top right. The title, in black, is balanced by a horizontal, slightly curved black line on top. And the participants are placed in a kind of circle around the central participant, which differs from the others in that it is not completely enclosed by a thick black line, but open at the bottom, so that the red colour, literally, drips out of it.

The title indicates what these participants represent. Their shapes and colours may be different, but they all represent 'thoughts'. What is a thought, according to this painting? Here we can make four observations. Thoughts are (1) differently coloured (red, blue and yellow); (2) differently shaped; (3) mostly enclosed by a thick, black crust (black, the colour of words!); and (4) sometimes not quite enclosed – in which case their content 'bleeds out of them', so to speak. These strongly saturated colours (the same palette as the Miró sculptures and the children's toys we discussed in the previous chapter) are 'more than real' and hence motivated by affect, rather than on naturalistic grounds (resemblance to reality) or conventionally (colour 'codes'). It is difficult to go into detail about the meanings of the different colours, though we have made an attempt to provide means for thinking about this in chapter 7. The literature on the 'emotive meanings' of colour is inconsistent. Some psychologists have reported that 'people' prefer saturated colour over unsaturated colour; others, that they prefer unsaturated colour over saturated colour. Blue has been described as 'depressing and sad' and as representing 'calm pleasure'. Goethe called yellow 'gay and softly charming', while Kandinsky said it 'never contains a profound meaning and is akin to utter waste'. One thing is certain, however: colour (and colour contrast) is used to realize affect in the sensory coding orientations that inform, for instance, certain types of art and art appreciation, certain forms of dress and interior decoration and their appreciation, and so on. In *Colourful Thoughts*, thoughts are thus represented as affects of different kinds: red, blue and yellow (among other things, for they also have a shape, a frame, etc.). As far as the enclosing black lines are concerned, we might perhaps say that the child represents thoughts as mostly 'dammed up', repressed, kept inside, except in the one, central case. On the shapes we will comment below.

The background may not be a concrete setting, but it is not a neutral background either: a green field, with yellow diagonal stripes and pink dots. It is difficult not to think of these stripes as downward vectors, going from top left to bottom right, particularly since there is, in the bottom right corner, a darkening of the green field in the form of an arrowhead: the painting as a whole thus converges towards the name of the artist, and might be seen as a kind of mental self-portrait. In conceptual visuals (maps, diagrams, heraldry) colours often have conventional meanings, and we would suggest reading these somewhat less saturated colours in this way: green as the colour of nature, pink as the colour of femininity. In other words, the strongly emotive, but bottled-up, thoughts of the child exist against a background of nature 'dotted with femininity'.

As far as the interpersonal meanings of the painting are concerned, the viewer is not positioned by any form of perspective, although there is a separation between foreground and background, through overlapping and through differences in colour saturation. Nor does the picture form a 'demand'. And as no human subject is represented, the issue of social distance does not arise. However 'colourful', the painting is, in many ways, 'objective'. It exists as an object in its own right, regardless of the viewer. Something can be said, however, about its modality. The painting abstracts from naturalistic depiction in almost every respect except one: the vibrant and strongly saturated colours. These colours, as we have noted already, are 'more than real', and thus suggest a coding orientation in which the affective forms the cornerstone of reality.

We turn, finally, to compositional, textual meanings. Three things can be noted. The painting is, first of all, a balanced composition with a strong sense of Centre and Margin. The child has, literally, balanced and centred her emotions in this picture. Second, the title is at the bottom, and so coded as, on the one hand, more concrete and real but, on the other hand, less valued and less 'ideal' than the visual element. At the top we find merely the shadow of this title: the colour, but not the substance of the verbal; its emotive quality, but not its overtly articulated content. Third, there is a difference between left and right – a difference in the shapes of the thoughts and a difference in colour (red is most strongly represented on the right).

On the meaning of this we can only speculate. It is tempting to read the shape of the participants on the left as phallic, and those on the right as, by contrast, representing the female. The centrality, and hence the mediating function (since left and right are polarized), of the central participant derives from this: the child herself is the central 'thought' in the middle, caught between the father and the mother. Remember also that the colour of the central participant (red) is most strongly represented on the right, the female side, and lies most clearly on the path of the vectors which lead to the artist's name.

We mentioned that the picture was painted as a gift to the father. In the picture the father is Given, the mother New. In other words, what the father, as the addressed viewer, is asked to pay attention to is the mother, the female, while the link between the two is formed by the 'thought' of the child, which, here – unlike all the other thoughts – escapes from its encapsulation and expresses itself in the act of producing the painting and giving it to the father.

Thus the child not only brings together choices from all the available resources of visual sign-making in a piece of intricate and complex visual thinking, but also fuses her thinking, her cognitive work, with her affects in an active process of working through some of the problems connected with her identity and subjectivity.

References

Allen, J. (1977) 'Self-reflexivity in documentary', *Cinetracts* 2: 37–44

Arnheim, R. (1969) *Visual Thinking*, Berkeley and Los Angeles, University of California Press

—— (1974) *Art and Visual Perception*, Berkeley and Los Angeles, University of California Press

—— (1982) *The Power of the Centre*, Berkeley and Los Angeles, University of California Press

Bakhtin, M. (1981) *The Dialogic Imagination*, Austin, University of Texas Press

—— (1984) *Problems of Dostoevsky's Poetics*, Manchester, Manchester University Press

Bal, M. (1985) *Narratology: Introduction to the Theory of Narrative*, Toronto, Toronto University Press

—— (1990) *Verf en Verderf: Lezen in Rembrandt*, Amsterdam, Prometheus

Barthes, R. (1967a) *Elements of Semiology*, London, Cape

—— (1967b) *Système de la Mode*, Paris, Seuil

—— (1970) *L'Empire des Signes*, Geneva, Skira

—— (1973) *Mythologies*, St Albans, Paladin

—— (1977) *Image–Music–Text*, London, Fontana

—— (1984) *Camera Lucida*, London, Fontana

Bassy, A.-M. (1975) 'Du texte à l'illustration', *Semiotica* 11(4): 297–335

Bazin, A. (1967) *What is Cinema?* vol. 1, Berkeley and Los Angeles, University of California Press

Bell, P. and van Leeuwen, T. (1994) *The Media Interview: Confession, Contest, Conversation*, Sydney, University of New South Wales Press

Belting, H. (1990) *The Image and its Public in the Middle Ages*, New Rochelle, NY, Aristide D. Caratzay

Bender, L. (1988) *France*, London, Macmillan

Benjamin, W. (1973) *Illuminations*, London, Fontana

Berger, J. (1972) *Ways of Seeing*, Harmondsworth, Penguin

Bernstein, B. (1981) 'Codes, modalities and the process of cultural reproduction: a model', *Language and Society* 10: 327–63

Bindon, H. and Williams, H. (1988) *Geography Research Projects: A Senior Student's Handbook*, Melbourne, Edward Arnold

Bogatyrev, P. (1971) *The Function of Folk Costume in Moravian Slovakia*, The Hague, Mouton

Bols, P., Houppermans, M., Krijger, C., Lentjes, W., Savelkouls, T., Terlingen, M. and Teune, P. (1986) *Werk aan de Wereld*, Den Bosch, Malmberg

Booth, W.C. (1961) *The Rhetoric of Fiction*, Chicago, Chicago University Press

Bourdieu, P. (1986) *Distinction: A Social Critique of the Judgement of Taste*, London, Routledge

Brecht, B. (1967) 'Über die Malerei der Chinesen', in *Gesammelte Werke*, vol. 18, Frankfurt-on-Main, Suhrkamp

Brown, C., Kelch, J. and Thiel, P.V. (1991) *Rembrandt: The Master and his Workshop*, New Haven, Yale University Press

Brown, T.M. (1958) *The Work of G. Rietveld, Architect*, Utrecht, A.W. Bruna

Bruna, D. (1988) *On My Walk*, London, Methuen Children's Books

Brunsden, C. and Morley, D. (1978) *Everyday Television: Nationwide*, London, BFI

Bryson, N. (ed.) (1990) *Visual Theory*, Cambridge, Polity Press

Burgin, V. (ed.) (1982) *Thinking Photography*, London, Macmillan

Chatman, S. (1978) *Story and Discourse*, Ithaca, NY, Cornell University Press

Clarke, G. (ed.) (1992) *The Portrait in Photography*, London, Reaktion Books

Comolli, J.L. (1971) 'Technique et idéologie: camera, perspective, profondeur du champ', *Cahiers du Cinéma* 229: 4–23

Coupe, S. and Andrews, M. (1984) *Their Ghosts May be Heard: Australia to 1900*, Melbourne, Cheshire

Dance, F.E.X. (1967) 'A helical model of communication', in F.E.X. Dance (ed.) *Human Communication Theory*, New York, Holt, Rinehart & Winston

Deleuze, G. (1992) *Cinema*, vol. 1, *The Movement Image*, London, Athlone Press

Dondis, D.A. (1973) *A Primer of Visual Literacy*, Cambridge, MA, MIT Press

Dragt, H., Hofland, W.A. and Tamsma, R. (1986) *De Geo Geordend*, Amsterdam, Meulenhoff

DSP (1991) *Arts Literacy*, Sydney, Disadvantaged Schools Programme Report

Dyer, G. (1982) *Advertising as Communication*, London, Methuen

Eco, U. (1976a) 'Articulations of the cinematic code', in B. Nichols (ed.) *Movies and Methods*, vol 1, Berkeley and Los Angeles, University of California Press

—— (1976b) *A Theory of Semiotics*, Bloomington, Indiana University Press

—— (1979) *The Role of the Reader*, Bloomington, Indiana University Press

Fairclough, N. (1992) *Discourse and Social Change*, Cambridge, Polity Press

—— (1993) 'Critical discourse analysis and the marketization of public discourse: the universities', *Discourse and Society* 4(2): 133–69

Finch, C. (1968) *Pop Art: Object and Image*, London, Studio Vista/ Dutton

Finnegan, R. (2002) *Communication*, London, Routledge

Fiske, J. (1982) *Introduction to Communication Studies*, London, Methuen

Fiske, J. and Hartley, J. (1979) *Reading Television*, London, Methuen

Fresnault-Deruelle, P. (1975) 'Du linéaire au tabulaire', *Communications* 24: 7–23

Gage, J. (1993) *Colour and Culture – Practice and Meaning from Antiquity to Abstraction*, London, Thames and Hudson

—— (1999) *Colour and Meaning – Art, Science and Symbolism*, London, Thames and Hudson

Gauthier, G. (1973) *Initiation à la sémiologie de l'image*, Paris, Cahiers de l'Audiovisuel

Genette, G. (1972) *Narrative Discourse*, Oxford, Blackwell

Ghaoui, C., George, S.M., Rada, R., Beer, M. and Gerta, J. (1992) 'Text to hypertext and back again'; in P. O'Brian Holt and N. Williams (eds) *Computers and Writing: State of the Art*, Dordrecht, Kluwer

Gledhill, C. (1994) 'Towards a genre of abstracting', paper presented at the 21st International Systemic Functional Congress, Gent, 1–5 August 1994

Goethe, J.W. von (1970 [1810]) *Theory of Colours*, Cambridge, MA, MIT Press

Goffman, E. (1976) *Gender Advertisements*, London, Macmillan

Gombrich, E. (1960) *Art and Illusion*, London, Phaidon

Goodman, N. (1969) *Languages of Art*, London, Oxford University Press

Goodman, S. and Graddol, D. (1996) *Redesigning English: New Texts, New Identities*, London, Routledge

Gregory, R.L. (1970) *The Intelligent Eye*, New York, McGraw-Hill

Habermas, J. (1984) *The Theory of Communicative Action*, vol. 1, Cambridge, Polity Press

Hall, E. (1964) 'Silent assumptions in social communication', *Disorders of Communication* 42: 41–55

—— (1966) *The Hidden Dimension*, New York, Doubleday

Hall, S. (1982) 'The determination of news photographs', in S. Cohen and J. Young (eds) *The Manufacture of News*, London, Constable

Halliday, M.A.K. (1978) *Language as Social Semiotic*, London, Edward Arnold

———— (1985) *An Introduction to Functional Grammar*, London, Edward Arnold

———— (1993) *Language in a Changing World*, Canberra, *ALAA Occasional Paper* 13

Halliday, M.A.K. and Martin, J.R. (1993) *Writing Science: Literacy and Discursive Power*, London, Falmer Press

Hartley, J. (1982) *Understanding News*, London, Methuen

Hauser, A. (1962) *The Social History of Art*, vol. 2, London, Routledge

Hermeren, G. (1969) *Representation and Meaning in the Visual Arts*, Lund, Scandinavian University Books

Hill, J. (1980) *Introductory Physics*, London, Macmillan

Hjelmslev, L. (1961) *Prolegomena to a Theory of Language*, Madison, University of Wisconsin Press

Hodge, R. and Kress, G. (1988) *Social Semiotics*, Cambridge, Polity Press

———— (1993) *Language as Ideology* (2nd revised edition), London, Routledge

Hogg, J. (ed.) (1969) *Psychology and the Visual Arts*, Harmondsworth, Penguin

Honzl, J. (1976) 'Dynamics of the sign in the theatre', in L. Matejka and I.R. Titunik (eds) *Semiotics of Art: Prague School Contributions*, Cambridge, MA, MIT Press

Hughes, R. (1969) *Heaven and Hell in Western Art*, London, Weidenfeld & Nicolson

Humphrey, S. (1992) 'Exploring the language of school geography', unpublished research report, Sydney, Disadvantaged Schools Programme

Iedema, R. *et al.* (1993) 'Media Literacy Report', unpublished research report, Sydney, Disadvantaged Schools Programme

—— (1994) 'The language of administration', unpublished research report, Sydney, Disadvantaged Schools Programme

Iser, W. (1978) *The Act of Reading*, Baltimore, MD, Johns Hopkins University Press

Itten, J. (1970) *The Elements of Colour*, New York, Van Nostrand Reinhold

Jaffé, H.L.C. (1967) *De Stijl: 1917–1931, Visions of Utopia*, Oxford, Phaidon

Jakobson, R. (1971) *Studies in Verbal Art*, Ann Arbor, Michigan University Press

Jakobson, R. and Halle, M. (1956) *Fundamentals of Language*, Mouton, The Hague

Jenkins, C. (1990) *Science Scene*, Book 1, Melbourne, Edward Arnold

Jennings, T. (1986) *The Young Geographer Investigates Mountains*, Oxford, Oxford University Press

Joos, M. (1967) *The Five Clocks of Language*, New York, Harcourt, Brace & World

Kandinksy, W. (1977 [1914]) *Concerning the Spiritual in Art*, New York, Dover Publications

Kress, G. (1977) 'Tense as modality', *UEA Papers in Linguistics* 5: 40–50

—— (1985) 'Ideological Structures in Discourse', in T.A. van Dijk (ed.) *Handbook of Discourse Analysis*, New York, Academic Press

—— (1987a) *Communication and Culture: An Introduction*, Sydney, University of New South Wales Press

—— (1987b) 'Educating readers: language in advertising', in J. Hawthorn (ed) *Propaganda, Persuasion and Polemic*, London, Edward Arnold

—— (1989) *Linguistic Processes in Socio-cultural Practice*, London, Oxford University Press

—— (1992) 'Explanation in visual communication', report to the ESPRIT II Basic Research Project on Explanation, Working Group 236

—— (1993a) 'Against arbitrariness: the social production of the sign as a foundational issue in critical discourse analysis', *Discourse and Society* 4(2): 169–93

—— (1993b) 'Media literacy as cultural technology in the age of transcultural media', in C. Bazalgette, E. Brevort and J. Savino (eds) *New Directions: Media Education Worldwide*, London and Paris, BFI/CLEMI

—— (1995) 'Representational resources and subjectivity', in C. Coulthard (ed.) *Critical Discourse Analysis*, London, Routledge

—— (1996) *Before Writing: Rethinking Paths into Literacy*, London, Routledge

—— (2000) 'Design and transformation', in B. Cope and M. Kalantzis (eds) *Multiliteracies*, London, Routledge

—— (2003) *Literacy in the New Media Age*, London, Routledge

Kress, G. and Trew, T. (1978) 'Ideological transformations of discourse: or, how the *Sunday Times* got its message across', *Sociological Review* 26: 755–76

Kress, G. and van Leeuwen, T. (1990) *Reading Images,* Geelong, Deakin University Press

———— (1992) 'Structures of Visual Representation', *Journal of Literary Semantics* 11(2): 91–117

———— (2001) *Multimodal Discourse – The Modes and Media of Contemporary Communication,* London, Edward Arnold

Lacy, M.L. (1996) *The Power of Colour to Heal the Environment,* London, Rainbow Bridge Publications

Lakoff, G. (1987) *Women, Fire and Dangerous Things: What Categories Reveal About the Mind,* Chicago, University of Chicago Press

Lakoff, G. and Johnson, M. (1980) *Metaphors We Live By,* Chicago, University of Chicago Press

Leibovitz, A. (1990) *Photographs 1970–1990,* New York, HarperCollins

Lindekens, R. (1971) *Eléments pour une sémiotique de la photographie,* Paris, Didier

Lupton, E. (1989) 'Reading isotype' in M. Victor (ed.) *Design Discourse – History/Theory/Criticism,* Chicago, University of Chicago Press

McKenzie, A.E.E. (1938) *Magnetism and Electricity,* Cambridge, Cambridge University Press

McQuail, D. and Windahl, S. (1993) *Communication Models,* London, Longman

Machin, D. and Suleiman, U. (2004) 'Two Computer War Games Set in Lebanon: The influence of a global technology on discourse', unpublished paper, Cardiff University

Martin, J.R. (1985) *Factual Writing,* Geelong, Deakin University Press

—— (1992) *English Text – System and Structure*, Amsterdam, Benjamins

Martin, J.R., Wignell, P., Eggins, S. and Rothery, J. (1988) 'Secret English: discourse technology in a junior secondary school', in L. Gerot, J. Oldenburgh and T. van Leeuwen (eds) *Language and Socialisation: Home and School*, Sydney, Macquarie University

Martin, M. (1968) *Le Langage Cinématographique*, Paris, Editions du Cerf

Martín, R.M. and Ellis, M. (2001) *Pasos*, Book 1, London, Hodder and Stoughton

Merritt, P.C. (ed.) (1984) *Book of Flowsheets*, New York, McGraw-Hill

Metz, C. (1974a) *Film Language*, New York, Oxford University Press

—— (1974b) *Language and Cinema*, The Hague, Mouton

Modley, R. and Lowenstein, D. (1952) *Pictographs and Graphs*, New York, Harper

Morris, D. (1977) *Manwatching*, London, Cape

Mukarovsky, J. (1976) 'Art as semiotic fact' and 'The essence of the visual arts', in L. Matejka and I.R. Titunik (eds) *Semiotics of Art: Prague School Contributions*, Cambridge, MA, MIT Press

Mumford, L. (1936) *Technics and Civilization*, New York, Harcourt, Brace & World

Myers, G. (1990) *Writing Biology*, Madison, University of Wisconsin Press

—— (1994) *Words in Ads*, London, Edward Arnold

Nash, J.M. (1974) *Cubism, Futurism and Constructivism*, London, Thames and Hudson

Nattiez, J.-J. (1976) *Fondéments d'une sémiologie musicale*, Paris, Uge

Nitzschke, V. (1990) *Politik: Lernen und Handeln für Heute und Morgen*, Frankfurt, Diesterweg

Novitz, D. (1977) *Pictures and their Use in Communication*, The Hague, Nijhoff

Oakley, M. *et al.* (1985) *Our Society and Others*, Sydney, McGraw-Hill

Ohman, C. (1989) *Historia*, Uppsala, Esselte Studium

Ong, W.J. (1982) *Orality and Literacy: The Technologising of the Word*, London, Methuen

Ostwald, W. (1935 [1916]) *Colour Science*, London, Windsor and Newton

O'Sullivan, T., Hartley, J., Saunders, D. and Fiske, J. (1983) *Key Concepts in Communication*, London, Methuen

O'Toole, M. (1994) *The Language of Displayed Art*, Leicester, Leicester University Press

Panofsky, E. (1953) *Early Netherlandish Painting*, New York, Harper and Row

———— (1970) *Meaning in the Visual Arts*, Harmondsworth, Penguin

Pask, R. and Bryant, M. (1982) *People in Australia: A Social Geography*, Melbourne, Edward Arnold

Pierce, J.R. (1972) 'Communication', *Scientific American* 227(3): 30–42

Poynton, C. (1985) *Language and Gender: Making the Difference*, Geelong, Deakin University Press

Prosser, R. (2000) *Leisure, Recreation and Tourism*, London, Collins Educational

Riley, J.W. and Riley, M.W. (1959) 'Mass communication and the social system', in R.K. Merton, L. Broom and S. Cottrell (eds) *Sociology Today*, New York, Basic Books

Rimmon-Kenan, S. (1983) *Narrative Fiction: Contemporary Poetics*, London, Methuen

Ringbom, S. (1965) *Icon to Narrative: The Rise of the Dramatic Close Up in Fifteenth Century Painting*, Abo, Abo Akademie

Rowley-Jolivet, E. (2004) 'Different visions, different visuals: a social semiotic analysis of field-specific visual composition in scientific conference presentations', *Visual Communication* 3(2): 145–77

Sacks, H. (1992) *Lectures on Conversation*, Oxford, Blackwell

Saint-Martin, F. (1987) *Semiotics of Visual Language*, Bloomington, Indiana University Press

Sale, C., Friedman, B. and Wilson, G. (1980) *Our Changing World*, Book I, Melbourne, Longman Cheshire

Saussure, F. de (1974 [1916]) *Course in General Linguistics*, London, Peter Owen

Scannell, P. (1994) 'Communicative intentionality in broadcasting', unpublished paper

Schapiro, M. (1973) *Words and Pictures*, The Hague, Mouton

Schramm, W. (1954) 'How communication works', in W. Schramm (ed.) *The Process and Effects of Mass Communication*, Urbana, University of Illinois Press

Scollon, R. and Scollon, S. (2003) *Discourses in Place: Language in the Material World*, London, Routledge

Selander, S. (1994) 'Pedagogiska texter och retorik', in S. Selander and B. Englund (eds) *Konsten att informera och övertyga*, Stockholm, HLS Förlag

Shannon, C. and Weaver, W. (1949) *The Mathematical Theory of Communication*, Urbana, University of Illinois Press

Sharples, M. and Pemberton, L. (1992) 'Representing writing: external representations and the writing process', in P. O'Brian Holt and N. Williams (eds) *Computers and Writing: State of the Art*, Dordrecht, Kluwer

Shepherd, J. (1977) 'The musical coding of ideologies', in J. Shepherd, P. Virden, G. Vulliamy and T. Wishart (eds) *Whose Music? A Sociology of Musical Languages*, London, Transaction Books

Sontag, S. (1977) *On Photography*, Harmondsworth, Penguin

Stefanescu-Goanga, F. (1912) 'Experimentelle Untersuchungen über die Gefühlsbetonung der Farbhelligkeiten und ihrer Combinationen', *Philosophische Studien* 10: 601–17

Theewen, G. (1993) *Joseph Beuys: Die Vitrinen*, Cologne, Walter König

Thibault, P. (1991) *Social Semiotics as Praxis*, Minneapolis, University of Minnesota Press

Thompson, P. and Davenport, P. (1982) *The Dictionary of Visual Language*, Harmondsworth, Penguin

Threadgold, T. (1988) 'Stories of race and gender: an unbounded discourse', in D. Birch and M. O'Toole (eds) *Functions of Style*, London, Pinter

Trew, T. (1979) 'Theory and ideology at work' and 'Linguistic variation and ideological difference', in R. Fowler, R. Hodge, G. Kress and T. Trew (eds) *Language and Control*, London, Routledge

Tufte, E.R. (1983) *The Visual Display of Quantitative Information*, Cheshire, CT, Graphics Press

Uspensky, B. (1973) *A poetics of composition*, Berkeley and Los Angeles, University of California Press

—— (1975) 'Left and right in icon painting', *Semiotica* 13(1): 33–41

van Leeuwen, T. (1985) 'Rhythmic structures of the film text', in T.A. van Dijk (ed.) *Discourse and Communication: New Approaches to the Analysis of Mass Media Discourse and Communication*, Berlin, Walter de Gruyter

—— (1986) 'Proxemics of the television interview', *Australian Journal of Screen Theory* 17/18: 125–41

—— (1988) 'Music and ideology: towards a sociosemiotics of mass media music', *SASSC Working Papers* 10(2): 199–220

—— (1989) 'Changed times, changed tunes: music and the ideology of the news', in J. Tulloch and G. Turner (eds) *Australian Television: Programs, Pleasures, Politics*, Sydney, Allen and Unwin

—— (1991a) 'Conjunctive structure in documentary film and television', *Continuum* 5(1): 76–115

—— (1991b) 'The sociosemiotics of easy listening music', *Social Semiotics* 1(1): 67–80

—— (1992) 'The schoolbook as multimodal text', *Internationale Schulbuchforschung* 14(1): 35–8

—— (1993) 'Genre and field in critical discourse analysis: a synopsis', *Discourse and Society* 4(2): 193–223

—— (1999) *Speech, Music, Sound*, London, Macmillan

—— (2003) 'A multimodal perspective on composition', in T. Ensink and C. Sauer (eds) *Framing and Perspectivising in Discourse*, Amsterdam, Benjamins

—— (2004) *Introducing Social Semiotics*, London, Routledge

van Leeuwen, T. and Caldas-Coulthard, C.R. (2004) 'The semiotics of kinetic design', in D. Banks (ed.) *Text and Texture – Systemic-*

Functional Viewpoints on the Nature and Structure of Text, Paris, L'Harmattan

van Leeuwen, T. and Humphrey, S. (1996) 'On learning to look through a geographer's eyes', in R. Hasan and G. Williams (eds) *Literacy in Society*, London, Longman

van Leeuwen, T., and Kress, G. (1992) 'Trampling all over our unspoilt spot: Barthes' "punctum" and the politics of the extra-semiotic', *Southern Review* 25(1): 27–38

——— (1995) 'Critical layout analysis', *Internationale Schulbuchforschung* 17(3): 25–43

van Leeuwen, T. and Selander, S. (1995) 'Picturing "our" heritage in the pedagogic text', *Journal of Curriculum Studies* 27(5): 501–23

van Sommers, P. (1984) *Drawing and Cognition*, Cambridge, Cambridge University Press

Veel, R. (1992) 'The language of school science', unpublished research report, Sydney, Disadvantaged Schools Programme

Voloshinov, V.N. (1973) *Marxism and the Philosophy of Language*, London, Seminar Press

Watson, J. and Hill, A. (1980) *A Dictionary of Communication and Media Studies*, London, Edward Arnold

Whorf, B.L. (1956) *Language, Thought and Reality*, Cambridge, MA, MIT Press

Wierzbicka, A. (1990) 'The meaning of colour terms: semantics, colour and cognition', *Cognitive Linguistics* 1: 99–150

Williams, N. and Holt, P. (eds) (1989) *Computers and Writing*, Norwood, NJ, Ablex

Williams, R. (1977) *Culture and Society 1780–1950*, Harmondsworth, Penguin

Williamson, J. (1978) *Decoding Advertisements*, London, Marion Boyars

Wolkers, J. (1965) *Een Roos van Vlees*, Amsterdam, Meulenhoff

Wollen, P. (1982) 'Godard and counter-cinema: vent d'est', in B. Nichols (ed.) *Movies and Methods*, vol. 2, Berkeley and Los Angeles, University of California Press

Index

Related titles from Routledge

Discourses in Place
Language in the Material World
Ron Scollon and Suzie Wong Scollon

'Written with directness and charm, and an abundance of persuasive examples, this book locates meaning not just in language but in the richness and complexity of the lived world ... its insights will start a generation of new thinking, and research. It marks a turning point in linguistics and semiotics alike.' – *Gunther Kress, Institute of Education, University of London, UK*

Discourses in Place develops the first systematic analysis of the ways we interpret language as it is materially placed in the world.

It argues that we can only interpret the meaning of public texts like road signs, notices and brand logos by considering the social and physical world that surrounds them. Drawing on a wide range of real examples, from signs in the Chinese mountains to urban centres in Austria, France, North America and Hong Kong, this textbook equips students with the methodology and models they need to undertake their own research in 'geosemiotics', and is essential reading for anyone with an interest in language and the ways in which we communicate.

ISBN10: 0–415–29048–1 (hbk)
ISBN10: 0–415–29049–X (pbk)
ISBN10: 0–203–42272–4 (ebk)

ISBN13: 9–78–0–415–29048–7 (hbk)
ISBN13: 9–78–0–415–29049–4 (pbk)
ISBN13: 9–78–0–203–42272–4 (ebk)

Available at all good bookshops
For ordering and further information please visit:
www.routledge.com